p68 - re Malamud

p50 poem of
false, childish
dreams

p51 - survivor
writing.

A DOUBLE DYING

A DOUBLE DYING
Reflections on Holocaust Literature

by ALVIN H. ROSENFELD

Bloomington & London

Indiana University Press

Selections from "Cut," "Lady Lazarus," and "Daddy" from ARIEL by Sylvia
Plath, published by Faber and Faber London,
copyright © 1965 by Ted Hughes.
Reprinted by permission of Harper & Row, Publishers, Inc.

Manufactured in the United States of America

Library of Congress Cataloging in Publication Data

Rosenfeld, Alvin Hirsch.
A double dying.

Bibliography: p.
1. Holocaust, Jewish (1939–1945), in literature. I. Title.
PN56.3.J4R6   809'.933   79–3006
ISBN 0–253–13337–8
1 2 3 4 5   84 83 82 81 80

To
My Mother,
Bertha Cohen Rosenfeld
and to
The Memory of My Father,
Max Rosenfeld

What of that special creature, the Holocaust writer?
Surely from the artistic point of view there is no simple
common denominator among all of us who deal with the
subject. . . . We are not at all of one school, nor do we
represent a particular esthetic tendency. Why then
do we feel so closely bound to each other . . . ?
Can dreams be involved here . . . ? After the Holocaust,
after the destruction, what sort of dreams do we have? For
myself, I know what my nightmares are. . . . I find such
traces even in books by Holocaust writers which do not treat
of the Holocaust at all. It would seem that one does not stop
being a Holocaust writer whatever one's theme is. Who
knows? Our souls may have been tattooed, along with
our hands.

—PIOTR RAWICZ

CONTENTS

Acknowledgments

I wish to express my gratitude to the following people, who read parts of this book in manuscript and offered various forms of advice and encouragement: Matei Calinescu, A. Roy Eckardt, Michael Morgan, Michael Rosenblum, and Sara Suleri. My friend and former chairman Kenneth Gros Louis, now Dean of the College of Arts and Sciences at Indiana University, generously allowed me to rearrange my teaching schedule at a decisive point in my writing, and I wish to thank him for his understanding and support. I also wish to acknowledge the assistance provided me by the American Council of Learned Societies, whose fellowship grant permitted me to pursue some of the research for this book during my sabbatical year in Israel.

Anyone who engages in serious study of the Holocaust owes a multitude of hidden debts to a small but unusually dedicated group of scholars, writers, and survivors who, at times through their work and at other times simply through being who they are, offer insight and encouragement when both are needed. These friends have had little, if anything, to do with this book in a direct way, and certainly are in no way responsible for whatever faults or flaws it may show, but I am sure that without them it could not have come about. Inasmuch as I feel myself a privileged part of their company, then, I wish to thank the following: Lucy Dawidowicz, Roy and Alice Eckardt, Yaffa Eliach, Emil and Rose Fackenheim, Irving and Blu Greenberg, Margit Kalina, Lawrence Langer, Shalom Lindenbaum, and Elie Wiesel.

Portions of this study previously have appeared in the following periodicals, and I thank the editors for permission to reprint: *American Poetry Review, Midstream, Moment,* and *Shoah.*

Finally, a special note of appreciation needs to be registered for Linda Sorisio, for typing, and for Erna, Gavriel, and Dalia, for enduring.

I. Reading and Writing after the Holocaust

Introduction

> Murder. Means nothing to the ear. In English it could even be glamorous. . . .
> Murder.
> And there are worse substitutes for feeling: Passed Away; Just Reward; A Long Illness.
> And the most inadequate word of them all: Holocaust. A nothing category; a eunuch of a word.
> A Jewish term, anyway. To them it has significance. To the rest of this numb world. . . . [1]

Despite its recent topicality, to the rest of the world "Holocaust" is without significant meaning, or at least without a compelling claim on any significant part of most people's lives. By contrast, the term, for all its admitted inadequacy, has come to occupy a central place in Jewish vocabulary, where it signifies the inexplicable and almost incomprehensible tragedy of European Jewry during the Nazi period. "Holocaust" implies not just death but total destruction; not murder, which carries with it some still lingering if dreaded sense of personal violation, but annihilation on so massive and indiscriminate a scale as to render death void of all personal characteristics, and hence virtually anonymous or absurd. Moreover, "Holocaust" suggests not only a brutally imposed death but an even more brutally imposed life of humiliation, deprivation, and degradation before the time of dying. The earlier Greek and Biblical connotations of sacrificial offering, while not altogether absent from the contemporary usage of the term, are submerged by the dominant political, racial, ideological, and technological strains of Nazism, which not only accompanied but seem to have dic-

3

tated the systematically planned elimination of the Jewish people. The resistance to that genocide, both physical and spiritual, also looks to find expression in "Holocaust," as do the elegiac and commemorative strains of remembrance itself. Finally, the incalculable damage done to our traditional concepts of God and man, of what it is that constitutes the norms and aspirations of social and cultural existence, begins to register in "Holocaust," even if all too weakly and imprecisely.

Clearly, no term available to us thus far is comprehensive enough or forceful enough to record a rupture in human history as severe as this. "Holocaust" alternates at times with the Yiddish *churbn* (from the Hebrew *Churban,* designating the destruction of the Second Temple and the dispersion of the Jews that followed it) and the Hebrew *Shoah* (meaning "catastrophe" or "destruction"). Such terms are suggestive and are in frequent use. But the fact is that we have no more precise or authoritative terminology than the phrase "the Holocaust." By adding the article we seem to be able to emphasize not merely an event but an epoch that is defined by that event: quite literally, the consummation by fire of one order of civilization and the beginnings of whatever it is that may succeed it.

While we may be without a unitary or commanding vocabulary of proper nouns, we hardly lack for words. The "War against the Jews," as Lucy Dawidowicz has called it, has been copiously recorded and never was a silent or hidden crime. Its prelude was explicitly, even vociferously announced; its progress did not go unnoticed; and its aftermath has resulted in a volume of literature that has already grown so large as to be beyond the reach of mastery. The extent of the persistent effort on the part of so many to articulate the Holocaust itself testifies to the magnitude of the event and emphasizes our common need to bring it under whatever control continued reflection may afford. This point, an important one for the present book,. needs further elaboration.

An age is known not only by the books it produces but by those it labors to preserve and pass on to succeeding generations. On both counts—that of original creation as well as that of vital cultural transmission—Holocaust literature must be counted among the most compelling literatures of our day. One would prefer to call the characteristic writings of a given period by more ennobling or more palatable names, but if we were to deny centrality to Holocaust literature, we would be falsifying not only the literary history of our time but a large part of its moral history as well. To say this, of course, is not to deny the presence over the last three or four decades of other kinds of writing that also demand and deserve our attention. There is, after all, always a simultaneity of literatures present in any given period, and, in our own highly syncretic culture, in which all kinds of things are going on at once, only a variety of expressive kinds could accurately reflect our lives. What, though, is needed to express our *deaths,* the characteristically violent, dehumanized deaths of the twentieth century? Is there any literature other than Holocaust literature that is capable of recording the unprecedented ways in which millions were sent to a heretofore unimaginable end? Such deaths take the strictest, most uncompromising measure of our lives, whether we like it or not or even whether we know it or not.

Holocaust literature insists that we know it. Moreover, it insists that we make our assessments of human conduct and our reassessments of every inherited metaphysical statement truthfully and at the very edges of historical conflagration. We would all wish it were otherwise, but the fact remains that just a short time ago countless numbers of human beings were incinerated while countless numbers more looked on or helped to feed the fires. In a terrible but undeniable way, that Holocaust marks out our time, so much so as to alter radically our conception of the human. For, as Elie Wiesel has convincingly stated it, "at Auschwitz, not only man died but also the idea of man."[2] Holocaust literature is our record of that dying—a double dying—and, at the same time, our hope for what might still live on or be newly born.

The present study will concentrate sharply on the implications of that double destruction, for language and literature and for whatever abiding sense we may still have of the humane. It will do so by raising and trying to provide answers to a number of fundamental questions about Holocaust literature. Who are its significant authors? What are its major themes, styles, and genres? Have we yet learned sufficiently well how to read it so as to begin to distinguish between its "good" and "bad" books, its most authentic or spurious and exploitative strains of expression? Can Holocaust literature be "literary" in the common and accepted senses of that term? Can it afford *not* to be literary? In what ways does it seem, almost unavoidably, to be a religious literature, perhaps even, as one of its writers has suggested, "the stories of a new Bible?" What is to be gained from reading Holocaust literature, which is bound to be distressing and frequently more than distressing, or what is to be lost from avoiding it? Can one avoid it and still remain honest to the times? If one cannot, how much Holocaust literature is "enough"? One book? Two? Three? Which ones? And by whom?

These are some of the questions that preoccupy scholars and critics who have set themselves the difficult but vastly important task of expounding the Holocaust through its literature. As with all questions that touch on this subject, answers are not always readily forthcoming, for, to cite Elie Wiesel once more, "the subject matter to be studied is made up of death and mystery, it slips away between our fingers, it runs faster than our perceptions."[3] Nevertheless, despite the difficulties, we are not altogether without means, and a serious critical address to such matters has begun.

Perhaps the first thing to recognize about Holocaust literature is that it is an international literature. That is not surprising, given the magnitude of the crime that swirls at its turbulent center, one whose circumference embraces all of Europe and virtually every non-European country where Jews have lived and where a triumphant Nazism might have worked its terror. The geographical compass of Holocaust literature, then, is unusually broad, as are the languages in which this literature has been written. These include all the major European languages; most of the minor ones; and, in an especially important way, the specifically Jewish languages, notably Hebrew and Yiddish. As a result, a rare degree of linguistic competence is required of any scholar who would hope to grasp Holocaust literature in its variety of original sources. Some of these writings have been made available in English translation, although much still remains accessible only to those who command Polish or Czech or Yiddish or any of a dozen other tongues.

Just as Holocaust literature occupies a multiplicity of languages, so too has it found its way into all of the generic forms of language. Thus the Holocaust has been addressed in novels and short stories; in poems and plays; in expository prose memoirs, diaries, and journals; in philosophical essays and midrashic exegeses; in parables, ballads, and songs. This literature has not occasioned any new kinds of writing, but it has greatly complicated all the literary forms it has occupied and seems to be in the process of breaking them down in an effort to find some new, more adequate measure of chronicling a radical evil and the range of human responses to it.

At this point it is too early to know precisely what language can and cannot do in expressing such extremity. One obligation of criticism, however, is to raise questions of the kind posed by Erich Kahler in *The Disintegration of Form in the Arts.* "What happens to artistic form," Kahler asserts, "seriously affects the human form, the form of man."[4] In light of the unprecedented distortions of humanity that were carried out under the impact of Nazism, this insight needs to be retained and reformulated in the following way: "How does what happens to human form, the form of man, seriously affect artistic form?" The question is difficult, yet the fact is even the first writers—a Chaim Kaplan, a Yitzhak Katznelson, or an Emmanuel Ringelblum—had to concern themselves, at the very moment of transcribing their eyewitness accounts of the atrocity, with the resources available to them in language for faithfully and credibly recording their own experiences. "It is beyond my pen to describe the destruction," Kaplan lamented over and over again in his *Warsaw Diary,* and yet his resolve to find the words to continue his writing usually proved stronger than silence. He faced more than occasional moments when language deserted him, though, and when he felt reduced to being a mere dumb bystander: "There is no strength left to cry; steady and continual weeping leads finally to silence. At first there is screaming; then wailing; and at last a bottomless sigh that does not leave even an echo."[5] Kaplan knew no greater imperative than to get beyond that expressionless despair, however, and if his diary continues to echo on powerfully into our own day, it is because more often than not he sought and found an artistic form that would be adequate to serve his needs as a writer, which is to say, preeminently as a *witness.*

As we distance ourselves in time from the event, though, and try to absorb it into consciousness, later writers—and readers as well—will find that the temptations to succumb to silence, avoidance, or even outright denial will be greater, and the "incredibility of the Holocaust," as Edward Alexander refers to it, will consequently grow to dangerous proportions.[6] Holocaust writers will have to overcome immense strains on the imagination. "How to write about it, yet how not to write about it?"—this query, which all along has been the dilemma of everyone who has been touched by the Holocaust, can only become more acute with time. Since the challenge is as much a moral one as a literary one—in this instance the ethical imperative and the aesthetic one conjoin—the means must be found or the human creature perish. Samuel Beckett, himself not a direct survivor of the death camps but someone whose imagination has absorbed more than a little of their impact, has formulated this issue as well as anyone has, and his words can be taken as implicitly part of the vocation of all Holocaust authors: "There is nothing to express, nothing with which to express, nothing from which to express, no power to express . . . together with the obligation to express."[7]

In each of the chapters that follows it is my intention to describe and assess the various ways in which writers have attempted to formulate and meet this obligation. In Chapter 1 the issues are defined in theoretical terms in an effort to begin to grasp the problematics of Holocaust literature. In the five chapters that follow, this literature is taken up within its major modes or genres. Chapter 2, devoted to a broad survey of diaries, memoirs, and journals, concentrates on problems of Holocaust and history. Chapter 3 reflects on the difficulties and achievements of fiction writers who have tried to move from documentation to art. And Chapters 4, 5, and 6 change the focus to poetry and an intensive investigation of "the sayable," especially in its relationship to problems of ontology and theology. The themes that are developed in these six chapters are various but generally center in the need to see Holocaust literature against the history that has produced it, a history that reduces the expressive powers of language almost to silence, yet at the same time obligates writers to speech. If one can talk about such a thing as a phenomenology of Holocaust literature, it would have to be in terms of this contradiction between the impossibility but also the necessity of writing about the death of the idea of man in order to sustain that idea. Each genre has its own difficulties living with this paradox but, as I try to show, each also demonstrates some unique strengths. In Chapters 7 and 8 my focus is on other matters: on the corruption of the German language under the Nazis as well as on the inevitable deceptions and distortions that result from inauthentic responses to the Holocaust. The literature examined in these later chapters is diverse and includes drama, fiction, and poetry; in one instance, it also includes film. Finally, as a brief concluding chapter, or epilogue, this study rounds out with a plea for sustained and authentic remembrance.

A word needs to be said about critical stance. While no literature is beyond judgment, the particular body of writings under review here does not cry out in the first place, in my opinion, for aesthetic evaluation. Ultimately such judgments will have to be made; from time to time an effort to make them will appear in the chapters that follow; but I admit that my principal interest is less in the "art of atrocity" than it is in other issues, most especially in trying to define the kind of knowledge that we acquire in reading the literature of the Holocaust and in weighing the consequent gains and losses that are ours in its aftermath. Much of the literature is painful and upsetting; at times it is disorienting; always, when it is authentic, it is humbling. Because of the particular history out of which it arises and the enormities of suffering and loss that it records, such writing tends initially to elicit extreme responses in readers. These are inevitable but cannot reasonably carry over into critical writing in any useful ways. My own hope has been to address the literature seriously and also intimately but without exhibiting any affective response other than that which belongs to attentive listening and sympathetic understanding. To what degree I may have succeeded in being both engaged and controlled in my readings, I do not know, but my aims have been to avoid as much as possible overdramatizing the literature by writing about it in rhetorical ways. It is inherently almost too strong and does not require any critical embellishments to accent its power. The ideal critical perspective would be close to the one described here by George Steiner:

> These books and the documents that have survived are not for "review." Not unless "review" signifies, as perhaps it should in these instances, a "seeing-again," over and over. As in some Borges fable, the only completely decent "review" of the *Warsaw Diary* or of Elie Wiesel's *Night* would be to re-copy the book, line by line, pausing at the names of the dead and the names of the children as the orthodox scribe pauses, when recopying the Bible, at the hallowed name of God. Until we know many of the words by *heart* (knowledge deeper than mind) and can repeat a few at the break of morning to remind ourselves that we live *after*. . . . [8]

Steiner's emphases, born as they are out of the highest kind of respect, seem to me unassailable, but they are almost impossible to sustain in an extended study of the literature. The discrepancy between honoring his ideal and fulfilling it in practice is a real one and poses critical problems that are not easy to solve.

It is likewise not easy to know how to meet those problems that relate to "audience." While some of the books and authors that I review in this study have become reasonably well known by now, others have gained only a small readership thus far, and some will be altogether new. That fact presents difficulties that are especially vexing. The author of any new book on Milton or Goethe, for instance, knows that he is writing by and large for specialists and makes his scholarly and critical assumptions accordingly. A book on the literature of the Holocaust, however, cannot make its primary address to other "scholars in the field," for at this point in Holocaust studies scholarship is very much still in its initial stages. Until the primary literature is more widely assimilated, much of the more detailed work that belongs to a secondary literature necessarily will give way to a criticism of broader definition. Some of the tasks I have set myself in the present study call for a finely tuned analysis; others require attention of a less intricate kind. As a result, one or two of the chapters that follow are of a frankly introductory nature, while the rest aim to pursue exposition and analysis of a closer and more refined sort. I can only hope that these variations in critical address will appear to readers less as discrepancies in method than as inherently proper and helpful for the particular body of literature under review.

Just which writers contribute most to making Holocaust literature what it is, and hence just which writers should be given prominence in such a study as this one, are matters still to be agreed upon. Needless to say, at this stage there is no "canon." Doubtless, my singling out of particular authors will please some readers and disappoint others, but such is inevitably the case whenever a large and diverse literature is studied selectively. The factors that have influenced my selections are not difficult to name, for beyond the more subjective matters of taste and judgment they reduce to two: linguistic competence and conceptual understanding. I have not included here such writers as Günter Grass, Jean-Paul Sartre, or Alexander Solzhenitsyn, for, while it is true that each of these writers has written importantly about war, I do not find that they have done so specifically and overwhelmingly under the impact of "the War against the Jews." As I will argue frequently in the following chapters, it is not warfare-in-general or even World War II in particular that is of primary concern to the writers of the Holocaust but Hitler's *Endlösung,* and that considered less as "theme" than grasped as a major turning point in history and the history of consciousness. Those writers that I do examine strike me as registering this history and reflecting its particular turn of awareness in some basic way; writers such as those three just named and others like them, for all their attractiveness or importance, occupy another sphere of literature and do not properly fall within the scope of this study. There are writers who do but who are absent from these pages. I regret in particular not including more of the Israeli poets and fiction writers of the Holocaust, who, it is hoped, will soon be made better known to American readers by other scholars. From the little one can glimpse of some of these writers through translation, they deserve a much wider readership than they have received thus far.

Otherwise, I will stand by my selections, considering them the best examples I have been able to find for the questions I am intent on raising. These center, as will soon become evident, in problems of language, and more particularly in what is felt almost universally to be a crisis of language after the Holocaust. Given the silencing power of that event, how can language faithfully record history? Credibly describe the trials of living and dying under an extreme and dehumanizing terror? Express the presence or absence of God? Finally, and as the result of all the foregoing, how does it express its own diminishment and near demise? Other issues will loom larger to historians or psychologists of the Holocaust, but to literary scholars these begin to seem the most compelling and the most needful of study.

"At the origin, there is language," as Edmond Jabès reminds us.[9] But what about at the end point: is language still *there*? After the Holocaust, that is a question that cannot be avoided, and I return to it time and again in this study.

CHAPTER I

The Problematics of Holocaust Literature

The most important literature of our day may well be that, from Kafka to Elie Wiesel, which predicts, records, interprets, or evaluates the experiences of those who foresaw or witnessed the Holocaust. Nothing, for instance, in the much publicized autobiographical writings of Anaïs Nin or in the *Journal* of André Gide can ever be, for future generations, of a moral or literary value that might compare with that of the diaries of Ithel witnesses of the agony of the Polish ghettos. . . . But our major literary critics, on the whole, have so far avoided facing this problem.

—EDOUARD RODITI

Just what is Holocaust literature? By that I mean a literature that is more than topical, as, say, a literature of the sea or a literature of warfare might be considered merely topical. For if by Holocaust literature all we have in mind is a large but loosely arranged collection of novels, poems, essays, and plays about a *subject,* even one so enormous and unnerving as the Nazi genocide against the Jews, then our concerns, while interesting and legitimate enough, are not truly compelling. Topical studies of all kinds—of the family, of slavery, of the environment, of World War I or World War II—abound today, and while they can be individually engaging, their value does not and cannot transcend the limitations inherent in their definitions *as* topical literatures.

By contrast—and the contrast must be conceived of as being one of the first degree—Holocaust literature occupies another sphere of study, one that is not only topical in interest but that extends so far as to force us to contemplate what may be fundamental changes in our modes of perception and expression, our altered way of being-in-the-world. Just as we designate and give validity to such concepts as "the Renaissance Mind" and "Romantic Sensibility" and "the Victorian Temper" to indicate earlier shifts in awareness and expression, so, too, should we begin to see that Holocaust literature is an attempt to express a new order of consciousness, a recognizable shift in being. The human imagination after Auschwitz is simply not the same as it was before. Put another way, the addition to our vocabulary of the very word Auschwitz means that today we *know* things that before could not even be imagined. Stunned by the awesomeness and pressure of event, the imagination comes to one of its periodic endings; undoubtedly, it also stands at the threshold of new and more difficult beginnings. Holocaust literature, situated at this point of threshold, is a chronicle of the human spirit's most turbulent strivings with an immense historical and metaphysical weight.

I use the term "human spirit" quite deliberately here, acknowledging in full the awkwardness and imprecision inherent in the term, because I cannot but conceive of Holocaust literature, when taken in its most encompassing definition, except as an attempt to retrieve some ongoing life—posit a future tense—for whatever it is of human definition that remains to us. The bodies—that is to say, the people—are gone and cannot be rescued back to life; neither can meaning in the old sense, nor absolute faith, nor old-fashioned humanism, nor even the senses intact. Yet writing itself, as we know from such a strongly determined work as Chaim Kaplan's diary, succeeded as an effective counterforce to nihilism, not so much an answer to death as an answer to barbarism, a last-ditch means of approximating and preserving the human in the face of a viciousness poised to destroy it. As a result, the vicious and the barbarous could win only partial victories, destroy the living but not altogether submerge life. What remains is less than what perished but more than that which wanted to conquer and prevail. We do have the books while the night has nothing but itself.

Given these considerations, what can we say about the attitude that denies the validity or even the possibility of a literature of the Holocaust? In one of its earliest and by now most famous formulations, that of the eminent critic T. W. Adorno, this position states that it is not only impossible but perhaps even immoral to attempt to write about the Holocaust.[1] Adorno had poetry specifically in mind, moreover, perhaps just a single poem, the "Todesfuge" of Paul Celan, which struck him as being incongruously, and perhaps even obscenely,

lyrical. As it happens, this poem is one of the great documents of
Holocaust literature, but to Adorno it was hopelessly out of touch with
its subject, as, he surmised, all such literature seemed destined to be.
That judgment is echoed by the German critic Reinhard Baumgart,
who objects to Holocaust literature on the grounds that it imposes artificial meaning on mass suffering, and, "by removing some of the horror, commits a grave injustice against the victims."[2] The point has also
been reaffirmed in a recent pronouncement of denunciation by Michael
Wyschogrod: "I firmly believe that art is not appropriate to the
holocaust. Art takes the sting out of suffering. . . . It is therefore forbidden to make fiction of the holocaust. . . . Any attempt to transform
the holocaust into art demeans the holocaust and must result in poor
art."[3]

Those who would know and could best judge the truth of this
assertion—the artists themselves—have, on occasion, spoken similarly,
even if out of a different ground and for different reasons. Thus Elie
Wiesel, whose writings perhaps more than any other's attest to the
continuing possibility of Holocaust literature, has newly and pointedly
spoken of its utter impossibility:

> One generation later, it can still be said and must now be affirmed:
> There is no such thing as a literature of the Holocaust, nor can there be.
> The very expression is a contradiction in terms. Auschwitz negates any
> form of literature, as it defies all systems, all doctrines. . . . A novel
> about Auschwitz is not a novel, or else it is not about Auschwitz. The
> very attempt to write such a novel is blasphemy. . . . [4]

The fact that such a view is put before us by an Elie Wiesel—and only
that fact—renders it understandable and respectable, even if not acceptable. We know, for more than a dozen books by Elie Wiesel alone have
now told us, that the Holocaust demands speech even as it threatens to
impose silence. But to let silence prevail would be tantamount to grant-
ing Hitler one more posthumous victory. If it is a blasphemy, then, to
attempt to write about the Holocaust, and an injustice against the victims, how much greater the injustice and more terrible the blasphemy
to remain silent.

What really is involved here is the deep anguish and immense frustration of the writer who confronts a subject that belittles and threatens
to overwhelm the resources of his language. The writer's position is, in
this respect, analogous to that of the man of faith, who is likewise beset

by frustration and anguish and, in just those moments when his spirit may yearn for the fullness of Presence, is forced to acknowledge the emptiness and silence of an imposed Absence. The life centers of the self—intelligence, imagination, assertiveness—undergo paralysis in such moments, which, if prolonged, have the effect of a total detachment or the profoundest despair. Yet to indulge in silence is to court madness or death. At just those points where, through some abiding and still operative reflex of language, silence converts once more into words—even into words about silence—Holocaust literature is born. Its birth must be seen as a miracle of some sort, not only an overcoming of mute despair but an assertion and affirmation of faith.

Faith in what? In some cases, perhaps in nothing more than human tenacity, the sheer standing fast of life in the face of a brutal death; in other cases, faith in the will to reject a final and wicked obliteration; in still others, faith in the persistent and all but uncanny strength of character to search out and find new beginnings. Given these dimensions of its existence and power, Holocaust literature, with all its acknowledged difficulties and imperfections, can be seen as occupying not only a legitimate place in modern letters but a central place. Long after much else in contemporary literature is forgotten, future generations of readers will continue to answer—by their very presence *as* readers—the question that ends Chaim Kaplan's diary: "If my life ends—what will become of my diary?" (p. 400). It will stand to the ages—and not by itself alone but with other accounts of what happened to man in the ghettos and camps of Europe—as a testament of our times.

If it is possible to reply to the view that would deny the existence or validity of Holocaust literature, it is much harder to know how to read such literature confidently or to assess it adequately. The problems are many and, in some cases, hardly manageable at all. There is the question of knowing how to respond to and comprehend the kinds of material that come before us. The stress here must fall on "kinds" because it is almost certain that we confront the works of survivors in markedly different ways than we do the works of those who perished, just as we assume still another reading stance for writings about the Holocaust by those who were not there. Knowing what we do know—but what the authors themselves could not when they wrote—about the ultimate fates of Chaim Kaplan or Emmanuel Ringelblum or Moshe Flinker, we do not take up their books with the same expectations and read them with the same kinds of responses as we do, say, the books of Primo Levi or Alexander Donat or Elie Wiesel. The difference is not reducible solely to the dimension of tragic irony implicit in the writings of the first group but absent from those of the second; nor is it just that we read, react to, and interpret the dead with a greater deference or solemnity than the living, for within the context of Holocaust literature the living often carry a knowledge of death more terrible in its intimacy than that ever recorded in the writings of the victims. Who, in fact, are the real victims here, the dead or those cursed back into life again, guilt-ridden and condemned by a fate that would not take them?

Is it not the case that the most lacerating writings often belong to those who survived, not perished in, the Holocaust? The concern here is with the problem of survivorship and with trying to determine the reader's role in Holocaust literature, a role that seems more difficult and anguished when confronting the living than the dead. When, for instance, we read the diary of young Moshe Flinker or Ringelblum's notebooks, we inevitably "complete" the narrative by bringing to the text material that it itself does not contain; we do that almost by reflex, filling in and interpreting with knowledge gained through biographical or historical notes. That is a wrenching but still possible act for the sympathetic imagination to perform. Oddly enough, the fact that it is we who are asked to perform it, and not the authors themselves, makes reading them somewhat more bearable, somewhat more possible. When, however, the task of not only recording but also interpreting, judging, and ever again suffering through the agony falls to a living writer—as it clearly does in the works of Elie Wiesel—then we no longer are talking about acts of sympathetic imagination but something else, something that we do not have a name for and hardly know how to grasp. The nightmare, in a word, is never-ending, and repeats itself over and over again.

It is not for nothing that the Holocaust seems to expel certain writers from its provenance after a single book, that they are, from this standpoint, one-book authors. Did the curse of obsessive recurrence lift from them (consider, for example, the writing careers of André Schwarz-Bart or Jerzy Kosinski) or merely change its terms? If they have found their way to new fictional territory, what was the purchase price for their release? Why can Elie Wiesel or Katzetnik or Arnost Lustig not pay it? These are problems—among other things, readers' problems—that we do not understand and have hardly even begun to take note of.

Here is a simple test: read Anne Frank's diary—one of the best known but, as such things go, one of the "easiest" and most antiseptic works of Holocaust literature—and then read Ernst Schnabel's *Anne Frank: A Profile in Courage,*[5] which "completes" the work by supplying the details of the young girl's ending in Auschwitz and Bergen-Belsen. You will never again be able to rid your understanding of the original text of dimensions of terror, degradation, and despair that it itself does not contain. We need, but do not have, a suitable hermeneutics to explain that phenomenon and render it intelligible, just as we need, but do not have, a working theory of the miraculous to explain the mere existence of other texts. That certain books have come down to us at all is nothing short of astonishing, and we can never distance ourselves from an accompanying and transfiguring sense of awe as we encounter them. A manuscript written secretly and at the daily risk of life in the Warsaw ghetto; buried in milk tins or transmitted through the ghetto walls at the last moment; finally transmitted to us—such a manuscript begins to carry with it the aura of a holy text. Surely we do not take it in our hands and read it as we do those books that reach us through the normal channels of composition and publication. But how *do* we read it? At this point in the study of Holocaust literature, the question remains open-ended.

As the years pass and direct access to events becomes impossible, the question of what constitutes legitimacy within the contexts of Holocaust literature promises to become increasingly important. The complexity of this issue has recently been heightened by Emil Fackenheim's suggestion that eyewitness accounts of events may at times be less credible than studies made after the fact and by people at some distance from it. Although Fackenheim was incarcerated briefly at Sachsenhausen and thus was given firsthand knowledge of that camp, it was not until he read a study of Sachsenhausen years later, he admits, that he felt he truly understood what had taken place there and what he himself had experienced.[6]

The issue in this case is not analogous to the one that always obtains when a personal and perhaps emotionally colored account of experience is weighed against the cooler and more objective kinds of information gathered after the fact by the working historian. For, as Fackenheim came to understand only much later, a built-in feature of the Nazi camp system was "deception of the victims," rendering accounts of the eyewitness in many cases less than reliable. The fictitious element of camp life—its pervasive irreality—was calculated to confuse and disarm the rational faculties, making the camp prisoners more pliable to their masters and hence more vulnerable to the diabolical system in which they were entrapped.

What does Fackenheim's case suggest about the relationship between proximity and authority in writings about the Holocaust? Normally, we are willing to grant a greater validity to the accounts of those who were there, and, in some measure, to withhold it from—or grant it only reluctantly to—the writings of those who were not. Fackenheim's questions may bring us to revise these notions and to reevaluate our measures not only of historical truth but of imaginative penetration and narrative effect as well.

And what about the truth of endings—writers' endings? Because Paul Celan or Tadeusz Borowski terminated their lives as they did, is it not the case that we are almost forced into a reader's stance *vis-à-vis* their stories and poems that we otherwise would not have and indeed do not want? Was suicide in each case an inevitable outcome of their work, a final and desperate conclusion to it, ultimately even a bitter evaluation of it? Was the self-destructive act of the man only and not of the writer? That such questions raise themselves at all means that we read these writers under a shadow of some kind—a different kind, incidentally, than the one that now hangs over the work of Sylvia Plath or John Berryman. (While their suicides also mediate between us and their books, one senses no historical determinism behind the personal anguish that must have led them to take their lives; the pressure to which they succumbed seems to have been biographically generated, its pain not larger than that of the single life.)

Kafka said that we are usually too easy on ourselves as readers, that we should choose books that ask more of us than we normally are willing to give. "We must have those books," he wrote, "which come upon us like ill-fortune, and distress us deeply, like the death of one we love better than ourselves, like suicide. A book must be an ice-axe to break the sea frozen inside us."[7] To make that formulation, Kafka must have been a great reader, as well as a great hungerer (in his case the two are really one), and yet, despite all his intense suffering and estrangement, he was spared the worst that the twentieth century was to bring upon writers such as Celan and Borowski. Had Kafka known them, could he still have spoken in the terms just cited above? When, in a writer's life, suicide becomes not a metaphor for something but the thing itself, we grow more cautious and defensive as readers and do not so readily welcome the kinds of hard blows that Kafka exhorts upon us.

Better to read warily and keep the seas of empathy inside us safely frozen a while longer.

By now the point should be clear: we lack a phenomenology of reading Holocaust literature, a series of maps that will guide us on our way as we pick up and variously try to comprehend the writings of the victims, the survivors, the survivors-who-become-victims, and the kinds-of-survivors, those who were never there but know more than the outlines of the place. Until we devise such maps, our understanding of Holocaust literature will be only partial, well below that which belongs to full knowledge.

One conclusion to these questions is that we are yet to develop the kind of practical criticism that will allow us to read, interpret, and evaluate Holocaust literature with any precision or confidence.[8] Older criticisms of whatever orientation or variety—Freudian, Marxist, formalist, structuralist, or linguistic—will not do here for any number of reasons. The largest is that the conception of man, or world view, embodied in psychoanalysis or dialectical theory or theories of aesthetic autonomy had almost no place in the ghettos and camps, which were governed by forces of an altogether different and far less refined nature. As a result, it would seem a radical misapplication of method and intentions to search through literary accounts of Auschwitz or the Warsaw Ghetto for covert Oedipal symbols, class struggle, revealing patterns of imagery and symbolism, mythic analogies, or deep grammatical structures. Auschwitz no more readily reduces to these considerations than does death itself.

Nor will it do to confine understanding within a framework of literary history that would tend to see Holocaust literature as part of the literature of warfare-in-general or even of World War II. There are novels eligible for such study, including Irwin Shaw's *The Young Lions,* Norman Mailer's *The Naked and the Dead,* and Herman Wouk's *The Caine Mutiny.* The distinction between these works and the works we shall be addressing—a hard one that needs to be held firmly in mind—has an illuminating parallel within historical writings about the period. In a newly published popular history of the Second World War written by A. J. P. Taylor, for instance, I find a total of two pages out of two hundred and thirty-five devoted to the Holocaust, this despite the fact that the author concludes his four-paragraph summary by stating that "the memory of Oświęcim and the other murder camps will remain when all the other achievements of the Nazi Empire are forgotten."[9] Given that view—a correct one—it seems shocking at first that Taylor would mention the Holocaust only, as it were, in passing. And yet he is not entirely wrong to do so, for to do otherwise would be to see the war against the Jews as an integral part of World War II. More and more it seems that it was not, neither in intention, nor in kind, nor in outcome. The war against the Jews may have occupied some of the same dimensions of time and space as World War II, but it was not always fought as a logical part of that war, nor can the literature it generated be compared to or profitably studied with the topical literature of the Second World War. Holocaust literature is simply and complexly something else, as the cataclysm that triggered it was something else, and not part of the general storm that swept over Europe four decades ago.

In referring to such extreme cases we tend to use the language of weather, but the analogy with earthquakes and storms will finally not hold; nor will most other analogies. That precisely is part of the problem. It supports the view that we must make distinctions between the literature of the Holocaust and the literature of general warfare. This is not to belittle those books that belong to this other literature or to suggest that the Great Wars of our century did not pose their own problems for writers. Clearly they did. The First World War in particular came with an enormous jolt and hardly presented itself to the grasping intelligence in neatly formed and easily apprehensible ways. Hemingway wrote that among the casualties of that war were "the words sacred, glorious, and sacrifice and the expression in vain," that these were words he "could not stand to hear," and that "finally only the names of places had dignity." Hemingway's loss was huge, the collapse of a whole idealistic code that once sustained life by giving it a measure of purpose and honor. In reading his fiction of the Great War, it does not take much to realize that Hemingway was saying farewell to far more than arms.

To what, though, was the young Elie Wiesel saying farewell when, in an often quoted and by now famous passage from *Night,* he wrote that he will never forget the flames that turned the bodies of children "into wreaths of smoke beneath a silent blue sky," the flames that consumed his faith forever?[10] What was his loss when, in turning the pages of an album of Holocaust photographs, he made this monstrous discovery:

At every page, in front of every image, I stop to catch my breath. And I tell myself: This is the end, they have reached the last limit; what follows can only be less horrible; surely it is impossible to invent suffering more naked, cruelty more refined. Moments later I admit my error: I underestimated the assassin's ingenuity. The progression into the inhuman transcends the exploration of the human. Evil, more than good, suggests infinity.[11]

For that plunge to the bottom of a final knowledge, we simply have no analogy, except perhaps to _hell_—a possibility that we shall have occasion to pursue a little later. For now, though, I think we must accept as a given the proposition that the Holocaust was something new in the world, without likeness or kind, a truth that was set forth years ago in a forceful and memorable poem by Uri Zvi Greenberg:

> Are there other analogies to this, our disaster that
>   came to us at their hands?
> There are no other analogies (all words are shades of
>   shadow)—
> Therein lies the horrifying phrase: No other analogies!
> For every cruel torture that man may yet do to man in
>   a Gentile country—
> He who comes to compare will state: He was tortured
>   like a Jew.
> Every fright, every terror, every loneliness, every
>   chagrin,
> Every murmuring, weeping in the world
> He who compares will say: This analogy is of the
>   Jewish kind.[12]

There have been attempts to find analogies—with Job, with the destruction of the Second Temple, with the *Akedah* (the binding of Isaac), with the concepts of *Kiddush ha-Shem* (martyrdom) or the Thirty-Six Righteous Men who uphold the world—and, to the extent that such allusions and antecedents have allowed certain writers at least a partial grasp of the tragedy, it would seem that we must qualify the notion that the Holocaust was altogether without parallels. On closer examination, however, it emerges in almost all cases that the gains in perspective are only temporary and provisional, for what inevitably emerges in Holocaust literature is that such analogies are introduced only to reveal their inadequacy, and they are in turn either refuted or rejected as being unworkable. Schwarz-Bart, for instance, ultimately shows us the *exhaustion* of the tradition of the *Lamed Vov* rather than its continuing usefulness, just as Elie Wiesel will time and again adopt the stance of a Job only to find that it will not serve. In the end, he will have to stand alone, rooted in a solitary ground that became his in the moment when he was struck by the isolating knowledge that "the Holocaust defies reference, analogy."[13] It must have been this realization more than any other that led Wiesel to remark that "by its nature, the Holocaust defies literature."[14]

As Wiesel's case shows, the implications of a literature without analogy are frightening in the extreme, for our whole conception of literature insists on recognizing its antecedents and, as such, affirms that writing grows as much from within a tradition as from within an individual. That is, a poem or a novel is not a new and wholly undetermined thing—a sudden and unprecedented appearance in the world—but bears some necessary relationship to other poems and novels that have gone before and, in some sense, have sired it. While every good piece of writing must be, in its way, an original act of creation, all literature is formed as much from reactions to an antecedent literature as from more direct or unmediated reaction to life. A poem descends from other poems, a novel from other novels, a play from other plays. Whether we know it or not, we read and understand literature exactly in this way, with implicit reference to and analogy with prior texts. Indeed, we could not begin to read at all, nor could writers write, if that were not so. Our whole fund of literacy, in short, comes into play in reading.

Yet when we confront those texts that are our concern here, we sooner or later find ourselves without these expected and necessary moorings in a familiar literary landscape, and, as a result, it is sometimes hardly possible to know how to proceed. Lost in a place whose dimensions we cannot easily recognize, let alone acknowledge as our own, we strive for orientation through intimacy with the common and familiar things of the world, but grasp only fog. The object in our hands looks like a book but seems to have turned into something else.

Some contrasting examples from past literature can be instructive here. Even a casual reader of Edgar Allan Poe or Franz Kafka, for instance, knows that a literature of terror and radical estrangement is not exclusively a product of the post–World War II decades. Read Poe's "The Pit and the Pendulum" or Kafka's "In the Penal Colony" and you will have all the terror you might want. Poe, in particular, relished macabre sensations and "the exquisite terror of the soul," and was gifted at finding precise literary correlatives for them. That is why still to this day the best of his stories possess the power to "thrill" and "haunt" us with simulations of extreme psychic torment. It was his subject, and he went about developing it with all the props and atmospherics of the Gothic romance or early symbolist fiction—a whole catalogue of literary horrors that will please and stimulate the imagination with fright. Yet at no time in reading Poe do we ever come to believe that the fantasy world we are invited to enter—his "dream kingdom"—is the "real" world, the phenomenal world of our day-to-day existence. We know that Poe is inventing, that at his best he is a gifted inventor, that his literary inventions possess a stark psychological power and can grip us, at times, mightily. In short, we pretty well know how to read him.

Kafka is a deeper and more complicated writer, one who is still far enough ahead of us to render his works less accessible to full and confident understanding. In his case, we may recognize affinities with an antecedent literature of the grotesque or absurd, but to read him in these terms does not carry us very far, just as it will not finally do to reduce his more enigmatic parables and stories to the critical categories of symbolism or expressionism or surrealism. While Kafka seems to embody elements of all of these, he simultaneously transcends them, so that in the end he is only what we have come to call, inadequately and at the risk of tautology, "Kafkaesque." Let us admit that we have not yet entirely caught up with him and, as a result, he is a far more dangerous writer for us than Poe.

Nevertheless, even in Kafka's case—as, say, in "In the Penal Colony" or "The Metamorphosis"—we are never led to abandon altogether our hold on a normative, stabilizing sense of things, on the saving power of the mundane. We may be released by his fiction into a universe of absurd and frightening proportions, but it is a highly composed universe, and while few would welcome a prolonged residence there, it is not a totally alien place. Kafka possessed the power, in fact, to domesticate us rather easily to his strange but familiar world, and we can cross back and forth between it and what we perhaps too comfortably call "reality" without paying an ultimate price in credulity. In its depictions of a mechanized or technological terror, of a reigning injustice, of brutal and systematic and causeless punishment, of an accepted guilt and passivity before annihilation, "In the Penal Colony" is an uncanny prefiguration of Holocaust literature, a premonitory text. Nevertheless, in reading it we are still a step or two away from a direct knowledge of *history* as Holocaust, and no reader of the novella would confuse the infernal torture machine that is its elaborate centerpiece with the actual machinery of Auschwitz or Treblinka, just as no reader of "The Metamorphosis" would accept Gregor Samsa's transformation into a giant insect as a change that could ever actually overtake him. We accept these intricate literary devices as complex acts of initiation—a series of bridges that we must cross to enter the Kafkaesque world— and once we acknowledge them as such, we are usually content to let the stories take over and develop in their own terms. Since we do not read Kafka within predominantly realistic or naturalistic frameworks, credulity is not unduly strained by these inventions, which we recognize as the components of a profoundly disturbing but nevertheless fictional universe.

What happens, though, when we enter *l'univers concentrationnaire* and come upon the kind of metamorphosis cited earlier, one in which living children are suddenly transformed into wreaths of smoke? What is our interpretive frame of reference for that? One finds nothing like it in Poe or Kafka or any other writer I know, including the Marquis de Sade. Since it is altogether too disorienting to acknowledge such writing as a piece of realism, one perhaps tries initially to shift the terms into the language of dreams—of some inverted symbolism or dark allegory. Yet these are evasive gestures, strategies of defense, and ultimately they must be abandoned in order to perform a reluctant and all but impossible act—reading—which in this case means acknowledging a truth that we do not want to be true. How, after all, can we accept a realism more extreme than any surrealism yet invented? It is one thing to grant Kafka the artistic liberty he needs to write "The Metamorphosis," changing a man into a bug, but it is something else again entirely—and altogether too much for rational belief—when Elie Wiesel writes of children being metamorphosed into smoke. Yet that is what is presented to us in *Night,* presented moreover in such a way as to permit us to read it on one level only—the literal one—the level of plainly declared, unencumbered truth. This, we are told, is what happened. It has no symbolic dimensions, carries no allegorical weight, possesses no apparent or covert meaning. Do not think about it in terms of Ovid or Poe or Kafka, for the mythical or metaphorical aspects of their writings do not come into play here; nor does anything else you have ever read before. Know only one thing—the truth of what happened—which sounds like this: "Not far from us, flames were leaping up from a ditch, gigantic flames. They were burning something. A lorry drew up at the pit and delivered—little children. Babies!

Yes, I saw it—saw it with my own eyes . . . those children in the flames."[15]

Has there ever before been a literature more dispiriting and forlorn, more scandalous than this? Who would not erase it at once from memory? Yet we must stay with these words, or with others like them, in an effort to determine one of the distinguishing characteristics of Holocaust literature.

In order to do that, I turn briefly from prose to poetry and present two short poems. The first was written in the nineteenth century by Henry David Thoreau; the second, written closer to our own day, is by the Yiddish poet Jacob Glatstein. The poems both carry the same title: "Smoke." Here is Thoreau's:

> Light-winged Smoke, Icarian bird,
> Melting thy pinions in thy upward flight,
> Lark without song, and messenger of dawn,
> Circling above the hamlets as thy nest;
> Or else, departing dream, and shadowy form
> Of midnight vision, gathering up thy skirts;
> By night star-veiling, and by day
> Darkening the light and blotting out the sun;
> Go thou my incense upward from this hearth,
> And ask the gods to pardon this clear flame.

Among the first observations one makes about this poem is that, in writing it, Thoreau had little interest in smoke as smoke but rather was attracted to it as the base for his transfiguring imagination, which loved to dissolve phenomena into fanciful patterns of thought. The poem, that is to say, employs its central figure in a clearly metaphorical sense, likening the smoke to other things—to birds, to the mythical Icarus, to dreams and clouds, finally to incense. Through this series of delicate imagistic changes, the poem develops the author's sense of the fugitive and transient quality of life. It is a finely wrought if uncomplicated poem, one that holds closely to classical patterns of poetic rhetoric, and therefore presents no particular problems to interpretation.

Compare it to Glatstein's "Smoke" ("Roikh" in the original Yiddish), given below in an English translation:

> From the crematory flue
> A Jew aspires to the Holy One.
> And when the smoke of him is gone,
> His wife and children filter through.

Above us, in the height of sky,
Saintly billows weep and wait.
God, wherever you may be,
There all of us are also not.[16]

This, too, is a fine poem, but what is it saying? In the opening lines
it describes a Jew ascending to his God through a chimney, followed
soon after by his wife and children passing upward in the same way.
The poem says that they do so by turning into smoke; moreover, it
says so with a certain jauntiness of rhythm—the hippety-hop of nurs-
ery school jingles—and the playfulness of rhyme. Is it a children's
poem of some kind? It is not inconceivable that a reader who chances
upon this poem a hundred years from now might ask such questions,
for there are elements here that call them forth. They do so, however,
only to disabuse us rather quickly of our innocence, for before very
long we would see that the sprightliness of rhythm and rhyme serves as
a trap, the apparent lightheartedness only a lure to draw us forward into
the poem's deadly center.

In searching to locate this center, we are soon brought to see that
the entire poem is predicated upon the author's certain knowledge that
we will recognize and be able to name the crime that resides behind or
before words, in the silence that the poem was written to break. The
unspoken but unmistakable ground of this poem, that is to say, is the
Holocaust.

Now we have just looked at a poem about smoke and recognized
that it served as a source of considerable metaphorical richness and
variety. Thoreau changed the smoke into birds and clouds and religious
incense, into a whole flock of wafting and melting and dissolving images. Glatstein, far from doing that, does the opposite: he changes the
Jew into smoke. Worse yet—and at this point the poem turns into
something else, something new in the history of poetry—he does so in
a way that has nothing at all to do with metaphor, a disabling fact that
he forces upon us from the start. To read this poem at all, we must
disown the figurative use of language, then, and interpret literally: the
Jew has become smoke and a similar fate will overtake his wife and
children. Thereafter Glatstein will add a religious dimension to his
poem, at which point we recognize play of another kind, that of Jewish
speculative theology. The poem ends, in fact, on a note of theological
paradox: the destroyed Jews will become absent company for an Absent
God. Their "aspiration," or ascent, however, must not be understood

in the first place in terms of paradox or fantasy or anything else that would detract from the brutal literalness of their end. For an exact parallel to their fate, recall that casual but unforgettable moment in Hochhuth's *The Deputy* when the Doctor remarks, quite matter-of-factly, that "On Tuesday, I piped the sister of Sigmund Freud up the chimney."[17]

It is all too strange but, at the same time, it is powerfully affecting. The poem, as we come to realize, is an assertion about a negation, a double negation: that of man and that of God. Both in this poem *are not*. Is there also a triple negation implied, the third loss being that of poetry itself? For what kind of poetry can we have that eschews the metaphorical use of language? The answer to this question compels us to recognize one of the deepest and most distinguishing characteristics of Holocaust literature and to state what may be one of its abiding laws: there are no metaphors for Auschwitz, just as Auschwitz is not a metaphor for anything else. Why is that the case? Because the flames were real flames, the ashes only ashes, the smoke always and only smoke. If one wants "meaning" out of that, it can only be this: at Auschwitz humanity incinerated its own heart.[18] Otherwise the burnings do not lend themselves to metaphor, simile, or symbol—to likeness or association with anything else. They can only "be" or "mean" what they in fact were: the death of the Jews.

The only knowledge we are left with, then, is this: in our own day, annihilation overleapt the bounds of metaphor and was enacted on earth. Is it possible to make poetry out of that? Insofar as it is a poem that has led us to the question, the answer, clearly, must be yes. Poetry—in this instance, a something about nothing, an assertion about a negation—survives to remind us of all that has been destroyed. And also to remind us of what has not been destroyed, for while it is true that Holocaust literature is nothing if not language in a condition of severe diminishment and decline, it is still capable of articulating powerful truths—if none other, then those that reflect life in its diminishment and decline. We have lost so much, but not yet the power to register what it is that has been taken from us.

Surely that is one of the major functions of Holocaust literature, to register and record the enormity of human loss. "For me," as Elie Wiesel once stated it, "writing is a *matzeva*, an invisible tombstone, erected to the memory of the dead unburied."[19] There is no denying the nobility of that conception of art or the importance of its execution. Yet a tombstone is at best only a minor literary genre, and part of the problem for Wiesel as a writer, as for all writers of the Holocaust, is to discover the literary forms most appropriate to representing the extremities of dehumanization and heroism that together begin to define what the Holocaust was.

In this connection, we must begin by recognizing that even before the advent of a literature of the Holocaust, the major literary genres were in a weakened state of flux and great uncertainty. Holocaust literature, which places its own heavy burdens on literary forms of all kinds, arrived, in fact, at a time when considerable doubt was already being raised about the ongoing viability of the narrative, dramatic, and lyrical modes. While it is not possible here to rehearse the troubled state of modern fiction, drama, and poetry, it can be stated that a large part of the trouble derives from an increasingly felt imbalance between what the world daily offers us as raw data and the mind's ability to make sense of it through its own conceptual and inventive capacities. In the ghettos and camps of Europe "reality" underwent so radical a distortion as to disarm and render no longer trustworthy the normal cognitive and expressive powers. As a result, reason seemed to give way to madness, as language did time and again to silence. When those thresholds dissolve, literature—a product of the composed mind and senses—is reduced to screams and whimpers: it decomposes. And there is no escaping the fact that, in part, Holocaust literature is a literature of decomposition. "No, this is not life!" runs the familiar refrain in Chaim Kaplan's diary. Although Kaplan had lived in Warsaw for forty years and must have come to know it well, its transformation under Nazi rule into a city of madness and slaughter disoriented him almost totally. "At times," he writes, "it seems to me that I am in an alien land, entirely unknown to me." At other times his sense of displacement exceeds anything even resembling the terrestrial, so that it appears "the ghetto was suspended over nothingness" (pp. 27, 34, 377).

That strain of irreality runs throughout Holocaust literature and continually undermines it. "Today at this very moment as I sit writing at a table, I am not convinced that these things really happened."[20] The confession in this instance is Primo Levi's, but it speaks a common truth, one known to all writers of the Holocaust and one as well that quite obviously subverts the writer's enterprise. For what literary means—what mere words—could possibly compete with the extravagant inventiveness of Nazism? In that time when day was ruled over by the twisted sun of the swastika and night by the dominant black of the Death's Head, life itself became a kind of macabre theatre. Nazism was far more than that, of course, was nothing less than an unrestrained plague of steel and flame, but it also worked in more subtle ways, preparing its ultimate terror by intermediary steps of manipulative distortion and deception. In this respect it might legitimately be grasped within the terms of literary fabrication, terms that a Joseph Goebbels or a Leni Riefenstahl were intimate with. Moreover, it is not difficult to locate the imaginative sources of this aspect of its genius. George Steiner pointed to them quite specifically and also quite accurately, I think, when he argued that Nazism was a literal staging of hell on earth, a perception confirmed by virtually all writers of Holocaust literature.[21] Hell as a prototype of the ghettos and death camps—that, it seems, was Christianity's distinctive contribution to the Final Solution, although one would hope to understand it as a Christianity turned against itself, in rebellion against itself and its own deepest principles.

In this paradigm of ethical and religious subversion, we may be able to discover a literary paradigm as well, one that is constant enough in Holocaust literature to constitute another of its governing laws. To grasp it, we must understand the revisionary and essentially antithetical nature of so much of Holocaust writing, which not only mimics and parodies but finally refutes and rejects its direct literary antecedents. The *Bildungsroman*, as Lawrence Langer has demonstrated, is one of these.[22] In such a book as *Night,* the traditional pattern of successfully initiating a young boy into social life and his own maturity is altogether reversed. Primo Levi's *Survival In Auschwitz,* which chronicles the devolution of a man, is a more complicated instance of the same thing. In both cases one sees not only the reversal of a familiar literary pattern but also a repudiation of the philosophical basis on which it rests. We recall Wiesel's pronouncement of the death of the idea of man. With the crumbling of that idea, all narrative forms that posit the reality of persons—rational, educable, morally responsible beings—are undermined and perhaps even invalidated. Yet such personal narratives of the Holocaust as the two just mentioned necessarily depend upon the traditional means of memoir, autobiography, and *Bildungsroman,* even though the stories they relate rewind the progress of growth backwards—from life toward death. I do not know that Wiesel and Levi consciously chose to counterpoint their terrifying accounts of dehumanization against forms that are essentially civilized and humane, but the effects of such a jarring contrast are unmistakable and strongly felt in their books.

In the case of Paul Celan, it is clear that an attitude of repudiation was specifically developed as a technique for writing post-Holocaust poetry. The evidence, as Jerry Glenn has shown,[23] is everywhere—in the ironically destructive allusions to the Song of Songs and Goethe's Faust in "Todesfuge"; in the radical undoing of Hölderlin's famous hymn "Patmos" in "Tenebrae"; in denial of the Genesis account of God's creation of man in "Psalm." In each of these cases (and many similar to them could be brought forward), Celan employs a technique of literary subversion that the German critic Gödtz Wienold has called a *"Widerruf."*[24] We have no precise English equivalent for the term— "repudiation" comes closest—but it is not difficult to explain.

Consider, for instance, this line from Chaim Kaplan's diary: "The enemy of Israel neither sleeps nor slumbers" (p. 208). Kaplan wrote that, almost certainly, not out of a mood of blasphemy but as an expression of genuine religious despair. It appears in his pages in an entry dated "October 12, 1940/End of Yom Kippur, 5701." On that very day the edict to establish the ghetto went into effect. The year before, at the end of Yom Kippur, 5700, Kaplan noted in his diary that "on the Day of Atonement the enemy displayed even greater might than usual," employing its artillery to destroy and kill at random. In the intervening year the bombardments got only worse, and it became clear to Kaplan that Warsaw Jewry was to face complete destruction. "Is this the way the Almighty looks after His dear ones?" he asks. "Has Israel no God?" He could not admit that, so on Yom Kippur, 5701, he gathered with his fellow Jews, "like Marranos in the fifteenth century," to pray secretly and illegally for God's forgiveness and mercy. What Jewish Warsaw received, however, was not the protection of the Guardian of Israel but the ghetto edict, which then and there effectively sealed the fate of hundreds of thousands of Polish Jews. Kaplan's profound shock at this reversal registers in that terrible line—"The enemy of Israel neither sleeps nor slumbers"—a radical rewriting of Psalm 121:4 that shows, in only a few words, a whole sustaining faith come crashing down. The entry for "October 24, 1949/The night of Simhat Torah, 5701" brings the matter to its bitter conclusion: "But he who sits in Heaven laughs."[25]

In Kaplan's case, it would make no sense to identify such expressions of forlornness and raw pain as examples of conscious "technique," if by that we imply a sustained literary method. Kaplan, a highly literate Jew, composed his diary in Hebrew and quite naturally thought in a language pervaded by Biblical and Talmudic passages. These influences never drop from his prose, but as he witnessed the level of Nazi barbarism rise in the ghetto, they undergo inversion, substitution, and reversals. In brief, they are destabilized, demoralized, subverted. Writing under this kind of pressure becomes counter-commentary.

The Yiddish poet Jacob Glatstein, like Celan, adopted these changes deliberately and developed them technically in his poems. I suspect that André Schwarz-Bart worked somewhat similarly in writing *The Last of the Just,* a novel that should be understood as an exhaustion not only of the Jewish tradition of the *Lamed-Vov* but of the Christian traditions of the saint's life and the *imitatio Christi* as well. In *The Painted Bird* Jerzy Kosinski will appropriate some of the language of the New Testament and Christian liturgy only to undermine it and invalidate its claims to permanent religious truth. Rolf Hochhuth will do the same in his highly charged and controversial play, which, among other things, offers itself as a contemporary rewriting of the lives of the Popes.

The common element in all these examples is the employment of the literary text as refutation and repudiation, a denial not only of an antecedent literary assertion but also of its implicit premises and explicit affirmations. In the main, Holocaust literature relies for its expression on the received languages and the established literary forms. It does so, however, in the profoundly revisionary way that we have been noticing, turning earlier literary models against themselves and, in the process, overturning the reigning conceptions of man and his world that speak in and through the major writings of our literary traditions. Levi, cognizant of these reversals and denials, suggests where they might lead us when he asks, "Our stories, . . . all different and all full of a tragic, disturbing necessity, . . . are they not themselves stories of a new Bible?" (p. 59). If we agree that they are, then Holocaust literature is at its heart of hearts revelatory in some new way, although of what we do not yet know.

There is something preposterous and even obscene about the notion of gross evil being inspiring, yet more than anything else, it is this crime, simultaneously searing and illuminating, that has inflicted the writer's vocation on the novelists and poets of the Holocaust. That it is an infliction is no longer open to doubt, for all survivors of this catas-

trophe who venture to write about it confess a disfiguration or impairment of one kind or another—a lapse in vision, a muteness of voice,
other vaguer disturbances of the sensorium. Think of how badly mutilated Ernie Levy is, how some of Celan's poems break down into
stammering, how pervasive the fear of blinding is in Kosinski's writings, how often Elie Wiesel's survivors seem to be struck dumb. For a
summarizing example, think most of all of that frightening line in one
of Nelly Sachs's late poems—the most costly *ars poetica* I know—"This
can be put on paper only / with one eyed ripped out."[26] No one touched
by the Holocaust is ever whole again—that much this literature makes
clear.

Yet that is not the whole truth, for while crime is impairing, it is
also powerfully vivifying, exposing the world as never before in all of
its most frightful detail. It is as if the fires that consumed so many also
carried with them a kind of wicked illumination. Yitzhak Katznelson's
description of his own pain, pairing as it does infirmity and insight, is
paradigmatic: "These last four years I have been shocked and confused
at what is being perpetrated so brazenly before the whole world. For
nearly a year now, I feel like one broken both in body and mind. . . .
My emotions are benumbed. . . . There are, however, terrible moments when I am acutely alert, when shafts of light pierce and hurt me
like sharp needles."[27] The Holocaust has worked on its authors in a
double way, then, simultaneously disabling them and enlarging their
vision, so that they see with an almost prophetic exactness. Holocaust
writers, in short, are one-eyed seers, men possessed of a double knowledge: cursed into knowing how perverse the human being can be to
create such barbarism and blessed by knowing how strong he can be to
survive it.

Saul Bellow expands upon this phenomenon in fine detail in his
characterization of Artur Sammler, who is, I believe, a prototype of the
Holocaust writer. A widower who lost his wife to the Nazis, Sammler
himself survives Hitler by escaping from a mass grave and then hiding
out in the forests, cellars, and cemeteries of Poland. Struck in the eye by
a German gun butt, he suffers a visual obstruction, but at the same time
the very nature of his experience has enlarged his sight, vivifying all
things and allowing him to make the subtlest kinds of distinctions
among them. His vocation, in other words, is that of a seer, a man of
unusual perception whose observations carry the ring of authority.

But, given the damage done to Mr. Sammler's sight, does he qualify as a trustworthy seer? From where or what does he derive his authority? He will raise this question himself more than once: "Of course since Poland, nineteen thirty-nine, my judgments are different. Altered. Like my eyesight."[28] To one of his interlocutors Sammler even apologizes for his "deformity," acknowledging that the abnormality of his experience during the war years brings him sometimes to suspect his own judgments: "My lot has been extreme. . . . One cannot come out intact" (p. 230).

Nevertheless, when it comes to determining "the true stature of a human being" (p. 232), Artur Sammler's point of view is fully informed and his vision the most delicate of recording systems. That is the case because after his experiences, he is able to look at life as one who has been inside death. His survival removed from him all distortions imposed by the fear of death and, in this sense, granted him not so much an exceptional vision but the only one that can properly see and assess life in the post-Holocaust period.

Such vision, as one soon comes to recognize in reading the Holocaust writers, has been purchased at an unusually high price. Physical injury, visual impairment, linguistic incapacity, the moral discouragements of listener lassitude and reader reluctance—what kind of literature can develop against such extreme countervailing forces? The answer is, a literature of fragments, of partial and provisional forms, no one of which by itself can suffice to express the Holocaust, but the totality of which begins to accumulate and register a coherent and powerful effect. On this one point all writers agree: the most that can ever be said individually will be nothing more than a beginning, a small opening into a large and barely imaginable truth. Historical research can begin to identify and gather some of the pieces, but literary forms that aim to be more encompassing and synthesizing inevitably come up against their limitations and fail, as they must, whenever inclusiveness or comprehensiveness is wanted. We have had no Milton or Tolstoy of the Holocaust and should not soon await one; in fact, it is wiser to discourage expectation of a literature of epic scope and look instead to its opposite, to the shards and fragments that reveal, in their separateness and brokenness, the uncountable small tragedies that together add up to something larger than the tragic sense implies.

If every broken head is a fragment of divinity, as one of the poets we shall be looking at later declares, then the most we can do as readers intent on glimpsing something close to wholeness is to assemble some of the shattered pieces. To make such an admission is not to deny the validity of a more holistic approach to knowledge or to discourage historical or critical efforts at integration, but rather to underline the importance of reading Holocaust writings as part of a composite literature, more impressive in the sum of its parts than as separate statements. The corporate impact far surpasses at this stage what any individual work can do.

If this view of Holocaust literature is correct, then one should read it with an ear attuned to its collective voices rather than to more isolated instances of expressive genius. To be sure, each of the writers we shall be concerned with may have written out his story or that of others in ways that are in some manner singular and distinct. Nevertheless, while amidst the general horror we are able to recognize individuated styles and concerns, for the most part we respond to them and learn from them as representative voices of a collective fate. The specific details of living and dying can never be lost or overlooked, but within the common features of this literature they do not easily overleap the boundaries of shared experience that a common history defines. As we shall see in the next chapter, this is especially true for the documentary literature, so much of which reaches us in diaries, journals, and memoirs that seem to be more the consecutive and often repetitive chapters of an ongoing, multi-authored story than the discrete narratives of single personalities. The individual cry is always recognizable, but as it echoes across a continent it is the assemblage of pain and rebellion that impresses itself upon us more than anything else. To hear it otherwise is in this instance to hear falsely.

II. Between Language and Silence

CHAPTER 2

Holocaust and History

Did we blind you? You continue to watch us. . . .
Speechless, speechless, you testify against us.

—Janós Pilinszky

If the Greeks invented tragedy, the Romans the epistle, and the
Renaissance the sonnet, our generation invented a new literature, that
of testimony.

—Elie Wiesel

In Maidanek, the extermination camp where he was to perish, the eminent Warsaw historian Dr. Ignacy Schipper spoke the following words to Alexander Donat. They point to a dilemma in Holocaust literature that we have never been able to resolve:

> . . . everything depends on who transmits our testament to future generations, on who writes the history of this period. History is usually written by the victor. What we know about murdered peoples is only what their murderers vaingloriously cared to say about them. Should our murderers be victorious, should *they* write the history of this war, our destruction will be presented as one of the most beautiful pages of world history, and future generations will pay tribute to them as dauntless crusaders. Their every word will be taken for gospel. Or they may wipe out our memory altogether, as if we had never existed, as if there had never been a Polish Jewry, a Ghetto in Warsaw, a Maidanek. Not even a dog will howl for us.
> But if *we* write the history of this period of blood and tears—and I firmly believe we will—who will believe us? Nobody will *want* to be-

lieve us, because our disaster is the disaster of the entire civilized world.
. . . We'll have the thankless job of proving to a reluctant world that we
are Abel, the murdered brother. . . . [1]

The problem that Schipper sets forth is not just one of point of
view, whereby a given history may look this way according to one
perspective and that way according to another, but more fundamentally
a problem of moral credibility and acceptance. Who will believe Abel's
story? Schipper does not ask who will accept responsibility for it, but,
less demandingly, who will believe it, simply assent to its reality? The
answer is, very few. Why is that so? Because to let in Abel's voice
would necessarily mean to hear the voice of Cain, one that may be too
uncomfortably familiar. Here, speaking through the mouth of Heinrich
Himmler, is what Cain sounds like:

> I also want to make reference before you here, in complete frankness, to
> a really grave matter. . . . I am referring to the evacuation of the Jews,
> the annihilation of the Jewish people. . . . Most of you must know what
> it means to see a hundred corpses lie side by side, or five hundred, or a
> thousand. To have stuck this out and—excepting cases of human
> weakness—to have kept our integrity, that is what has made us hard. In
> our history this is an unwritten and never-to-be-written page of
> glory. . . .[2]

Himmler addressed his words to a group of SS-*Gruppenführer*
(lieutenant-generals) on October 4, 1943. By that time the Warsaw
Ghetto had already been liquidated, its remaining Jews sent off to Treblinka or Maidanek. Alexander Donat was among them, but, through a
series of opportunities found and made, he was to survive and to write
his story, a harrowing guide to "The Holocaust Kingdom." His book is
one page of Abel's testament, a piece of the history of blood and tears
that Himmler vowed would never be written. In defiance of that vow,
though, it *has* been written—by Donat, by Kaplan, by Levi, by
Flinker, by Ringelblum, by Wiesel, by Wells, and by dozens of others.
    Hitler assumed power in 1933. In 1935 the infamous Nuremberg
laws were passed, severely restricting Jewish rights of all kinds. In
November of 1938, during "Kristallnacht," the largest anti-Jewish pogrom in modern European history broke out in towns and cities
throughout Germany and Austria. The following year the German
army, which had previously annexed Austria and occupied Czechoslovakia, invaded Poland and World War II began. For the Jews it was

to mean systematic mass destruction of a kind never before known and hardly to be imagined. Chaim Kaplan foresaw what was to come and recorded in the very first entry of his diary his doubt "that we will live through this carnage" (p. 19). The date of the entry was September 1, 1939, the beginning of the war and, for the Jews of Europe, the beginning of the end of a thousand-year civilization.

The Jewish defenses against the genocide that was being planned for them were worse than meager, for the Jews lacked not only arms and faithful allies but also a collective awareness of what was in store for them. Even while orders were being issued by Heydrich to establish ghettos in occupied Poland and by Himmler to begin building extermination camps at Auschwitz and elsewhere, the Jews remained for the most part in the dark about the violent end that was to be their lot. By November of 1940, however, when virtually overnight teams of masons began erecting the high walls around them, people like Kaplan were shocked into an awareness that far more than the Warsaw Ghetto was being sealed off. Indeed, nothing less than the fate of Polish Jewry—a community of some 3,300,000 people—was being sealed. Yet what could they do? Penned in behind the ghetto walls of Warsaw, Lodz, Vilna, Kovno, Bialystok, and numerous other centers of Jewish concentration, millions of Jews were condemned to a life so miserably constricted as to allow for release only through death, which might come in the form of slow starvation or disease within the ghettos or more violently under the gas of the death camps to which so many were to be deported. As these options became clear, and as the stories of the open slaughter of entire Jewish communities by mobile German killing squads spread, a passion to register every detail of Nazi brutality and Jewish suffering grew. "*Record, record!*" became the motivating impulse of the day, and while the liquidation of Polish Jewry could not be halted by the writer's pen, at the least it could be chronicled and remembered. To get it all down on paper, without exaggeration or distortion, became nothing short of a sacred task. "It is difficult to write," attests Kaplan, more often than not cut off from electricity and his hands frozen for lack of heat, "but I consider it an obligation and am determined to fulfill it with my last ounce of energy. I will write a scroll of agony in order to remember the past in the future" (p. 30).

I

The Warsaw Diary of Chaim Kaplan, written in Hebrew, runs from September 1, 1939, to August 4, 1942. It is as full and detailed a document of this crucial period in the life-and-death of Polish Jewry as we might hope to have and provides not only a remarkably objective record of the terror of the Nazi occupation but also a closely observant and intensely analytic portrait of the Jewish will to hold up under impossible conditions. As these conditions worsened—and they did so in ways that most of us can hardly comprehend—Kaplan's commitment to record deepened, his intellect pitted against the daily barbarism and a stalking death. The match, of course, was a preposterously uneven one, which he could only lose, but for as long as breath and ink held out Kaplan persisted in writing his diary. His resolve "not to let a single day go by without making an entry" was strong, but if ever a writer's will was to be tested by the enormity of events, Kaplan's was. His purpose was clearly defined from the start—"I sense within me the magnitude of this hour, and my responsibility toward it . . . continuing this diary to the very end of my physical and spiritual strength is a historical mission which must not be abandoned" (p. 104)—but as the horror of daily life in the ghetto increased, the diarist often found himself hard put for words. "It is beyond my pen to describe what befell us last night"; "Dante's description of the Inferno is mild compared to the inferno raging in the streets of Warsaw"; "I haven't the strength to hold a pen in my hand, I'm broken, shattered" (pp. 27, 29, 41)—such confessions of impotence and verbal paralysis thread themselves through the pages of *The Warsaw Diary* as intimations of some imminent and inevitable collapse. Remarkably, it never comes. What does, in almost four hundred pages of finely wrought, lucidly registered prose, is a work of testimony rare for both its documentary value and its refined intelligence, a record of frightful times yet of a mind refusing easily to succumb to them.

Kaplan's focus, from beginning to end, is always threefold: on the relentless and sadistic cruelty of the Nazi conquerors; on the helplessness and misery of their Jewish victims; and on the dispiriting passivity and acquiescence of the majority of the Poles. Nazi barbarism, exhibited openly and with growing ostentation, is recorded in all its revolting detail and analyzed as a form of national psychosis that surpasses in its tyrannical and perverted drive anything previously experienced. From the evidence all around him, Kaplan soon enough came to understand that the Germans were planning the complete extermination of the Jews, but the extent of the spiritual destruction they would first have to undergo before being sent to their deaths shocked and dismayed him. What would explain the obvious pleasure the Nazis took in humiliating and degrading their victims before killing them? Consider just two examples among many:

> In Lodz some Jewish girls were seized for forced labor. Women are not given hard work, but instead perform various services, generally in homes. These girls were compelled to clean a latrine—to remove the excrement and clean it. But they received no utensils. To their question: "With what?" the Nazis replied: "With your blouses." The girls removed their blouses and cleaned the excrement with them. When the job was done they received their reward: the Nazis wrapped their faces in the blouses, filthy with the remains of excrement, and laughed uproariously. And all this because "Jewish England" is fighting against the Führer with the help of the *Juden.*
>
> There was another incident, of a rabbi in Lodz who was forced to spit on a Torah scroll that was in the Holy Ark. In fear of his life, he complied and desecrated that which is holy to him and his people. After a short while he had no more saliva, his mouth was dry. To the Nazi's question, why did he stop spitting, the rabbi replied that his mouth was dry. Then the son of the "superior race" began to spit into the rabbi's open mouth, and the rabbi continued to spit on the Torah. (P. 87)

To understand such cruelty in psychological terms alone—as instances of aberrant or even psychotic behavior—is hardly to understand it at all. Kaplan's perceptions run deeper than that and inform him, correctly, that such viciousness is born more out of ideological than psychological necessity, and that in the eyes of Nazi ideology the Jews were "outside the category of human beings." "I fear such people!" he exclaims, because they are armed with "both book and sword. . . . Here lies the source of the evil. Ideological filth is hard to vanquish. . . . There is war which is nothing but power and worldliness, and there is war whose source is in the spirit—and it is self-evident that this Nazi war is no less than a war whose roots are inspired with spirit" (p. 107).

How does one fight such a war, especially if one lacks not only arms but allies? For that was precisely the situation of the Polish Jews, who had neither a standing army nor, as Kaplan makes abundantly clear, the active sympathies of most of their Polish neighbors. This question comes to overwhelm all other concerns in the diary. For while individually every death might be recorded as a personal loss, it is the threat to the communal or national destiny of the Jews that troubles Kaplan most of all. "Almighty God!" he cries out, "are you making an end to the remnant of Polish Jewry?" (p. 54). The answer, he feared, was "yes," that the God of Israel had abandoned his people. The result of this anguished awareness, confirmed daily as the level of carnage rose, is to bring a brooding, mournful quality to many of Kaplan's entries.

At the same time he was aware of the considerable cultural and religious activity in the ghetto, and innumerable entries allow us to glimpse the manifold expression of spiritual resistance. Clandestine schools operated to educate the children; lectures and musical programs were organized for adults; prayer quorums formed "illegally" for the observance of Sabbath and all the holidays; political action groups arose; and, despite the ban against it, smuggling continued briskly, often carried out by children. Such activities helped to keep life going and constituted, before the armed uprising in the spring of 1943, as effective a reply to oppression as the Jews could muster. "Every spark of light," Kaplan notes, "is a potential breach in the kingdom of darkness of bestial Nazism" (p. 68).

His own contribution to maintaining that light was, of course, the diary itself. He began it in order to record daily events that might "serve as source material for the future historian" (p. 104), but while the documentary value of *The Warsaw Diary* is great, one reads it today as much for its intellectual and literary interests as for its historical ones. To give the diary this emphasis is not to "aestheticize" it but simply to begin to see what writing itself meant in such a time. What we learn from Kaplan is that it could be nothing less than a form of heroism, an assertion of dignity and even nobility in the face of death. For by now it should be clear that the choice the Jews of Warsaw had was not one between life and death; Polish Jewry was doomed—there was no longer any question about that; rather, the question was: to live and die on whose terms, theirs or ours? Would the Nazis prevail so far as to dictate not only death but all the conditions of living and dying? A totalitarian definition of power requires that kind of comprehensiveness, not only in political terms but in spiritual ones as well. That is

why the Nazis sought to degrade and to dehumanize their victims before destroying them. And that is why any withholding of assent, any
retention of personal definition, threatened them and ultimately would
defeat them. In Kaplan's case, then, heroism comes to be defined in
terms of intellectual opposition, a withstanding of Nazi prevalence and
oppression through the exercise of mind. The entry for December 16,
1940, presents us with the terms of the struggle:

> My inkwell lay dormant for a few days because of my mental dis-
> tress. Every hour there is a new edict, every moment a frightening tide
> of Job. Every so often I remember that I am a prisoner in the ghetto;
> that I am penned within a piece of land four or five kilometers in size,
> without contact with anyone outside; that by law I am not allowed to
> buy or even to read a book in a foreign language. When I remember all
> this I become desperate, ready to break my pen and throw it away.
>
> But this despair does not last forever. The spirit of dedication
> which had left me in my moments of spiritual agony returns, as though
> some hidden force were ordering me: Record! (Pp. 232–33).

We need not guess about the nature of this hidden force, for Kaplan
refers to it explicitly whenever he reflects on piercing the darkness of
Nazi bestiality with the light of human deed. Every flexing of Jewish
will was an act of sabotage. The Hasidim praying were radical dis-
senters; the children learning or smuggling were active conspirators;
even those who passed their time in frivolous ways, dancing while their
stomachs were groaning, were effective saboteurs, for "the more one
dances," Kaplan notes approvingly, "the more it is a sign of his belief in
'the eternity of Israel.' Every dance is a protest against our oppressors"
(pp. 244–45). "A certain invisible power is imbedded in us," he
confirms, "and it is this secret that keeps us alive and preserves us . . . ;
as evidence, we don't have cases of suicide" (p. 131).

What preserved Kaplan, neither a dancer nor a smuggler or even,
apparently, despite his considerable attachment to the tradition, an especially devout Jew, was the diary, his "friend and ally," as he refers to
his journal. "I would be lost without it," he confesses. "I pour my
innermost thoughts and feelings into it, and this brings relief" (p. 278).
There came a time, though, when no amount of opposition could be
effective and no relief could be had, when the daily death toll by starvation, typhus, and murder simply was not rising rapidly enough to suit
the Germans, and the liquidation of the ghetto was ordered. *The War-*

saw Diary, an overwhelmingly elegiac piece of literature throughout, becomes in the end the despondent chronicle of Polish Jewry in its death throes. "Blessed is the eye that has not beheld all this!" (p. 36) is almost its summarizing exclamation. The literary merit of Kaplan's writing is consistently high but never more so than in those moments of seemingly unrelieved bleakness when the diarist's dirgelike prose weds him inseparably to the long tradition of Jewish lamentation literature, which echoes powerfully through his pages. In one of his final entries, shortly before he and his wife were transported to their deaths in Treblinka, Kaplan, who earlier referred to himself as "the grandson of Isaiah the prophet" (p. 159), proves that the prophetic vocation—and what was it if not an earlier expression of Jewish protest, dissent, and heroic affirmation?—was still alive:

> The terrible events have engulfed me; the horrible deeds committed in the ghetto have so frightened and stunned me that I have not the power, either physical or spiritual, to review these events and perpetuate them with the pen of a scribe. I have no words to express what has happened to us since the day the expulsion was ordered. Those people who have gotten some notion of historical expulsions from books know nothing. We, the inhabitants of the Warsaw ghetto, are now experiencing the reality. . . .
>
> Some of my friends and acquaintances who know the secret of my diary urge me, in their despair, to stop writing. "Why? For what purpose? Will you live to see it published? Will these words of yours reach the ears of future generations? How? If you are deported you won't be able to take it with you because the Nazis will watch your every move, and even if you succeed in hiding it when you leave Warsaw, you will undoubtedly die for lack of strength, you will die by the Nazi sword. For not a single deportee will be able to hold out to the end of the war."
>
> And yet in spite of it all I refuse to listen to them. I feel that continuing this diary to the very end of my physical and spiritual strength is a historical mission which must not be abandoned. My mind is still clear, my need to record unstilled, though it is now five days since any real food has passed my lips. Therefore I will not silence my diary! (Pp. 383–84)

If Chaim Kaplan was the elegist of the Warsaw Ghetto, Emmanuel Ringelblum was its principal archivist. A professional historian before the war, Ringelblum organized an underground group of researchers (the "Oneg Shabbat," or Sabbath Celebrants) who devoted themselves to collecting and preserving as complete a record of the everyday affairs of the ghetto as they could manage. The result, written chiefly in Yiddish and spanning the period from January 1940 to December 1942, is the important journal *Notes from the Warsaw Ghetto* (the English version is, unfortunately, only a selection from a much longer two-volume work originally published in Poland).[3] While the *Notes* are still too preliminary and fragmentary to be regarded as a full history (Ringelblum had planned to expand them for such a work, but time and conditions never permitted him to do so), they stand nevertheless as an invaluable record of the ghetto years. Written in a terse manner, frequently clipped and telegraphic in style, sometimes even employing code ("Muni" is Ringelblum, "Horowitz" is Hitler, "Moses" is Mussolini, etc.), the *Notes* are replete with the most varied details of social and political life in the ghetto and serve as a complement to Chaim Kaplan's equally informative but far more personal testament.

Writing rapidly, in a style controlled by objectivity and understatement, Ringelblum itemizes the innumerable occurrences of cruelty and heroism, degradation and resistance that constituted the daily round of living and dying in Jewish Warsaw. These are presented matter-of-factly and without comment or evaluation by the author, who regarded himself more as a reporter than an interpreter of events:

> The mother of someone killed in January hit a German in the street, then took poison. (P. 45)
>
> At the funeral for the small children from the Wolska Street orphanage, the children from the home placed a wreath at the monument with the inscription: "To the Children Who Have Died from Hunger—From the Children Who Are Hungry." (P. 52)
>
> A police chief came to the apartment of a Jewish family, wanted to take some things away. The woman cried that she was a widow with a child. The chief said he'd take nothing if she could guess which one of his eyes was the artificial one. She guessed the left eye. She was asked how she knew. "Because that one," she answered, "had a human look." (P. 84)
>
> A man came along with a pass. The watchmen on Grzybowska Street took him into the guardroom, tortured him there for two hours, forced him to drink urine, have sex relations with a Gentile woman. They beat him over the head, then cleaned the wounds with a broom. The next day, they treated him humanely, gave him food and drink, took him to his destination, on the way saying that Jews are people, too. (Pp. 109–10)
>
> In the prayer house of the Pietists from Braclaw on Nowolipie Street there is a large sign: Jews, Never Despair! The Pietists dance there

with the same religious fervor as they did before the war. After prayers
one day, a Jew danced there whose daughter had died the day before.
(P. 125)

Death lies in every street. The children are no longer afraid of
death. In one courtyard, the children played a game tickling a corpse.
(P. 174)

These things speak for themselves and, as Ringelblum surely realized, require no elaboration. When life itself becomes this bizarre,
what is there to say about it additionally? The *Notes,* in their spare,
fragmentary, often episodic character, reveal nothing so much as the
disconnections and erosions of normal existence, of life broken into discordant moments and glimpsed just at the point where it is slipping
away. Ringelblum presents some of the details of the work of Jewish
self-help agencies, and a kind of gallows humor, exemplified by some
memorable jokes, helps to relieve the grim picture, but otherwise a
reader of these pages is carried along on a drift toward madness and
death. "In a refugee center an eight-year-old child went mad.
Screamed, 'I want to steal, I want to rob, I want to eat, I want to be a
German'" (p. 39). This episode is one of the countless, almost char-
acterless instances of extreme anguish that hastened the dissolution of
the ghetto's population. It is fitting that Ringelblum does not give the
child's name, his father's occupation, the look on his mother's face at
the moment when she came to realize he was lost. These "novelistic
details" probably would have seemed out of place and inconsequential
to him, registering as they do a time less destitute and grotesque. Such
details are glimpsed from time to time in the *Notes,* but for the most
part Ringelblum's record is a concise and sober one, hinting at no
superfluity except that of suffering, and conveying, as he wished, a tone
of "epic calm . . . the calm of the graveyard" (p. xxiii).

Fully aware of the significance of his labors but sensing that he
might in fact not ever present them personally to the world,
Ringelblum carefully sealed his manuscripts in rubberized milk cans and
buried them in the ground of Jewish Warsaw. Although he managed to
survive the ghetto uprising, he was discovered in hiding with his wife
and young son and, with them, summarily executed outside his bunker.
His journal, found in the ruins of the ghetto after the war, is, like Kaplan's *Diary* (which was surreptitiously transmitted through the ghetto
walls and later recovered), an unexpected legacy to us from the dead.

While these two books have emerged as among the most important we have on the Warsaw Ghetto, they are by no means all we have. An extensive literature on ghettoization has by now accumulated, much of it centering on Warsaw, the largest and most renowned of the European ghettos. The young Mary Berg commenced taking notes on events in October of 1939 (she was sixteen at the time) and continued writing more or less regularly for the next three and a half years. Her *Warsaw Ghetto: A Diary,* translated from the Polish, appeared in 1945, one of the first eyewitness accounts to reach the West.[4] Like the works already mentioned, though, this diary ends too soon to be able to tell us very much firsthand about the revolt that began in April 1943 (the author, the daughter of an American citizen, managed to win her release from the ghetto and to reach France by that time, and consequently could report only some hearsay information that had reached her there). The opening chapters of Alexander Donat's wide-ranging memoir, *The Holocaust Kingdom,* are devoted to Warsaw, as is much of Yitzhak Katznelson's despondent *Vittel Diary,* and these begin to convey a bit more about the uprising of the Jewish fighters. For fuller and more detailed accounts of this heroic action, which is remembered today not only as the most spectacular instance of Jewish resistance in the war but also as the first occurrence of civilian armed resistance anywhere in Nazi-occupied Europe, we are indebted to such books as Marek Edelman's *The Ghetto Fights,* Bernard Goldstein's *The Stars Bear Witness,* Vladka Meed's *On Both Sides of the Wall,* and Ber Mark's *Uprising in the Warsaw Ghetto.*[5] Written by survivors of the ghetto's brave, if tragic, ending, these works are all highly readable accounts of Jewish Warsaw's final agony.

No review of the literature on Warsaw could be made without some mention of Janusz Korczak, the martyred director of the Dom Sierot, an orphan home that catered to the welfare of some two hundred Jewish children. The death march of those children has become legendary, as has the man who led it, for virtually all accounts of the Warsaw Ghetto allude to this much venerated pediatrician and educator. The recent publication of the *Ghetto Diary*[6] of Janusz Korczak now allows us to gain a more intimate sense of the man in his final months.

Korczak wrote his diary between May and August 1942. It is striking both for its general lack of specific reference to the war and for its highly personal, allusive, elliptical style. Writing usually late at night, when his children and staff workers were asleep and he himself was all but exhausted from sickness and the trials of the day, Korczak filled his pages with insights of the most varied sort, ranging as they do from reflections on history to self-analysis, from experiments with educational theory to meditations on aging, writing, playing, medicine, drinking, and hunger. Diffuse, impulsive, and fragmented in its jottings, the diary is more an occasional day-book than anything else, a register of quizzical, often macabre moments that suddenly break into lucidity. An effort to gain some much-needed psychological detachment from the strains of the war is only partially successful, for while Korczak wishes to avoid dwelling on the daily ravagements of ghetto life, believing as he does that to describe "someone else's pain resembles thieving, preying upon misfortune" (p. 87), an awareness of the waning, hopeless life of his children inevitably intrudes.

"Children?" he queries at one point; "they send us here the mere leavings of children" (pp. 148–49). A little later: "The children moon about. Only the outer appearances are normal. Underneath lurks weariness, discouragement, anger, mutiny, mistrust, resentment, longing" (p. 166). He would feed them as best he could, weigh them periodically, administer to the seriously ill whatever medicines he could find, tell them stories and put on plays, but the persecutions, however much he might want to ignore them, had their own wasting effects: "The body of a dead boy lies on the sidewalk. Nearby, three boys are playing horses and drivers. At one point they notice the body, move a few steps to the side, go on playing" (p. 121). Famine and typhus were taking their toll, and not only on the poor, the young, and the very old. Korczak had long feared madness, "a hereditary affliction," as he referred to it (his father had gone insane), and his prose time and again reflects the precarious state of his own mind:

> The look of this district is changing from day to day.
> 1. A prison
> 2. A plague-stricken area
> 3. A mating ground
> 4. A lunatic asylum
> 5. A casino. Monaco. The stake—your head. (P. 185)

A mere list, but enough to record the fearfulness that Korczak felt all around. A kindly, eccentric, devoted man who longed to establish the world's first "Children's Republic," he hardly knew at times how to contain his astonishment at the poverty and cruelty that had overtaken his dreams. Where Kaplan lamented and Katznelson cursed wildly, Korczak either winced in muted tones or turned against himself in a humor of self-lacerating irony:

A chimney sweep must be smeared with soot.
A butcher must be stained with blood (a surgeon, too).
A cesspool cleaner stinks.
A waiter must be crafty. If he is not, woe be unto him.
I feel all smeared, blood-stained, stinking. And crafty,
since I am alive—I sleep, eat and, occasionally, I even joke. (P. 149)

"Why am I writing all this?" he asks himself more than once. Whatever his other reasons, Korczak undoubtedly wrote in an effort to contain his pain and keep his balance. His diary does not resemble the historical chronicle that Ringelblum and his dedicated associates looked to assemble. It is too introspective and too personal for that. Neither is it at all like Kaplan's diary, for Korczak was too remote from Jewish tradition to carry over the learned discourse and elegiac tones of classical Hebrew lamentation. Rather, he left behind something closer to a Kafkaesque sketch, a collection of disparate reflections on discordancy and the absurd, some of them hardly moving beyond the initial stages of bafflement. Was it part of his strength or of his weakness that he could not raise his voice in protest against the violence being committed all around him? "I never wish anyone ill. I cannot. I don't know how it's done" (p. 188). By temperament not knowing how to go into opposition, or not caring to, Janusz Korczak quietly prepared his children and himself for what the Germans euphemistically called "resettlement," and when, on August 5, 1942, their time came, he led his two hundred youngsters into the boxcars that would take them to the gas chambers of Treblinka. Although he himself was offered a reprieve, he chose to remain with his children and accompanied them to the end. His diary, entrusted to a young friend for safekeeping the day before the transport, reveals nothing so much as the estrangement that this "sculptor of the child's soul" (p. 113) felt toward the ruin that life in the adult world had become. The awful wonderment "that all this did happen" (p. 185) is what echoes on beyond the final words of his diary:

I am watering the flowers. My bald head in the window. What a splendid target.
He has a rifle. Why is he standing and looking on calmly?
He has no orders to shoot.
And perhaps he was a village teacher in civilian life, or a notary, a street sweeper in Leipzig, a waiter in Cologne?
What would he do if I nodded to him? Waved my hand in a friendly gesture?
Perhaps he doesn't even know that things are—as they are?
He may have arrived only yesterday, from far away. . . . (P. 189)

Other towns and cities found their own chroniclers and commemorators, who wrote as persistently and as honestly as they could,
even if not always with the learning or distinction of a Kaplan or a
Ringelblum or the Kafkaesque ironies of a Korczak. Yitzkhok
Rudashevski's *The Diary of the Vilna Ghetto* presents the hopes and fears
of a Jewish youngster caught in the downfall of the city that was once
prized as the "Jerusalem of the East." *The Diary of Éva Heyman,* written
by another child, offers a somewhat analogous record, this time set in
Hungary during the early months of 1944.[7] Not unexpectedly, both
books mingle childhood perceptions with an otherwise remarkably mature grasp of events. Most of all, they show the pitiable defenselessness
of Jewish children in the ghettos. One reads diaries like these, in fact,
with a growing and almost unbearable sense of tragic irony, for today
we know all too well what the young authors of such narratives could
not possibly know as they still wrote—the infinitely harsher terror that
was still to await them. Rudashevski, aged fifteen, was murdered with
his family at Ponar, the site of destruction for much of Vilna Jewry.
Éva Heyman, two years his junior, perished at Auschwitz.

Holocaust diaries written by children or young adolescents seem
almost to constitute a distinctive subgenre of the literature of incarceration. In most cases certain recognizable patterns repeat themselves—
wonderment over the extreme violence and open viciousness of the
adult world; bafflement over Jewish isolation and suffering and of the
gentile world's seemingly uncaring abandonment of them; an instinctive eagerness to resume the more peaceful round of childhood duties
and pleasures; an imaginative indulgence in the future, where interesting careers or romantic marriages lie promisingly in wait just beyond
the end of the war; a growing fear that the war might, in fact, not
quickly end, or at least not end well for the Jews, so that the postwar
future, whatever it might hold for others, may not include them at all;
and the terrible fright that comes with such realizations, themselves the
premature and unwelcome signs of a suddenly realized and all-too-
vulnerable mortality.

Such apprehensions, detailed and given point by each new day's
hopelessness, are not the normal lot of children, at least not of children
born into normal times, for a heavy premonition of human finitude is
usually no part of childhood awareness. For the Jewish children of the
Holocaust, though, such dread became a familiar and finally inescapable
emotion and was recorded copiously in the pages of their diaries. It is

probable, in fact, that a principal purpose for keeping a diary in the first place was to exorcise this unwanted sense of dread, to find some means of coping with the unexpected but very tangible fearfulness all around. While adults more typically wrote for the public record, to broadcast to the world at large the atrocities being committed against them, the younger diarists seemed to write for more private reasons, reasons of the heart or of an intellect that needed to contain the overpowering enormities of experience in some manageable space, which might mean nothing more than the space of a blank page. A certain measure of consolation and companionship could be found by filling those pages each day, and some much-needed encouragement in imagining oneself, in some better time, an author or a statesman or a professional photographer.

These, or something like them, are the characteristic emotions that one finds time and again in the diaries written by children, and in none so much as Anne Frank's *The Diary of a Young Girl.*[8] One finds them as well, although greatly complicated by the tormented searchings of a young religious Jew, in *Young Moshe's Diary.* In contrast to the literature mentioned thus far, all of it originating in Eastern Europe and, as such, on intimate terms with extreme dehumanization and the spectre of mass death, the diaries of Anne Frank and Moshe Flinker were composed in Holland and Belgium under relatively "easier" conditions. To say this, of course, is not to suggest that *The Diary of a Young Girl* and *Young Moshe's Diary* are in any way "comforting" books or that they are untrue to their authors' situations, but that these situations, for all their difficulties, were still several steps removed in experiential terms from the fate that the Nazis were drawing up for the Jews of Europe in their planned "Final Solution." As a result, to limit one's understanding of the Holocaust to such a book as Anne Frank's diary is to grasp only the most preliminary outline of the coming war against the Jews.

Anne Frank, the daughter of Jewish refugees from Germany, composed her diary in Dutch between the summer of 1942 and the summer of 1944 while in hiding in Amsterdam. Her story, freshly and vividly told, describes a double war that was taking place during this two-year period—a war within and the war without. The latter, while more than a casual backdrop to Anne's domestic and subjective preoccupations, is nevertheless subordinate to them, for the major part of her writing is given over to reflections on the restrictions of life in their cramped "Secret Annexe" hideaway, on the inevitable daily frictions with mem-

bers of her family, and on her own budding maturity as a young girl
yearning her way into womanhood. Anne Frank fancied herself an
author, and it is hardly to be doubted that, had she lived, she might
indeed have gone on to write novels, for her diary is quickened by a
descriptive prose that succeeds in portraying "the extraordinary things
[that] can happen to people who go into hiding." It was part of the
author's saving temperament as a writer that allowed her, at least for
part of the time, to imagine her family's situation in hiding as an adventure story of sorts, one that tested their resourcefulness in the art of
living with handicaps, which were unwanted but, given some discipline, cheerfulness, and luck, might be managed. *The Diary of Anne
Frank* is also a love story and, as such, is alive as well with the poetry of
adolescent romance. And insofar as the young girl embraced and apparently managed to hold onto a naïve humanism, the diary is, in part, a
testament of hope. Nevertheless, it is not without its more realistic and
even fatalistic side, and its premonitions of a bad end, recorded more
than once after the young girl peeked through her curtain of fancy onto
the dark streets beyond, came to be borne out in a brutal way.

   Moshe Flinker's story, while in some ways comparable, is, in tone
as in philosophical outlook, a strongly contrasting one, for *Young
Moshe's Diary*[9] contains almost none of the gaiety and brightness that
characterize *The Diary of a Young Girl*. Instead, one encounters in its
brooding, tormented pages the most difficult of questions that a religious person can raise—questions that arise when faith is caught in the
impossible dilemma of trying to reconcile the promise of divine justice
with the extremities of human suffering, the redeeming God of Israel
with his dying people. As a traditionally educated and fully committed
member of that people, Moshe Flinker was beset not only by the personal difficulties he and his family faced as Jews in occupied Belgium
but also by religious despair, and theodicy is a recurring problem in the
pages of his diary. "What can God mean by all that is befalling us and
by not preventing it from happening?" (p. 26) he queries continually,
and while he strives for answers, none satisfies him sufficiently. His
only hope is that the war might soon end and he be allowed to fulfill his
dream of starting life anew as a Jewish statesman in Palestine. To that
end, he labored to perfect his Hebrew, the language in which he composed his diary during a ten-month period in 1942 and 1943, and to
learn Arabic as well. As he looked around, though, and each day saw
Jews being seized and transported out of the city to the east, the sky

appeared to him "covered with bloody clouds" (p. 121), and he seemed to anticipate that the Zion of his yearnings lay too far beyond the horizon of war for him ever to reach it. He would continue to recite psalms of hope until the end, although, as he confessed on the last page of his diary, he already felt "as if I were dead" (p. 123). Not long after, he was—at age sixteen, another youthful victim of Auschwitz.

Diaries are, almost by definition, provisional forms of writing, notes and drafts that are designed to serve—in some later, more leisurely day—the larger and more refined ends of composition. For most of the diarists, no such day was ever to come again, and as a result Ringelblum's expanded history and the novels that Anne Frank planned to write are books we will never have. The books we do have, though, carry a considerable authority, and while they may be fragmented and still unfinished, the Holocaust diaries are immensely moving and simply irreplaceable documents. As compilations and reflections on an impossible time, they are, to be sure, incomplete and less than exhaustive, but that only means they speak out of the truth of their moment—itself a broken and almost incomprehensible one.

II

In turning from the diaries to the memoirs of the Holocaust, one turns away from the imminence of human extinction to an experience that, paradoxically, is in some ways more punishingly cruel for being more extended in its anguish—survivorship.[10] For those who managed to outwit or outlast the ghettos and camps, surviving often takes on an aspect of life-after-death, not so much a gift of rebirth in the coveted religious sense but rather a life afflicted by guilt, absurdity, and irreality. In psychological terms, the victory over destruction often gets translated into its opposite—the prolonged distress of an unwanted, unearned life. In moral terms, the survivor frequently feels himself indicted for unspecified but unforgivable crimes—chief among them the "crime" of having returned to the living while others, and often one's "betters," went to their deaths. In literary terms, the memoirist finds himself beset by a double burden, then: that of recollection, which is painful enough, but also that of psychic restoration and moral reconciliation, which may be simply impossible. The first forces him back into his most discordant, nightmarish experiences, which he must try to order into some kind of patterned narration simply to appear credible to his readers; the second lacks not only an inherent order but any apparent *meaning,* and certainly is without any inner logic or secure metaphysical implication. Yet, despite these difficulties, the memoirist must get his story told, both for the obvious didactic reasons—so that the world may know—and to commemorate the dead and make his own life-after-death somewhat more manageable.

Autobiographical accounts by survivors of the ghettos and camps began to appear almost immediately after the war ended and continue to be written to this day. Given the strong confessional urge behind so much of this literature, it is not surprising that the corpus of such writings has grown to be both large and unusually compelling. It is also diverse and ranges in narrative kinds from more or less unembellished exposition and analysis to more imaginative forms that mingle documentary statement with elements of fiction. In an effort to recall their experiences faithfully and without any adornment, some memoirists have aimed for strict narrative realism; others, believing that these same experiences were almost other-worldly in their strangeness and brutality, have tried to simulate them in a prose that is itself wrenched and estranging. Thus, we have on the one hand the recollections of a Josef Katz (*One Who Came Back*) presented in diary fashion, in this case an adopted or "invented" form, for the author, a German Jew transported to the camps of Nazi-occupied Latvia, did not actually transcribe his thoughts day by day during his period of incarceration but came to compose them only after liberation. The effort in this instance, quite obviously, was to reproduce the onset and gradual unfolding of the Holocaust in linear, chronological terms. On the other hand, in more complex and more highly literary books, such as David Rousset's *The Other Kingdom* and Charlotte Delbo's *None of Us Will Return,* we encounter memoirs that are in some ways the analogues of prose poetry and the impressionistic essay and that draw heavily upon the techniques of symbolist and even surrealistic fiction to reproduce coherent "moments" of an otherwise incoherent nightmare.[11] Neither point of view will, by itself, yield any more or less of the truth, to which all survivors are equally dedicated, but the manner of transmission will shape one's sense of events differently and will leave a varied impact on readers. As with all serious writing, then, it becomes important to observe not only *what* a given writer is telling us but *how* he goes about ordering and presenting his tale.

In some cases—and this tends to be true of several of the memoirs

written by doctors—there is an attempt to write from a tightly controlled and even clinical point of view, as exemplified by such books as
Bruno Bettelheim's *The Informed Heart* and, in substantial portion, Victor Frankl's *Man's Search for Meaning* (a revision and expansion of his
earlier *From Death-Camp to Existentialism*). Both draw upon personal
experience in the camps to study the psychology of resistance and survival, but whatever the value of such study—and it has been much
debated by later scholars—it is clear that by quickly moving to convert
the most painful of subjective experiences into scientific "data," the
memoirist is distancing himself and his readers from the full blow of
atrocity. The clinical perspective, in other words, is a kind of defensive
strategy, one that we see at work as well, although tempered by feelings of guilt, in Miklos Nyiszli's *Auschwitz: A Doctor's Eyewitness Account* (the memoir of the chief physician of the camp crematoria) and
Elie A. Cohen's *The Abyss: A Confession* (written by a Dutch physician
who worked as a prison-doctor at Westerbork and later at Auschwitz).[12]

The narrative point of view becomes more intensely subjective in a
grouping of excellent books that recommend themselves to us both as
historical sources and as personal testimonies. These include Alexander
Donat's *The Holocaust Kingdom,* Eugene Heimler's *Night of the Mist,*
Gerda Klein's *All But My Life,* Seweryna Szmaglewska's *Smoke Over
Birkenau,* Rudolf Vrba's *I Cannot Forgive,* and Leon Wells's *The
Janowska Road.*[13] In all these works one encounters an order of experience that, in its daily round of gratuitous cruelty, extreme deprivation,
and constant terror, so far surpassed anything previously known as to
make writing about it a next-to-impossible task. The concentrationary
universe, as it has been called, was, in the words of David Rousset, "a
universe apart, totally cut off, the weird kingdom of an unlikely fatal-
ity" (pp. 10–11). "Even I," Rousset confessed, "after more than a year
there, cannot talk about it without feeling as if I were making it all up.
Either that, or telling a dream that someone else had dreamed" (p. 41).
All memoirists have known this sense of radical self-estrangement,
which handicaps any thinking and writing about the Holocaust, but
which their books themselves are written to break.

Two that have broken it with uncommon force are Primo Levi's
Survival in Auschwitz (previously published as *If This Is a Man*) and Elie
Wiesel's *Night*. Both are first-person accounts by survivors of Ausch-
witz, the first written by an Italian chemist whose reflections on his

period "in hell" are everywhere influenced by the traditions of Western humanistic learning and especially by a close knowledge of Dante; the second by a young, pious Hungarian Jew who presents his anguished story in the terms of classical Judaism—in this instance, a vocabulary of high ethical and devotional living severely undermined by atrocity and no longer readily applicable to the interpretation and judgment of experience.

Levi's account, a portrait of the human being *in extremis*—of man "on the bottom"—is pervaded by the manifold ironies of the literature of absurdity, a literature that renders the utter senselessness of happenings. Grounded in a humane intelligence and persistently curious and observant, it is turned toward whatever remains of the human face after it has been pummeled and befouled by the crime of the camps, barbarized almost beyond recognition but, in rare instances here and there, still retaining a countenance of fraternal decency and brightness.

Levi's story spans the period (December 1943–January 1945) of the author's incarceration in Auschwitz, a year that seemed "a journey toward nothingness" (p. 13). A man of intellect and civilized manner, who thought in Cartesian categories and once believed that he inhabited a sensible world, Levi found himself suddenly in a place so radically deformed as to disarm thought itself. There is water at the camp, but men and women dying of thirst are forbidden to drink it. Their bunks are made and stand before them, but the dead-weary inmates are not permitted to occupy them. "Warum?" he asks a guard, and receives in reply: "Heir ist kein warum" ("Why?" "Here there is no why") (p. 25). As the blows begin and herds of people are marched off to their deaths, a band plays *Rosamunda*. A brightly illuminated sign across the door reads "Arbeit Macht Frei," but the workers are clearly slaves and most of what they do is senseless, unproductive labor. It all seems some "colossal farce in Teutonic taste" (p. 25). Of what use are the disciplines of intellect in such a world? "Better," Levi concludes, "not to think" (p. 32).

For a man trained in thought and guided by its habits, that loss was a drastic one, but it proved to be only one of many deprivations. Stripped of his clothing, his shoes, his hair, even his name, the inmate of Auschwitz soon became, as Levi learned, "a hollow man, reduced to suffering and needs, forgetful of dignity and restraint" (p. 23). Even language, perhaps the final protest against full expropriation, was disarmed and emptied of its normal capacities to function, for in the "perpetual Babel" of the camps "no one listens to you" (p. 33). Dispossession, in sum, was all but total.

The literary form that Levi's memoir takes to convey this radical reduction of the human is an intricate and especially interesting one, for the author has written a kind of reverse *Erziehungsroman,* a narrative of *mis*education or an unlearning and relearning of human possibilities. A rationalist inhabiting a place governed by absolute irrationality, Levi sees life devolving to its most elementary forms, all of them to be mastered in order to withstand the camp's clearly perceived plan: "to annihilate us first as men in order to kill us more slowly afterwards" (p. 45). As a matter of basic self-defense, then, the inmates, removed as they are from the social patterns of the civilized order, travel a route that takes them from an accomplished adulthood back to the earliest of childhood beginnings, learning all over again how to eat, how to wash, how to relieve themselves, how to stand, how to dress, how to stay warm, how to sleep, even newly how to talk the special language of the camp. Those who failed at their lessons almost certainly would perish. Those who learned them well and could apply them consistently became attuned to what was "essential and what adventitious to the conduct of the human animal in the struggle for life" (p. 79) and had a chance to go on.

The language here is naturalistic, yet Levi does not place his final perceptions in a merely Darwinian notion of human survival. Given the social structure of the camp, according to which "the privileged oppress the unprivileged," he understood early that survival depended on "the struggle of each one against all" (pp. 38, 39). At the same time, he learned two other lessons that were likewise basic yet transcended the brute nature of the war of the fit against the less fit. Both illustrate the necessities of moral survival, even though they might involve nothing more than a washing of one's hands or the simplest gestures of kindness. Each strengthened the will to resist deprivation and avoid succumbing to the degradation that precedes and announces death. In Levi's case, as is made clear in the quotations below, they are what helped to keep him not only alive but human:

> In this place it is practically pointless to wash every day in the tur
> bid water of the filthy washbasins for purposes of cleanliness and health;
> but it is most important as a symptom of remaining vitality, and neces
> sary as an instrument of moral survival.

I must confess it: after only one week of prison, the instinct for cleanliness disappeared in me. I wander aimlessly around the washroom when I suddenly see Steinlauf, my friend aged almost fifty, with nude torso, scrub his neck and shoulders with little success (he has no soap) but great energy. Steinlauf sees me and greets me, and without preamble asks me severely why I do not wash. Why should I? . . . Washing one's face in our condition seems a stupid feat, even frivolous: a mechanical habit, or worse, a dismal repetition of an extinct rite. . . .

But Steinlauf interrupts me . . . and administers me a complete lesson. . . . Precisely because the Lager was a great machine to reduce us to beasts, we must not become beasts; that even in this place, one can survive, and therefore one must want to survive, to tell the story, to bear witness; and that to survive we must force ourselves to save at least the skeleton, the scaffolding, the form of civilization. We are slaves, deprived of every right, exposed to every insult, condemned to certain death, but we still possess one power, and we must defend it with all our strength for it is the last—the power to refuse our consent. So we must certainly wash our faces without soap in dirty water and dry ourselves on our jackets. We must polish our shoes, not because the regulation states it, but for dignity and propriety. We must walk erect, without dragging our feet, not in homage to Prussian discipline but to remain alive, not to begin to die. (Pp. 35–36)

While on the face of it a ritual washing in filthy water seemed an absurd act, it proved to be just the opposite, a defiant reply to absurd conditions, a stubborn retention of civilized ways. Yet Steinlauf's wisdom, grounded in the ceremonies of self-reliance that flourished "on the other side of the Alps," was not enough for the Italian Levi, whose social needs required something more than Spartan discipline. Fortunately for him a human connection, modest enough but altogether devoted, supplied them in the person of Lorenzo:

The story of my relationship with Lorenzo . . . in concrete terms it amounts to little: an Italian civilian worker brought me a piece of bread and the remainder of his ration every day for six months; he gave me a vest of his, full of patches; he wrote a postcard on my behalf to Italy and brought me the reply. For all this he neither asked nor accepted any reward, because he was good and simple and did not think that one did good for a reward. . . . I believe that it was really due to Lorenzo that I am alive today; and not so much for his material aid, as for his having constantly reminded me by his presence, by his natural and plain manner of being good, that there still existed a just world outside our own, something and someone still pure and whole, not corrupt, not savage, extraneous to hatred and terror; something difficult to define, a remote

possibility of good, but for which it was worth surviving. . . . Thanks
to Lorenzo, I managed not to forget that I myself was a man. (Pp.
109–11)

The narrator of *Night* underwent many of the same trials recorded
by Primo Levi but sustained an additional one as well: the trial of a
tormented and finally broken faith. Elie Wiesel's restrained but agonizing memoir succeeds, as few other books do, in calling attention to the
specifically Jewish dimensions of the Holocaust, for it relates the personal and communal sufferings of the victims within the traditional
terms of theological reflection. It does so, moreover, with a moral
authority so pronounced and so rarely found in our day that, to grasp
it, one has to bypass almost all of modern literature and seek for interpretive parallels in the Bible and its major commentaries. For, among
other things, *Night* is a contemporary rendering of the *Akedah*, told by
an Isaac who looked up to heaven from under the knife but saw no
restraining angel coming, just as it is a fervent Jobean accusation against
the God who would permit such murder to go unchecked. In narrating
his memoir from the standpoint of the most enduring of theological
issues, Wiesel undoubtedly raised more questions than he could easily
answer in one slim volume of autobiographical reflection, but he has
left in the minds of all his readers—who now number in the
millions—a powerful truth: that "man defines himself by what disturbs
him and not by what reassures him." No one can put down *Night* and
not realize the massive disturbance that the Holocaust poses to all our
traditional ways of thinking and believing, just as no one can regard the
mirror in which the young survivor of Auschwitz peers at himself un-
believingly at the book's end and not see reflected back, in more ways
than we might care to acknowledge, our common face.

Elie A. Cohen, who subtitled his own memoir "a confession," relates that when his camp was liberated and the inmates stormed the SS
storehouses in search of goods, he carried off a typewriter, paper, and
envelopes. His fellow prisoners must have thought him a little mad for
doing that, for in the exhausted condition most were in, it was hardly
possible to write anything. Nevertheless, Cohen's "theft" was more
than a symbolic act, for he correctly sensed even then that full liberation, if it was to come at all, would require more than physical release
from the camps. The writing impulse was as primary as it was to be
redeeming, and in exercising it the memoirists of the Holocaust have

not only informed us about history's worst moment but revealed, through their variety of confessional writings, that ultimately to be at liberty one must be able to tell one's tale.

III

The dozen or so titles reviewed in these pages constitute only a small section of the historical record of the Holocaust. Numerous diaries exist in addition to those mentioned here, and literally thousands of survivor accounts have been written (the YIVO Institute in New York lists over two thousand such titles; Jerusalem's Yad Vashem lists even more; and many others are housed in major documentation centers elsewhere around the world). As Lucy Dawidowicz attests, the sources available to us for the history of the Holocaust "surpass in quantity and comprehensiveness the records of any other historical era."[14] The literature of testimony is indeed vast and, in its most comprehensive definition, would have to include not only the more or less "completed" books looked at here but that much larger corpus of individual letters, handbills, proclamations, account books, government decrees, diplomatic and business reports, corporate files, memoranda, etc. In its bureaucratic and legal expression, this literature would have to include such things as the Nuremberg laws, which deprived the Jews of Germany of most of their rights, and the minutes of the Wannsee Conference, where plans for the Final Solution apparently were concluded. As eyewitness accounts, it would embrace the papers of the *Sonderkommando* at Auschwitz, Kurt Gerstein's deposition describing the gassings at Belzec, Yankel Wiernik's reports on the gas chambers and crematoria at Treblinka, and Rivka Yosselevscka's testimony at the Eichmann trial about the killings by the *Einsatzgruppen* in Russia. As examples of the literature of heroism and defiance, it takes in the calls to resistance among the Jews in the ghettos of Eastern Europe; the last testament of Mordecai Anilewicz, who led the revolt in Warsaw; and, almost as a unique genre, the suicide notes of people like Samuel Zygelbojm, the Polish Jewish leader who took his life in London in a vain attempt to jolt the indifference of the Western powers and stir them into action in behalf of the Jews. One should not neglect the jottings and pictures of children and the medical records compiled by doctors in the ghettos who studied the wasting effects of typhus and starvation. As part of the literature of fraud and deception, or self-defeating artifacts, baptismal certificates and the omnipresent, always changing German *Schein* have to be considered. And we must not ignore that most minimal but most telling of confessional forms—the fragment—such as the one marked on the walls of a cellar in Cologne where Jews were hiding. "I believe in God," it reads in part, "even when He is silent."

This last, brief inscription, recalling as it does the words of Dr. Schipper, returns us almost full circle to the Biblical contest with which this chapter began. It should end, however, not with the voice of Abel—a fading one—but with that of Cain, always a bolder, more insistent, more dissembling voice. In the literature of self-incriminating testimony, is there anything more revealing than that of Himmler's "Final Summation"?

> We shall never be brutal and heartless where it is not necessary— obviously not. We Germans, the only people in the world who have a decent attitude toward animals, will also take a decent attitude toward these human animals. But it is a crime against our own blood to worry about them and to give them ideals that will make it still harder for our sons and grandsons to cope with them. . . . We had the moral right, we had the duty toward our people, to kill this people which wanted to kill us. . . . And in all, we can say that we have carried out this heaviest of our tasks in a spirit of love for our people. And our inward being, our soul, our character has not suffered injury from it.[15]

By the time Himmler made this speech to his SS officers, Chaim Kaplan, who feared the Nazis as much for their spirit of idealism as for their sword, was dead, as Emmanuel Ringelblum, Anne Frank, Moshe Flinker, Éva Heyman, Yitzhak Katznelson, and Janusz Korczak were soon to be. In the endless contest between testimony and counter-testimony, their words, like the blood of Abel, cry out to us from the earth.

CHAPTER 3

Imagination in Extremis

Our old culture in which humanity transmitted its common life
from one generation to the next was a moral culture, and the ethical
was supreme: no greater good than good, no greater evil than evil.
The death of our old culture came about when the evil greater than
evil occurred—which is the terror.

—Isaac Rosenfeld

"Terror," Isaac Rosenfeld said, "is today the main reality because it is
the model reality." If reality in the 1940s was defined by terror, its
source was not difficult to locate: "The concentration camp is the model
educational system and the model form of government."[1] What it educated toward, as we observed in looking at Primo Levi's memoir and
the diaries and memoirs of some of the other writers, was the degradation and devolution of human types. What is presided over and governed was death and the forms that death might take. The "evil greater
than evil" occurred when death was adorned by the most hellish kinds
of invention:

> The Untersturmführer returns from his vacation. . . . He has come
> back with a new idea; we must have music, a lot of it, to lift our
> morale. We must have it when we go out to work and when we return.
> . . . For this he brings us a fiddle and a harmonica.
> The Untersturmführer has another idea too. He now orders the
> three leather craftsmen in the brigade to make the fire chief and his
> assistant two hats with horns, like those of a devil. From then on, we
> march to work with the fire chief and his assistant leading us, wearing
> their horns and carrying the hooks they used to stir the fire. The two

men were always singed from the fire, and this gave them a charred, blackened look . . . ; with their horned hats, they truly looked like devils. Our Untersturmführer was determined to lighten our mood. (P. 187)

This description of the fire chief and his assistant is not taken from a medieval morality play or from a modern fantasy about hell but from Leon Wells's memoir, *The Janowska Road*. The author has no interest in rivaling the literature of macabre or surrealist invention but is simply trying to relate episodes from his life as a member of a death brigade, whose work it was to obliterate, with bonfires and bone-crushers, some of the millions of corpses produced by the Third Reich. Here, again in Mr. Wells's words, is a description of his "work":

> The fire is burning; the smoke stings our eyes and the smell chokes us. The fire crackles and sizzles. Some of the bodies in the fire have their hands extended. It looks as if they are pleading to be taken out. Many bodies are lying around with open mouths. Could they be trying to say: "We are your own mothers, fathers, who raised you and took care of you. Now you are burning us." If they could have spoken, maybe they would have said this, but they are forbidden to talk too—they are guarded. Maybe they would forgive us. They know that we are being forced to do this by the same murderers that killed them. We are under their whips and machine guns. They would forgive us, they are our fathers and mothers. . . . (Pp. 141–42)

The Untersturmführer, knowing what pressures his men are under, comes to their aid not only with the revelry of music and costume but, more practically, with the kinds of tools that will at least lighten their labors, if not also their mood:

> One day a machine is brought to the site. It looks like a cement mixer, and is run by a diesel engine. Inside the body of this mixer are large iron balls. These at last successfully crush the bones. At the bottom of the mixer is a sieve that filters out the fine bone dust, holding back the still uncrushed pieces of bone, which are then returned to the mouth of the mixer. The fine dust is strewn in the neighboring fields. (P. 187)

As we observed earlier, one finds such machines, or others remotely like them, in Poe and in Kafka, and any number of variations of them in gothic or horror narratives. They belong to the literature of terror, where they seem to satisfy whatever appetites readers have for vicariously experiencing hell. Leon Wells seems actually to have *lived* through hell, as these few quotations from his memoir reveal appallingly enough, and has returned from the place to tell us what his period of residence there was like. To round out the human landscape of that inferno, here is one last citation from his account, this time describing the living and not the dead:

> Mothers undress their children, and the naked mother carries her child in her arms to the fire. However, sometimes a mother will undress herself but will fail to undress the child, or the child refuses to let itself be undressed out of panic. When this happens, we can hear the voices of the children. "What for?" or "Mother, mother, I'm scared! No! No!" In these cases, one of the German SD's takes the child by its small feet, swings it, crushing its head against the nearest tree, then carries it over to the fire and tosses it in. This is all done in front of the mother. When the mother reacts to this, which happens a few times, even if only by saying something, she is beaten and afterwards hung by her feet from a tree with her head down until she dies. (P. 206)

What is the point of reproducing these passages? What was Wells's intention in writing them? He says that it is "to let the world know what happened." But how can the "world"—meaning, in this instance, we as readers—possibly respond to what he relates in any way other than out of shock and revulsion followed soon after by numbness? Such responses do not belong to the normal experience of reading, at least not of reading literature. Is *The Janowska Road,* then, not a piece of literature? One can only answer this question in a mixed way, just as one can only read such a book with mixed responses. "In the presence of extraordinary actuality," Wallace Stevens wrote, "consciousness takes the place of imagination."[2] Inasmuch as Wells's memoir is a piece of writing chastened by the most severe exertion of consciousness, it is literary, although only in the special way that such other highly restrained Holocaust documents as those we looked at in the previous chapter also help to form a literature. It is not "literary" in the more inventive sense of making imaginative projections, however, and, as we discussed earlier, it is certainly not part of the traditional literature of terror. The imagination of disaster that we find in the authors of gothic and grotesque fiction never included anything remotely resembling the Janowska camp of Auschwitz, nor could it have, for prior to the rise of Nazism there were no precedents, literary-wise (with the possible exception of a Kafka story) or otherwise, for such depraved and terror-ridden places. The Christian conception of hell seems to anticipate them, but its punishing fires were to be located somewhere beyond the grave and obscurely under the earth, not in Middle Europe. For man-made factories of death actually to be situated in the countryside of Poland and near the populated towns and villages of Czechoslovakia, Austria, and Germany simply passes beyond novelistic conception of any kind previously known to us. Life, in these instances, presents itself as the least probable of fictions.

As a result, those writers who have attempted to compose fiction about the Holocaust have been faced with a new kind of problem, one that defies the traditional as well as the more experimental modes of narrative representation. For when fact itself surpasses fiction, what is there left for the novel and short story to do? In one way or another, all the writers to be considerd here have had to struggle with this question, which in its extreme perplexity belongs to the ways of the post-Auschwitz imagination.

One way of defining this cast of imagination is to follow Stevens's suggestion and understand the writer's task as one in which conscious-ness asserts itself defensively before the pressures of an extraordinary reality. Literature, in these terms, is "a violence from within that pro-tects us from a violence from without. It is the imagination pressing back against the pressure of reality."[3] In Wells's case, as also in the cases of others who were directly caught up in the turbulence of the war years, writing assumed just such a function. To maintain consciousness at anything like its normal levels, Wells read whatever he could get his hands on and began to compose his memoirs. At a time when "the world as a whole had no reality or meaning," writing itself constituted a central act of survival. Upon his liberation, he notes, his only posses-sion was "a package of papers tied together with a piece of string and fastened to my belt by a short length of rope. This was the day-to-day record I had kept of my experiences in the concentration camp and the Death Brigade" (p. 249). This tableau of the author walking away from the camp with his manuscript tied to his belt is a perfect emblem of the Holocaust survivor-as-writer, one who pitted the life of the mind against the daily wastings of death and, in this case, lived to tell his tale.

What, though, about those writers to whom this emblem does not apply, either because they never personally lived through the ghettos and the camps or did but emerged with no chronicle of their experiences? In the absence of firsthand documentation, how, in other words, can fiction—the imaginative reproductions or transformations of experience—begin to register meaningfully "a world that had no reality or meaning"?

A possible way of coping with such a problem is to have fiction *appear* as the literal transcript of fact, a strategy adopted by John Hersey in *The Wall* and Leon Uris in *Mila 18*. Both novels are about the Warsaw Ghetto uprising and both employ as a central part of their narrative technique the "recovery" of historical records, in the first instance the "Levinson Archive" (apparently modeled after Ringelblum's *Notes*) and, in the second, pages from the "Journal of Alexander Brandel" (similarly modeled). Both Hersey and Uris, in projecting fictionalized "historians" of the ghetto as their frame narrators, have obviously aimed to capture something of the authority that belongs to the eyewitness account of events that we find in the best of the diaries and journals. "What a wonder of documentation!" Hersey exclaims in his "Editor's Prologue," in this manner inviting his readers to enter the fictional world he is about to present to them as if it were part of the historical record. "Levinson was too scrupulous to imagine *anything*," Hersey assures us, and then goes on, as he must, to imagine *everything*. We are not to take his book as "made up," however, but "retrieved" (as the writings by Ringelblum, Kaplan, Frank, Katznelson, and numerous others were in fact retrieved). *The Wall*, "edited" by John Hersey, claims as its "true author" a lost ghetto historian, and it is to his words that the reader seemingly will be turning in beginning the novel: "It is time to let Noach Levinson speak for himself."[4]

In the cases of Hersey and Uris, then, the tensions and contradictions that exist between the history and fiction of the Holocaust are overcome by having fiction simulate the historical record, or pose as fact. Whatever the dramatic interests of these novels, the implications of such a narrative conception would seem to be that the literary imagination cannot gain a sufficient authority in its own terms but must yield to the terms of legitimacy that belong to documentary evidence, in which case readers might prefer to turn directly to the actual historical testimonies we do have.

A second category of fiction chooses to imagine the Holocaust more obliquely, once more from the perspective of history but the history of earlier and perhaps anticipatory events. The implications this time are that we cannot confront a Janov, an Auschwitz, or a Buchenwald head-on and hope to comprehend it, but that their foreshadowings might be glimpsed in the profound sufferings of antecedent eras—that of Chmielnicki, perhaps, or of pre-Revolutionary Russia. I. B. Singer, in setting *The Slave* in seventeenth-century Poland, chose the first of these options; Bernard Malamud, in establishing *The Fixer* at the end of the Czarist era, chose the second.

Prior to the Nazi period, the single greatest slaughter of the Jews in Europe occurred during the Chmielnicki massacres, an extended and especially brutal pogrom that devastated entire communities of Jews in Eastern Europe. *The Slave,* which is set in the immediate aftermath of this tragedy, raises many of the same questions that one finds in the writings of a Chaim Kaplan or an Elie Wiesel:

> There was a limit to what the human mind could accept. It was beyond the power of any man to contemplate all these atrocities and mourn them adequately.

> It was difficult to believe in God's mercy when murderers buried children alive.

> There was not a prayer, law, passage in the Talmud that did not seem altered to him.

These passages are of a kind that arises only after periods of intense communal suffering, and while such calamitous experience is not unknown to Jewish history prior to this century, it does not seem likely that a modern author could compose fiction about Jewish catastrophe in Poland and not have the ghettos and death camps in mind. *The Slave,* then, while ostensibly an historical romance set in the seventeenth century, seems almost inevitably—although obliquely—to be a novel about the Holocaust.

In crucial ways, Malamud's historical novel, *The Fixer,* presents us with an analogous example, for this is a portrayal not only of the prolonged sufferings of an unjustly incarcerated Jew (a strongly representative Jew, whose name, Jakov Bok, carries the connotations of "Israel the Scapegoat") but also of the political manipulation of antisemitism on a mass scale. Moreover, the antisemitism is of a racial as well as a religious kind, which strikes against all Jews indiscriminately. To Jakov's protestations that he was "a Jew [but] otherwise he was innocent," there comes a reply of absolute and lethal accusation: "No Jew is innocent." Given such a formula for total entrapment—a warrant for genocide directed against an entire people—is it possible that Malamud, writing in the 1960s, could have composed such a passage as the following and not have had Hitler in mind? "After a short time of sunlight you awake in a black and bloody world. Overnight a madman is born who thinks Jewish blood is water. Overnight life becomes worthless. The innocent are born without innocence. The human body is worth less than its substance. A person is shit. Those Jews who escape with their lives live in memory's eternal pain."

While these reflections occur within a fictional context of pre-Revolutionary Russia, they project several decades forward and assume a place in consciousness that derives from the 1930s and 1940s. As with Singer's book, then, we seem once more to be confronting the Holocaust unmistakably, even if indirectly.[5]

The point is this: all novels about Jewish suffering written in the post-Holocaust period must implicate the Holocaust, whether it is expressly named as such or not. An especially artful writer, such as a Singer or a Malamud, might succeed in oblique or indirect representation of this most horrific of all Jewish tragedies, but whatever the overt terms of their fictions, covertly the Holocaust will make itself strongly felt. As indeed it must, for Jewish consciousness today has been so fundamentally transformed under the impact of the ghettos and death camps as to refer virtually all earlier instances of Jewish agony to Auschwitz. The *churbn* gathers into one consuming flame the destruction of the first and second Temples *and* the destruction of European Jewry. That Holocaust, as central to our common awareness now as it is inescapable, casts its shadow backwards as well as forwards, then, seeing in Chmielnicki and Petlura the certain forerunners of Hitler, just as in an earlier period Amalek was taken to be the prototype of Haman and Haman the type of all arch antisemites who would succeed him. The phenomenology of Jewish suffering makes such identifications inevitable. By the same token, a phenomenology of reading Holocaust literature necessitates including such books as *The Slave* and *The Fixer* within the same field of awareness, albeit in obviously altered terms, as *The Janowska Road* or *The Last of the Just*.

With André Schwarz-Bart's novel fiction moves backward from history to legend in order to advance forward into the very heart of the chamber of destruction. While to arrive there is ultimately to participate in a distinctly twentieth-century order of death, the dying itself as Schwarz-Bart conceives of it began a long time ago, at least as far back as the anti-Jewish persecutions of medieval Europe. "The true story of Ernie Levy," we learn from the opening paragraph of *The Last of the Just,* "begins much earlier, toward the year 1000 of our era, in the old Anglican city of York."[6] There, in the midst of a church-inspired pogrom, Rabbi Yom Tov Levy and a small group of his followers chose to martyr themselves rather than submit to forced baptism. This *Kiddush Ha-Shem* established a line of *Lamed-Vovnikim,* or "just men," in the Levy family, the last of whom, Ernie, is swallowed up in the gas chambers of Auschwitz. As Schwarz-Bart sees it and presents it, then, the Nazi Holocaust of our time is the culmination of a long history of anti-Jewish violence in Europe that began almost a thousand years before. This historical perspective, whether demonstrably sound or not, greatly enriches the novel, for it allows the author not only to place the contemporary fate of the Jews within the broader frame of a centuries-old hostility but also to depict, through the descendants of Rabbi Yom Tov Levy, a variety of Jewish responses to both the Christian and secular-political animus directed against them. These responses range from martyrdom and exile to a crafty evasion and a naïve and compliant accommodation. At times active resistance is portrayed, although Schwarz-Bart is sharply aware of the pitiful defenselessness of the Jews and at no point highlights open warfare on a mass scale as a realistic option.

Rather, his sympathies are strongly with the exercise of spiritual resistance, a quieter form of power that derives from religious faith and finds reinforcement in some of the heroic motives of myth and legend as well as in historical examples. *The Last of the Just,* rooted as it is in two of the most imaginative and hallowed of Jewish religious and folk sources—*Kiddush Ha-Shem* and *Lamed-Vov*[7]—advanced beyond most previous attempts at fictionalizing the Holocaust by projecting a possible *meaningfulness* to Jewish suffering and even a measure of freedom within it. Both are ultimately driven to their limits, to be sure, for both are predicated on the finalities of Jewish martyrdom, yet Schwarz-Bart succeeded far more than he failed in showing the courage, dignity, grace, and compassion that can attend such tragic action. His point in doing so, clearly, is to affirm that, even in impossible circumstances, one can choose death rather than be altogether terrorized and victimized by it. To die on one's own terms and not succumb to the meanness and viciousness of the slaughterer, in other words, is to die at the height of spiritual resistance to oppression.

Despite some attempts to see "a Christian message" in *The Last of the Just,* though, it should be stressed that there is no expiation or redemption in Ernie Levy's ending, no "salvation" that will result from it. Schwarz-Bart makes the point emphatic on the last page of his book when he cautions against such hopefulness: "This story will not finish with some tomb to be visited in memoriam. For the smoke that rises from crematoriums obeys physical laws like any other: the particles come together and disperse according to the wind that propels them. The only pilgrimage, estimable reader, would be to look with sadness at a stormy sky now and then" (p. 374). If one is intent in seeing in this horror a symbolism of religious ascension, one will be disappointed, for all that might be detected of the burnt remains of Ernie Levy and the millions of others like him is ash and smoke. And such debris, far from carrying any salvific assurances, reduces the spirit as well as the body to mere waste.

It may be this perception of a final futility that has brought most other writers to avoid taking Schwarz-Bart's lead and following him back into history. On the one hand it seems clear that an awareness of earlier periods of antisemitic violence can lend a perspective for understanding and narrating the Holocaust, but only if the latter is conceived as being part of some historical continuum. If, however, it is felt as being *sui generis,* not the result of a long-standing "antisemitism," then the interpretive vocabulary provided by earlier periods in Jewish history obviously will not serve. Elie Wiesel pointedly registered this sense of a large-scale inadequacy of perspective when he refused the consolations tendered him by the Lubavitcher Rebbe, who tried but failed to get the survivor to grasp Jewish fate under the Nazis within the broader terms of the *Churban:*

> [Here is] a nice story from the Talmud. . . . It was about either Rabbi Johanan Ben Zakkai or Rabbi Eleazar; when his son died, his disciples came to console him, and they said, "You know, Rabbi, when Adam's son Abel died, even he was consoled. Why aren't you consoled?" So he said, "My friends, don't you think I am sad enough with my own tragedy? Why do you add the tragedy of Adam too?" So they said, "Remember Aaron the high priest: when his sons died even he was consoled." And he said, "Don't you think I am sad enough with what happened to me, why do you add the sorrow of Aaron?" And so on and so on. What does that mean? That pain is accumulative. One does *not* negate the other, but one is being *added* to the other. This is the answer that I gave to the Lubavitcher Rebbe. . . . When he tried to tell me that

the Churban, the first Churban of the Temple two thousand years ago, already posed the problem, I said, "but these two tragedies add to each other and the problem is already more enhanced, more grave, more serious."[8]

Implicit in this rejection of analogous or antecedent example is the necessity to begin all over again, to place whatever understanding or representation of the Holocaust may be possible within its own terms. Just what these may be will vary from novelist to novelist, but the task for the writer would seem to involve either some form of fictional realism, in which the charge will be to re-create what life and death were like in almost naturalistic terms, or some form of surrealism, in which the Holocaust is transmuted into more abstract visions of agony, absurdity, or mythic suffering. Writers such as Borowski, Kuznetsov, Lustig, Semprun, and J. F. Steiner exemplify the first of these two possibilities; writers such as Delbo, Gascar, Kosinsky, Lind, and Rawicz exemplify the second. If there is a third option, it would include a fiction of post-Holocaust implication, as illustrated by *Mr. Sammler's Planet,* already noted earlier, as well as such novels as Norma Rosen's *Touching Evil,* I. B. Singer's *Enemies: A Love Story,* and some of the retrospective fiction of Wiesel. There are gains and losses to be had through each of these modes, and individual writers have written interestingly out of each of them; no one, however, has yet produced a fiction encompassing enough or compelling enough to be wholly adequate to its task, that being, in Isaac Rosenfeld's terms, to comprehend the terror "which begins, far beyond the point—already outside the human world—where our old evil left off" (p. 199).

The problem with these terms, which are otherwise useful, is that they still continue either to imply a moral world or, acknowledging the displacement or destruction of moral categories, to suggest an order of experience that was otherworldly. The Holocaust, rather, existed somewhere between these two poles, its locus an extreme disjunction between familiar and remote or uncanny situations. In the fiction defined by the first category of writers, narrative representation is grounded in historical and moral realities that we can all recognize easily enough, although we will have difficulty comprehending the extreme harshness to which these were subjected. In the second category of fiction, we have already crossed over to some other side, not yet beyond the boundaries of recognition but at the same time not to be comprehended within the terms of normative experience. In both cases it is a disjunction brought on by incipient or overt terror that draws our attention and, by forcing perspective out of its normal alignments, upsets our balance.

More than anything else, perhaps, it is perspective that is the crucial problem for the fiction writer to solve. Hersey and Uris, as we observed earlier, chose a documentary perspective, as Schwarz-Bart did an historical one. In the case of such an engaged writer as Jorge Semprun, whose protagonist in *The Long Voyage* is a fighter from the Spanish Civil War, politics provides a central ideological perspective just as a Proustian handling of time provides a central structural one.[9] Each of these is viable enough, although each is also predictable. It is only when, in the realistic mode, we encounter a Borowski that we are met and disarmed by surprise, for the point of view this writer adopts for most of the stories in *This Way for the Gas, Ladies and Gentlemen* is unusual enough to be virtually without precedent.[10]

What Borowski has done, quite simply, is to show how the evil of the concentration camp system can coopt the narrative perspective to such a degree as to take it over wholesale. In his own words (from "Auschwitz, Our Home"), "we are not evoking evil irresponsibly or in vain, for we have now become a part of it . . ." (p. 113). Czeslaw Milosz spells out precisely how this attitude has shaped Borowski's stories:

> In the abundant literature of atrocity of the twentieth century, one rarely finds an account written from the point of view of an accessory to the crime. Authors are usually ashamed of this role. But collaboration is an empty word as applied to a concentration camp. . . . [Borowski] is a nihilist in his stories, but by that I do not mean that he is amoral. . . . He wants to go the limit in describing what he saw; he wants to depict with complete accuracy a world in which there is no longer any place for indignation. The human species is *naked* in his stories, stripped of those tendencies toward good which last only so long as the habit of civilization lasts. But the habit of civilization is fragile; a sudden change in circumstances, and humanity reverts to its primeval savagery.[11]

Indignation is absent from this fiction for it implies distance or detachment, an attitude of moral separation. Shock, wonderment, revulsion, or compassion, likewise all absent, do the same. To keep these civilized responses alive would be to portray the savagery of the concentration camp as a thing apart, and Borowski, who is nothing if not the opposite of a sentimentalist, is intent on showing how terror quickly becomes domesticated and soon enough can define the circumstances of Auschwitz as "home." That is a stance that belongs to the veteran observer, one who long ago gave up the sense of the camp being an extraordinary mutation of reality and not the thing itself. One does not fight against it so much as for one's place within it—as soft and as privileged a place as one can acquire, and by whatever means necessary to make the acquisition secure. Of course that is to be complicitous, which of course means to be "an accessory to the crime," but there is only the crime. Borowski, who by all accounts conducted himself with exemplary behavior during his incarceration in Auschwitz, chose to narrate his stories from the viewpoint of complicitous criminality, which, more than anything else, is what makes them so terrifying. His narrator eats well while others starve; dresses in silk shirts and expensive shoes while others go exposed and begin to freeze; catches as much sleep as he can while others rave in the agony of their death throes. The aim is to stay alive admidst all the death, moral survival not being the point at issue so much as physical survival itself. Such an attitude is shocking to the reader, but little shock at all registers within the stories themselves, in which the protagonist can walk away from a selection "humming a popular camp tango called 'Cremo'" (p. 55).

The contrast in narrative perspective with such a moralist as Schwarz-Bart, for instance, is extreme and helps to reveal just how severe, and accomplished, a realist Borowski is. *The Last of the Just* is ultimately a novel about spiritual resistance, whose final form—martyrdom—is portrayed as the better option to moral compromise. Everything turns on this insight: "Not to abandon a world that has abandoned you is to add madness to your misfortune" (p. 116). Ernie Levy, who in effect is a voluntary suicide, lives and dies by this code, showing himself in the process to be a man of noble, even sacrificial, ideals. No such idealism informs Borowski's fiction, which exists to show an opposite attitude, one in which heroism plays no role whatsoever. Far from voluntarily "abandoning" the world, Borowski's narrator through most of the stories in *This Way for the Gas* looks to reap profit from it, getting himself the most rewarding jobs, feeding and clothing himself as lavishly as he can, avoiding the gas. "Work is not unpleasant when one has eaten a breakfast of smoked bacon with bread and garlic and washed it down with a tin of evaporated milk," he says—this while some of his bunkmates are literally starving to death (p. 58). While a soccer game is being played, "between two throw-ins . . . , right behind my back, three thousand people had been put to death" (p. 84). These are the women, old men, and children of a new transport, who walk to their deaths while, "at the gate, a band was playing foxtrots and tangos" (p. 84). Such events are discordant, even obscene in their juxtapositions, but everything at Auschwitz exists in gross disjunction with the earlier life; and, seeing things this way, Borowski is sternly correct in his refusal to attempt a resolution between the two. Life in such a place is purchased at whatever price is asked, and death is attended by "no hocus-pocus, no poison, no hypnosis. Only several men directing traffic to keep operations running smoothly, and the thousands flow along like water from an open tap" (p. 112). To express sympathy for these dead or outrage at their fate would be to give vent to a humanism at odds with Borowski's controlling point of view, which maintains the cool detachment of the uninvolved. Within the context of these stories, anything else would appear sentimental and subvert the peculiar "concentration-camp mentality" that this fiction was written to expose (p. 176). Here it is spelled out at its most explicit:

> . . . they are really quite amusing, these civilians. They react to the camp as a wild boar reacts to firearms. Understanding nothing of how it functions, they look upon it as something inexplicable, almost abnormal. . . .
>
> Today, having become totally familiar with the inexplicable and the abnormal; having learned to live on intimate terms with the crematoria, the itch and the tuberculosis . . . ; having, so to say, daily broken bread with the beast—I look at these civilians with a certain indulgence, the way a scientist regards a layman, or the initiated an outsider. (Pp. 111–12)

As readers we are necessarily outsiders, although somewhat less so after suffering the stories of *This Way for the Gas, Ladies and Gentlemen,* whose hard look at camp life, uncompromised by pity or fear, brings the terror almost unbearably close. Borowski knew, of course, that readers, being "civilians," would only begin to understand if he could disabuse them of civilized habits, these being the same reflexes of humane expectation that so quickly dropped away under the pressure of camp life. He manages to convince us of their fragility not by direct assault but in far more subtle ways, by showing, for instance, how hope—the father of all illusions—subverted both consciousness and will and made so many pliable for death.[12] Such indulgence had to give way or, as was usually the case, life would trickle away in the endless stream that carried millions to the gas. Borowski effects his act of disillusionment by adopting a narrative perspective stripped of most of the human affections—the only point of view, he was convinced, that would not deceive. "I do not know whether we shall survive," he wrote in "Auschwitz, Our Home," "but I like to think that one day we shall have the courage to tell the whole truth and call it by its proper name" (p. 122).

Borowski did survive, both Auschwitz and Dachau, and, while still a very young man, wrote and published his stories. In one of them he notes that, if he were to survive, he would come away from the camps "marked for life" (p. 122). Following the war years and a period of time in Munich, he returned to Poland and took up writing political journalism of a heavily compromised kind, which earned him positions of high standing in government circles but also the dismay of some of his literary friends. According to both Czeslaw Milosz and Jan Kott, Polish emigré scholars who have written intimate portraits of Borowski's career, the writer began to grow despondent and, like Mayakovsky before him, to acknowledge that he had "stepped on the throat of his own song."[13] A half dozen years after his liberation from Dachau, Borowski, not yet thirty, turned on the gas jets in his Warsaw apartment and took his own life.

Most realistic fiction of the Holocaust, grounded as it is, at least initially, in traditional moral concepts, makes strict divisions between the victims and the executioners, just as it distinguishes between the past and the present, normal and abnormal behavior, sanity and madness. The terror, as it is usually portrayed in these novels, is something directed against the innocent by an agent of evil while others may look on aghast or be simply indifferent. These divisions dissolve in Borowski's fiction, which portrays the three almost as one, the terror being a total force that quickly breaks down all former distinctions. The dominant sense in Borowski is not of the hunter and the hunted but only of the hunt. That is why among the fictional realists his is the strongest case, for it is the least bound by moral concepts of the old evil, which cannot encompass or begin to explain the new.

For this same reason, Kosinski may be the strongest example

among the fabulists of the Holocaust, although at their best Lind and
Rawicz begin to rival him. Rawicz, in fact, can be used to provide a
helpful introduction to one of the key ways that Kosinski has worked in
writing *The Painted Bird*. "All mutilation is holy," Rawicz writes, "so
holy that it passes the contagion of its holiness on to the One who
mutilates. From the wedding between the holy Mutilator and the holy
Mutilated are born children in shapes hitherto unknown. . . ."[14] That
vision of absolute contamination and desecration informs the narrative
perspective of Kosinski's novel throughout, far more so indeed than the
author's own judgment that he has portrayed man "in his most vulnerable sense, as a child, and society in its most deadly form, in a state of
war." In this case, Kosinski the critic is not the best guide to Kosinski
the novelist, for while *The Painted Bird* may in some loose thematic way
involve a confrontation between "the defenseless individual and overpowering society," it is far closer to the modern bestiary that Rawicz
points us toward and hardly at all a book about the contests between
self and society.[15]

The most compelling, and disturbing, aspect of Kosinski's
achievement, in fact, is that it has been won almost altogether at the
expense of individual and societal norms. Its series of grotesque and
revolting scenes do not find their coordinates naturalistically within the
historical frame of the war years but emerge in front of them as
metaphors of an evil so rampant as to be virtually unanchored in history
and unexplainable by historical criteria. The level of deviance is so high
and so constant in Kosinski, in fact, as to appear almost gratuitous,
leading readers to question whether *The Painted Bird* is a terrifying and
obscene book or a book about the terrors and obscenities of the Nazi
period. My own sense of it is that it is more the latter than the former,
which is to say that it is in its mode the furthest extension we have so
far of terror portrayed in its absolute dimensions, glimpsed at those
points where it begins to evolve into myth.

Such portrayals, far from establishing the categories of "self" and
"society," reflect their wholesale contamination and hence their ruin. If
ever there was a book that confirms Wiesel's contention that in the
Holocaust not only man died but also the idea of man, *The Painted Bird*
is it. Its power, which becomes almost allegorical, derives from the
author's ability to detach his visions of degraded life and violent death
from the historical matrix of the Holocaust and have them appear pre-
ternatural, as if they are universally abiding forces that are not to be

placated or even understood, at least not understood in human terms. From its initial invocation of Mayakovsky—"and only God, / omnipotent indeed, / knew they were mammals / of a different breed"—to the apocalyptic detonation of the trains at the end by the Silent One, the accent is on human types of estranged and sordid character performing the most improbable and repellent deeds. As these evolve over the course of the narrative, and they do so randomly and often inexplicably, the effect is one of accumulating terror, as if no action was so awful that its wickedness could not be surpassed. That is to register effectively the dominating sense of the Holocaust as a series of relentless thrusts against any lingering traces of human definition, but inasmuch as Kosinski has transcribed this vision in terms that are largely ahistorical, we are left gazing upon Rawicz's "shapes hitherto unknown" and not the more common and recognizable human species.

The single reference in *The Painted Bird* that implicates the Holocaust directly, in fact, is the one that is exploded at the novel's end. Earlier in the book there is a glimpse of the trains carrying the Jews to their deaths; later the unnamed boy who is the protagonist in the novel practices gaining a mastery over the trains by lying down between the tracks and letting the engine roll over him. If one recalls Marx's definition of war being the locomotive of history (and more than one reference in the novel gives emphasis to Marxian concepts), then one can understand the boy's action as being as much a challenge to history's evil as to death itself. The boy experiences exhilaration of the highest sort each time he passes the dangerous test he sets for himself: as he says, "by comparison with the fear that filled me when I waited for an approaching train, all other terrors appeared insignificant" (pp. 218–19). Being bypassed by that death train, after voluntarily subjecting oneself to it, is not, as in Schwarz-Bart's moral universe, to choose martyrdom but, in Kosinski's nihilistic one, to gain the upper hand over the power that shapes events. When at the novel's end that same hand helps detonate the explosives that will send the train screaming off its tracks, history is subjugated. For at the moment when that occurs, the boy recalls "the trains carrying people to the gas chambers and crematories" and begins to feel within himself "the magnificent sensation" of knowing he controlled the power over life and death (p. 220). Given the movement of this novel, however, which indulges explanations only to discard them rapidly, the boy's victory can only be regarded as a temporary one. The apocalyptic shattering of history, which haunts

Kosinski's writing from first to last, finds a strong metaphor in this final scene of the train's perilous derailment, but that is only to show once more, albeit in a culminating way, that all the dehumanizing forces of death and destruction remain out of control, as they have been throughout the nightmare world of *The Painted Bird*. The whole novel, in fact, ends up being one large metaphor for an unchecked terrorism whose mutilating violence twists the human being out of shape. At the ugly center of so much raw barbarism is the Nazi Holocaust, but depicted in its more abstract strains of inflicting gratuitous cruelty and unrelieved pain. Kosinski's art lies in this ability to transmute history into mythic forms, made all the more frightening for being made somewhat harder to see.

The fictions of Borowski and Kosinski single themselves out as unusually strong books largely through their presentations of what is least acceptable to us emerging as what is now most accessible to consciousness and hence unavoidable. Other novels and short stories show the many faces of the same terror, but none in such sustained and consistently menacing ways. In part that may be owing to the felt need of any number of writers to document or otherwise support the "truthfulness" or "reality" of their fictions or, conversely, the failure on their part to demonstrate convincingly the "irreality" of the Holocaust. The issue once more centers in problems of perspective. Piotr Rawicz, for instance, begins his novel as if it were to consist of transcripts of a survivor's historical narrative but closes it with a "Postscript" in which he disavows any documentary intentions:

> *This book is not a historical record.*
>
> If the notion of chance (like most other notions) did not strike the author as absurd, he would gladly say that any reference to a particular period, territory, or race is purely coincidental.
>
> The events that he describes could crop up in any place, at any time, in the mind of any man, planet, mineral. . . . [16]

Even allowing for the obvious irony in this disclaimer, it does not sit well with the claim to veracity that opens *Blood from the Sky* and tends to throw into uncertainty the matter of just how it is we are to read this book. That is not our problem with Kuznetsov, who goes out of his way to stress the historical accuracy of his novel, subtitling *Babi Yar* "A Document in the Form of a Novel" and foreswearing, in his author's preface, "the slightest element of literary invention." In an interview in the *New York Times Book Review,* Kuznetsov even claimed he invented the term "documentary novel" to signify his fidelity as a fiction writer to the historical record. Three years later, when the author was already living outside of his native Soviet Union, where *Babi Yar* first appeared in a bowdlerized version, Kuznetsov republished the novel in a "complete" and uncensored edition, which carried new material but the very same disclaimers of "leaving nothing out and making nothing up." As a result the same problem that one encounters in reading Hersey and Uris is compounded by new difficulties about what is and isn't "true."[17]

Similarly, Charlotte Delbo's *None of Us Will Return* concludes, at least in its new American edition, with these words: "I am no longer sure that what I have written is true, but I am sure that it happened," a confession that recalls Wiesel's statement, in the introduction to *Legends of Our Time,* that "some events do take place but are not true; others are—although they never occurred." Such problems are exacerbated when efforts are made to "re-create" historical figures in fiction (an Eichmann, a Himmler, a Höss, a Mengele) and then to have them mingle with the products of literary invention, as in Gerald Green's novel *Holocaust* and William Styron's *Sophie's Choice.* Solutions are not truly forthcoming when "testimonials" to the accuracy or historical validity of fictions are attached to the novels, as, for instance, with J. F. Steiner's *Treblinka,* which is "accredited," so to speak, by Simone de Beauvoir; or Manès Sperber's *. . . than a tear in the sea,* which is prefaced by a long historical reflection by the author.[18] This need to place documentary or expository prose in apposition to works of fiction is quite common in Holocaust writings and would seem to indicate an awareness that imaginative literature on this subject does not carry a sufficient authority in its own right and needs support from without. This hesitation to let fiction speak for itself almost certainly grows out of a sense of double insecurity, on the one hand cognitive—"Did these things really happen?"—and on the other expressive—"Given the meager means of language, how can I convincingly relate them?" Both are seen clearly enough in the following brief passage from Carlo Levi's *The Watch,* which poses a challenge to Holocaust fiction, especially of the realistic mode, that few writers have been able to meet satisfactorily: "What sort of novel do you want after Auschwitz and Buchenwald? Did you see the photographs of women weeping as they buried pieces of soap made from the bodies of their husbands and sons? That's the

way the confusion ended. The individual exchanged for the whole. . . .
There you are! Your *tranche de vie*—a piece of soap."[19]

So much, this passage says ringingly enough, for literary naturalism. Sensing the inferior status of fiction next to such Holocaust artifacts or even photographs of them, it is little wonder that most writers
have expressed at some point feelings of linguistic inadequacy that are
close to despair. Rawicz, recognizing the futility of transcribing the terror through metaphor and analogy, resolves in the middle of his novel
"to kill comparisons, to expunge them all, . . . and to engage in mere
recounting, mere enumerating" (pp. 183–84). Schwarz-Bart, in one of
the most revealing moments in *The Last of the Just,* interrupts his narrative to lament authorially, "I am so weary that my pen can no longer
write. 'Man, strip off thy garments, cover thy head with ashes, run into
the streets and dance in thy madness . . .'" (p. 370). Far from seeming
an intrusion, this admission of the near-collapse of narrative power carries with it an honesty that is affecting and adds to rather than detracts
from the veracity of the novel.

Such veracity does not finally depend, however, on any exact
fidelity to history so much as it does on the writer's ability to absorb
history into myth or legend. In reviewing the fiction of the Holocaust,
one is struck by the fact that it often is most memorable when it departs
from the traditional ways of the novel and begins to approach the condition of poetry. What lingers on frequently has less to do with the
narrative elements of plot development and character portrayal than
with the presentation of feeling through certain brilliant images, which
can be in their way as crystallizing and as lucid as the photographs that
so overwhelm Carlo Levi. Rawicz is especially inventive in this respect,
for he is a writer capable of momentary thrusts into a highly developed
image-making. Delbo, Borowski, Kosinski, Schwarz-Bart, and Semprun are, at key moments in their novels, similarly capable. No one
who has read these authors at all carefully will soon forget the visual
analogues of grief and anguish that they are able to present—the field of
human heads turning like rotting cabbages in *Blood from the Sky*; the
dead children, carried away from the boxcars "like chickens," several
held in each hand, in *This Way for the Gas, Ladies and Gentlemen*; the
slaughter of the butterflies in *The Last of the Just*; the crumbling of the
crematoria and their fading from memory in *The Long Voyage*. I choose
to end here, though, with a passage from Arnost Lustig's *A Prayer for
Katerina Horovitzova*,[20] which perhaps best expresses the power of fic-

tive image-making by showing what must be the end point of all images of the Holocaust:

> His eyes reiterated something which had nothing to do with his work—that these ashes would be indestructible and immutable, they would not burn up into nothingness because they themselves were remnants of fire. They would not freeze, but simply mingle with the snow and ice, never drying under the sun's hot glare because there's nothing more to dry out of ashes. No one living would ever be able to escape them; these ashes would be contained in the milk that will be drunk by babies yet unborn and in the breasts their mothers offer them; the ashes will linger in the flowers which will grow out of them and in the pollen with which they will be fertilized by bees; they will be in the depths of the earth too, where rotted woodlands transform themselves into coal, and in the heights of heaven, where every human gaze, equipped with a telescope, encounters the invisible layers which envelop this wormy terrestrial apple of ours. These ashes will be contained in the breath and expression of every one of us and the next time anybody asks what the air he breathes is made of, he will have to think about these ashes; they will be contained in books which haven't yet been written and will be found in the remotest regions of the earth where no human foot has ever trod; no one will be able to get rid of them, for they will be the fond, nagging ashes of the dead who died in innocence.

CHAPTER 4

Poetics of Expiration

Hush and hush—no sound be heard.
Bow in grief and say no word.
Black as pain and white as death,
Hush and hush and hold your breath.
—MANI LEIB

Poetry, it was once widely believed, resided naturally in certain areas of experience as well as formally in a certain use of language. Some subjects seemed inherently poetic just as certain conventions of language likewise served the ends of poetry and carried it into the world. All this—the definitions of what constituted a natural subject matter for poetry and the formal means by which it was to be embodied—began to change a long time ago, so that by the mid-twentieth century poetry had already opened up broadly to include a much wider range of subjects in far looser, less conventional modes of language than ever before. From at least the time of the French Symbolists, dismal landscapes, unheroic figures, and unelevated feeling became commonplace features of poetry and even began to define anew "the poetic" for us, which need not any longer appear in the formal dress of rhyme, a regulated meter, or traditional stanzaic patterns. Poetry was what our most gifted poets made of the world with their words, and if the world no longer looked or felt like it had in the past, poetry had to change to register the new circumstances. If it failed to reflect such changes, or if it sought to convey them in the conventional language of former periods, poetry declined into a genteel pastime—a cultivated hobby for skilled rhetoricians, perhaps, but not the vital speech of the day. For to be living, poetry must continually change, even as it remains the voice of constancy within change.

For the most part, the one abiding constant of all poetry at all times has been a belief in the potential of language to serve the poet's endless expressional quest. This belief, which is necessarily anchored in another constancy—that of some recognizable, commonly accepted human scale—was severely challenged by the Nazi terror, so much so that it was forcibly turned into something that begins to look like its opposite: the belief that human life could be, and in select instances even should be, undone, that people were trash and might be disposed of as such. A counterpoetics stands behind this nihilistic creed, one that was formulated with a memorable exactness in Rolf Hochhuth's play *The Deputy:*

> The truth is, Auschwitz refutes
> creator, creation, and the creature.
> Life as an idea is dead.
> This may well be the beginning
> of a great new era,
> a redemption from suffering.
> From this point of view only one crime
> remains: cursed be he who creates life.
> I cremate life. That is modern
> humanitarianism—the sole salvation from the future.
>
> (P. 248)

This speech, given to the doctor in the play (a character modeled on the notorious Dr. Mengele), is spoken with a notable eloquence, but is there any *poetry* possible in the view of life and death that is espoused here? Dying itself, as we know from centuries of literature that have been occasioned by it, is among the most powerful inducements to affective language, but death as a willed de-creation—a savage and systematic undoing of the human species—is not of the same order of dying at all and cannot be embraced within any concepts of poetry known to us thus far. A search through the annals of past poetry will reveal some compelling satanic figures, but one would have to search long and hard to find an undefeated, triumphant satanism, let alone one based on historical models. The satanic impulse greatly draws poets of a certain imaginative cast, but has any ever celebrated a satanic movement? Nazism was such a movement, particularly in its murderous campaign against those it considered *Untermenschen,* but while it was effectively promoted by a kind of epic street theater and popular cinema (cleverly managed, in spectacular pomp and precision, by Joseph Goebbels and his colleagues in the manipulative arts), it failed to produce a single poet of merit. What it did do was send into flight some of

Europe's best writers and silence others who remained. Nevertheless, as with writers in the other literary forms, poets have emerged out of and after the ghettos and camps, and these and others have joined voices in developing a poetry of the Holocaust.

This poetry is as various as the individual experiences, styles, and nationalities of the writers themselves. By now their numbers are too great and their efforts and achievements too mixed and uneven to allow them to be considered as one coherent or corporate entity. They include the popular songwriters and balladeers, some of them known to us by name, whose compositions circulated freely in occupied Eastern Europe. Among poets who wrote in German they include Celan, Kolmar, and Sachs; among the Yiddish poets, Glatstein, Grade, Katznelson, Leivick, Manger, Molodowsky, Sutzkever, and Zeitlin; and among the Hebrew poets, Alterman, Gilboa, Greenberg, Kovner, and Pagis. There are additional poets of interest in each of these groupings, just as there are also occasional poems by such writers as Feldman, Hecht, Hill Layton, Levertov, Milosz, Pilinszky, Plath, Radnoti, Reznikoff, Rozewicz, Simpson, and Yevtushenko. Two recent books by younger American poets, William Heyen's *The Swastika Poems* (1977) and W. D. Snodgrass's *The Führer Bunker* (1978), indicate that an effort to gain poetic access to the Holocaust is continuing even by writers as far removed in time, place, and experience from the European tragedy itself as these two.

The poetry of the Holocaust, then, is both large and diverse, too much so, in fact, to be considered here in its detailed variety. It seems preferable instead to reflect on what may be unique to at least some of this poetry, especially if we might gain thereby some closer knowledge of the poetic vocation itself in the post-Holocaust period.

I

Most accounts of poetic origins are based in one way or another on some version of the idea of inspiration. An animating agent, either external to the poet or within him, is at work to trigger the *furor poeticus,* which brings language to birth as poetry or song. This inspiring force may be called the Muse or Apollo, the Holy Spirit, Psyche, or the Unconscious, but whatever its name it tends always to move in more or less the same way, visiting the poet at unexpected moments and surprising him into utterance. "One hears—one does not seek; one takes—

one does not ask who gives," as Nietzsche described the composition of *Thus Spake Zarathustra*. "The idea simply comes," T. S. Eliot said. "It will come if it is there and if you will let it come," confirmed Gertrude Stein. And Mallarmé: "Words rise up unaided and in ecstasy." Whatever explains it, this great but unbidden gift, which occurs, as Nietzsche testified, "as if in an eruption of freedom, independence, power, and divinity," arrives as an invigorating and informing force, providing the poet with new energy and new knowledge. It is impossible, in fact, to divorce the idea of inspiration from either respiration or revelation, a second breath and second sight. That is why poetry is conceived as being both *animus* and *spiritus*, the world inhaled anew as revisioned power, exhaled as revitalized form.

Given the concerns that we have been pursuing up to this point, though, it is necessary to examine a poetics that runs counter to the idea of inspiration and, as we begin to glimpse it in the writings of certain poets of the Holocaust, has the effect of seeming to displace it or even to refute it. I refer to a development that becomes particularly apparent in some of the late work of Paul Celan and Nelly Sachs. If I read them at all correctly they seem to announce, in some of their most moving poems, a poetics of *expiration*. To clarify what I mean by that term, it will be useful to glance briefly at a passage in Celan's *Der Meridian*—the poet's acceptance speech on receiving the Georg Büchner Prize in 1960—and then to turn to some poems by him and Nelly Sachs.

In discussing Büchner's art, Celan refers to a challenge that he himself felt acutely as a poet. Reflecting on what happens to language under assault, he notes that, under conditions of great stress, the word "is no longer a word; it is a terrible falling silent; it takes away [the poet's] breath and word, and ours, too. Poetry: it can signify a turning of the breath."[1] Poetry always relies upon breath's turning, by which we mean—or at least have meant in the past—breath's *re*turning, its resumption and reorientation under the influence of inspiration. In its most minimal definition, poetry's possibility, as life's own, is dependent upon the grace of breath's rhythmic occurrence. The word "is," in fact, was thought at one time to come from the Indo-European root *as,* meaning "to breathe."[2] Poets, the "shepherds of being," as Heidegger called them, have always sought the words that might allow them a closer understanding of this correlation and usually have formulated it in terms of hovering spirits, animating breezes, or inspiring winds. Think of Shelley invoking the West Wind to descend upon him and scatter his verse abroad in a great prophetic blast; or of Wordsworth, gentler in spirit but no less eager to be quickened by "the sweet breath of Heaven," that "mild creative breeze," as he reflects on it in the *Prelude,* which gave renewed life to his songs.[3] This reference to "Heaven's breath" is not gratuitous or merely an example of conventional poetic diction, for in this context we are drawn most of all to recall that most sublime—and most literal—of inspirations, the original moment of creation itself when God breathed into the nostrils of man "the breath of life; and man became a living soul." As we learn of his origins in Genesis, man, we might even say, is God's poem, the dust of the earth elevated to human form when inspired by the divine breath. *"Ruach"* in Hebrew, in fact, signifies not only "breath" and "wind" and "spirit," but "soul," that spark of divinity in the creature that ties him to his Creator. In countless ways the Hebrew Bible reinforces this primary connection between God's inspiring force and man's vital being. "Remember that my life is a breath," Job says (7:7). As a richly poetic example, recall as well the verses in Ezekiel 37 that describe the restoration of the dry bones: "Then said He unto me: 'Prophesy unto the breath, prophesy, son of man, and say to the breath: Thus saith the Lord God: Come from the four winds, O breath, and breathe upon these slain, that they may live. . . . and the breath came into them, and they lived, and stood upon their feet, an exceeding great host."

This is majestic, visionary poetry, foreseeing as it does nothing less than a reversal of the processes of human finitude, the reconstitution of living form from its crumbling into dust. Needless to say, such poetry is no longer so available to us today. As far as we know, our dead— and in the European catastrophe they numbered many times more than the "exceeding great host" lamented by Ezekiel—remain dead, their breath literally choked off in their throats, their cry a mouthful of silence. No heavens have opened to reveal God's breath returning to the slain house of Israel; nor would we easily tolerate a poetic voice that would proclaim such things: it would probably seem muddle-headed, blasphemous, insane. As a result, Ezekiel's vision of restitution comes, if it comes at all in the post-Holocaust period, as bitter parody, as in Dan Pagis's "Draft of a Reparations Agreement":

> All right, gentlemen who cry blue murder as always,
> nagging miracle-makers,
> quiet!
> Everything will be returned to its place,
> paragraph after paragraph.

The scream back into the throat.
The gold teeth back into the gums.
The terror.
The smoke back to the tin chimney and further on and inside
back to the hollow of the bones,
and already you will be covered with skin and sinews and you will live,
look, you will have your lives back,
sit in the living room, read the evening paper.
Here you are. Nothing is too late.
As to the yellow star: immediately
it will be torn from your chest
and will emigrate
to the sky.[4]

As if in some manipulative cinema—a crazy backwards winding of
the camera—Pagis returns the scream to the throat. Celan, less prone to
follow this vein of irony, remains closer to the awful experience itself,
registering the moment of breath's constriction, its turning away from
any sources of reparation or revivification, its winding down toward
expiration. There is a terrifying mimesis at work in his poems, so much
so that as we read them we are almost forced to descend several degrees
on the scale of animated being—to lessen our pulses, lower our rate of
breathing, generally reduce our vital signs. For he seems to have written many of his poems perilously close to some threshold beyond
which life is all but snuffed out, or where it is conceived as never having been at all: "It is / I know, not true / that we lived, it was / simply a
breath passing blindly / between There and Not-Here and At-Times."[5]
If we pursue such passage to its end point—and his poetry tends to
compel us to do so—more often than not we arrive at "the No-
longer-nameable": at silence. Robbed of its breath, the word—"hot /
audible in the mouth"—remains unspoken, so that the voice you hear
is "No one's voice, again." Here is how "No one's voice" sounds in a
poem, the quiet but magnificent "Psalm":

No one kneads us again out of earth and clay,
no one breathes into our dust.
no one.

Praise be to you, No One.
To please you
we want to bloom
toward
you.

A Nothing
we were, we are, we
shall remain, blooming:
the Nothing's rose, the
No One's rose.

With
the style, bright of soul,
with the filament, deserted of heaven,
with the corolla red
from the crimson-word we sang
over—ah!—over
the thorn.[6]

In the imagery of Jewish religious thought, Israel is often portrayed as a rose growing with its heart toward heaven, a symbol of the nation's repentance before God. Celan not only retains this traditional imagery but uses it as the centerpiece of his poem; yet in it there is no mention of God's name, only a reference to "No One." It is because God has become "the no-longer-nameable"? There is much in "Psalm" that *implies* him, yet the poem is dominated by his absence: "No one kneads us again out of earth and clay, / no one breathes into our dust." This is unmistakably God-language, but in the negative: it is a decomposition of the very same verses in Genesis that we noted earlier in remarking on the creation of man as God's poem. In the Holocaust that "poem" was radically and systematically undone, its once-divine image reduced to ash.

In the poem "Chymisch" ("Chemical"), Celan elegizes "all the cremated names" as "so many ashes to bless" (p. 187). In "Psalm," that post-Holocaust poem of praise, he turns toward the Lord of names and addresses him, not at all mockingly, as "No One": the expired Inspirer. For with the demise of the creature, it is as if the Creator himself has been taken out of language, his life-giving Name negated. What remains, in this strangely beautiful poem, is Jewish stubbornness—a lingering and defiant piety—expressed in the devotional yearnings of a bloodied remnant bending still faithfully toward the source of its original bloom.

That is to read Celan at his most reverent. To be sure, his is a reverence marked by the most extreme of paradoxes, that of an almost destroyed people still reaching toward a deserted heaven and an absent God. Nevertheless, the devotional quality of such a poem as "Psalm" is not to be doubted. And there are others like it, among them "Stehen" ("To Stand") and "Einmal" ("Once") from Celan's sixth volume of poetry, *Atemwende* ("Breath's-Turning," 1967). These are all brief lyrical poems, however, and although they are finely wrought, they do not begin to match in extended reflection such earlier and lengthier rehearsals of destruction as "Todesfuge" ("Death Fugue") and "Engführung" ("Stretto"). As one moves into Celan's later volumes, in fact, his poems tend to become more clipped and elliptical, their forms frequently abbreviated and narrowed on the page, their language often intensely private and even hermetic. Words get broken up into their separate syllables, syntax is occasionally twisted, the breath runs short and, at times, in gasps. Colors, never abundant in this poet's work, are blanched to shades of white and gray, as if something under the eyelids has broken; sounds echo more faintly and seem to arise from places deeply recessed or off in the remote distance; the world becomes more and more illegible as things change their shapes and recede from touch; experience itself eludes easy comprehensibility and is less and less translatable into language. The self, as Celan divined its coming fate in "Heimkehr" ("Homecoming"), is "slip[ping] into dumbness"(p. 93).

"Homecoming": to Celan it seems to have been predicated upon a poetics of expiration. The far and away called to him luringly, and ultimately drew him out of language. His late poems refer to mudchoking, to submergence, to drowned images; to bloody phalluses, mute stones, and riven skies; to landscapes that are frosted over and located somewhere outside of the workings of time; to the abstract realms of above and below and beyond; to Babel. "I hear," he writes only half-whimsically in one of these late poems, "I hear that they call life / our only refuge."[7] And again—but more chillingly—in a poem that encompasses all of three lines:

> You were my death:
> you I could hold
> When all fell away from me[8]

Finally, in "Fadensonnen" ("Thread-Suns"), the poem that gave its title to the last volume that Celan was to publish while still alive, the conviction, at once affirmative and despairing, that "there are / still songs to sing beyond / mankind" (p. 223). Breath, withdrawing, pointed the poet elsewhere, toward some irreality that most of us prefer not to know about firsthand, but which Celan seemed ultimately drawn to enter and explore, never to return:

> Deep
> in the time-crevasse,
> by the
> honey-comb ice,
> there waits, as a breath-crystal,
> your unimpeachable
> testimony.

(P. 227)

II

As in the work of Celan, one can observe in the writings of Nelly Sachs a poetics of expiration working itself out in ways that are both thematic and mimetic of the Holocaust. By that I mean, of course, the Holocaust as it has had its most lasting impact—on consciousness, not flesh. For those who actually perished, no words are adequate. Much of Holocaust literature, consequently, might be described more accurately as "post-Holocaust literature," the expression of those who come after. For those who were swallowed up by the night, there is only "the throat's terrible silence before death," as Nelly Sachs put it in one of her poems ("Lange schon fielen die Schatten," "The Shadows Fell Long Ago").[9] Yet in just so putting it, she herself begins to move toward the victims, and in a poetry of mimetic forms recapitulates something of the ineffable terror that must have marked their fate. Poetry's weakness and its force oddly come together in this drift toward silence, through which language both depletes and replenishes itself.

The themes of the Holocaust are explicit and not at all difficult to locate in Nelly Sachs's poetry, especially in the early volumes, which contain those many choruses of lamentation and beseeching—"Chorus of the Dead," "Chorus of the Rescued," "Chorus of the Orphans," etc. The language of these poems is typically direct (in many cases, perhaps too direct); their images—of burning chimneys, smoke-blackened stars, unsheathed knives, torn skin—are undisguised and equally direct; their tone, a mingling of elegiac sorrow and pained, ceaseless yearning. It is impossible, in other words, to read the early poetry of Nelly Sachs and not recognize the aptness of the poet's dedicatory inscription to her first book, *In den Wohnungen des Todes* ("In the Dwellings of Death")—

"for my dead brothers and sisters." Feeling her kinship to the dead as personal loss and national tragedy, she sets out consciously and quite determinedly to commemorate them, and in poem after poem she intones her mournful, tender, always respectful dirge. Such poetry is, in her own words, a prolonged "music of agony" (p. 343)—grief-stricken, openly and effusively bereaved, the pained utterance of a wound that will not close until death itself arrives to heal it over.

While one can admire the nobility and tenacity of her undertaking in these early volumes, Nelly Sachs's most striking work is found elsewhere. For especially in her two final volumes—*Noch feiert Tod das Leben* ("Death Still Celebrates Life," 1965) and *Glühende Rätsel* ("Glowing Enigmas," 1963–66)—the Holocaust shows its impact on her not only thematically but in poems whose language and forms begin to more closely approximate and reproduce her descent into night. To observe that happening, it may be helpful to reflect briefly on another remark made by Celan in *Der Meridian*. "Poetry today," he writes all too knowingly, "shows a strong inclination towards silence."[10] Now it needs to be acknowledged that such a statement could have been made by any of a number of other writers, some of whom may have lived before the Holocaust or had nothing at all to do with it. A "literature of silence," in fact, begins to make its appearance well before the period of World War II and may be traceable even as far back as the nineteenth century. Nevertheless, this tendency toward the wordless—toward poetry's surcease—not only reaches its climax in Holocaust literature but shows, in ways not to be seen so clearly and profoundly elsewhere, history's implication in the etiology of silence and, most importantly, the implications of radical evil for humanistic and theological self-understanding.

"When the great terror came / I fell dumb,"[11] begins one of Nelly Sachs's poems in the *Glühende Rätsel* series, and no reader sensitive to the contexts out of which she wrote could possibly miss her reference point here or fail to grasp her intended meaning. The declaration, so far from being metaphorical, seems actually to have been physiologically true, for the poet apparently suffered through a period in her life when she was literally voiceless, without the ability to speak at all. Her way of representing this state of terror-stricken dumbness relies on metaphor, often that of a fish with mutilated gills, "its deathly side / turned upward," desperately struggling for breath. The image effectively serves to portray the poet's feelings of helplessness and torment before a violence so brutal that it took the breath away and reduced her to a state of speechless seeking.

Seeking for what? For the victims who were torn away into nothingness and, so that their loss would not be total, for the poet's means to retrieve them, at least for memory. That double search set her on her course—"to write the first letter / of the wordless language,"[12] as she described it. To do that, she had to articulate a new poetics, one so far removed from traditional concepts of inspiration as to take place "behind the lips." "Hinter den Lippen": it is in a poem with this very title that we begin to see Nelly Sachs searching for ways to reproduce "the throat's terrible silence before death":

Behind the lips
waits the ineffable
tears at the words'
umbilical cords

Martyrdom of the letters
in the urn of the mouth
spiritual ascension
of incisive pain—

But the breath of the inner speech
through the wailing-wall air
breathes confession delivered of all its secrets
sinks into the asylum
of the world wound
it had gleaned from God
even in its ruin—[13]

From this point on—the point of "inner speech"—the equation in Nelly Sachs's poetry between silence and a new kind of breathing—a breathing "already without voice" (p. 265)—becomes clear. "The graveless sighs in the air / . . . creep into our breath" (p. 87), she writes in one poem. And, in another, she announces her vocation as that of gathering the homeless dead into "the sanctuary of [her] breath" (p. 151). That is an altogether uncanny inspiration, one whose rhythmic ebb and flow depend upon a music meant "not for the ear" but for the soul's "seed whispering / in death" (p. 303). Is it possible to hear such music and, beyond hearing, reproduce it anew in poetry? Yes, so her final poems seem to tell us, if listening is attuned to silence and the voice empowered by a wind of waning currents.

"A sigh / is that the soul?" she queries. To find out, and to follow its fading music, she felt she had to stand in the very center of the world's wound. Only there might silence grant her its song, she believed. For in her day, after what she called "the sorrow-stone tragedy" (p. 225), language was to be retrieved, if at all, only by descending again into the darkness that precedes creation. That was her sphere as a poet and, in those late poems of all but total dispossession, Nelly Sachs returned to it time and again, with grace and a lingering beauty, carrying her quest to the very edge of articulation. There, at "the last breathing point of life" (p. 303), just before the soul's sigh escaped into nothingness, she pursued and seemingly solved the most enigmatic of riddles: how language, expiring, can still find a voice: how "death still celebrates life." "Wait," she promises, "Wait till the breath ends / it will sing for you as well" (p. 373).

III

The Bible does not tell us what Adam did in the moment after his creation, but we almost certainly know what he did: he spoke. Whether he spoke to praise his Maker or in wonder at being alive, we do not know, but it is hardly to be doubted that, feeling life within him, he uttered words. Is that not, in fact, the way of any newborn child, who wails his way into the world with the first breath he takes? The wail is his announcement of arrival: "I am here," or, simply, "I am." Every poet does the same, and, to the degree that every man is equally the recipient of breath, all are at least incipient poets. Life's equation, understood in these terms, then, is this: "to breathe" is "to be" is " to speak." And so Adam, the first in the line of human creation, must have spoken.

What about the *last* in the line? And the one who comes just before him, close enough to witness his end? We cannot easily imagine our own termination, let alone life's, but as we read further and further into Holocaust literature an awareness of human ending becomes unavoidable. Here Scripture at one time could be of more direct, interpretive help, as we see, for example, in Psalm 104:29: "Thou hidest Thy face, they vanish; / Thou withdrawest their breath, they perish, / And return to the dust." These verses take their place naturally enough in the biblical scheme of things, within which it is not at all difficult to accept the idea that he who created man out of the dust of the earth by breathing into his nostrils returns him to dust when breath is withdrawn. For millennia, indeed, men and women grasped the mystery of human expiration in these terms, and just as they recited psalms to celebrate their comings, so they had prayers with which to mourn their goings.

Within Jewish tradition, the dead are commemorated by recitation of the *kaddish,* which, oddly enough, makes no mention of them. It is, instead, said in praise of the Creator who gives us our life and preserves us in peace and well-being, a virtual thanksgiving prayer. The thrust of the *kaddish,* in other words, is psalmic in a celebratory sense.

Yet such recitations and sanctifications as the *kaddish* were severely undermined, if not altogether shattered, in the Holocaust. Praise may still be forthcoming, as we saw in Celan's "Psalm," but its divine object, as we likewise saw, has vanished. Instead of an exaltation of "the name of the Holy One, blessed be He," the Holocaust poet recites his praise to "No One." Or, as Elie Wiesel tells it in "The Death of My Father," that agonizing autobiographical postscript to *Night,* he may hardly be able to bring himself to utter words at all. For what relationship did the elder Wiesel's death in a Nazi concentration camp have to the life he had formerly led, the person he had formerly been? Here is how Elie Wiesel describes his father's ending:

> Stretched out on a plank of wood amid a multitude of blood-covered corpses, fear frozen in his eyes, a mask of suffering on the bearded, stricken mask that was his face, my father gave back his soul at Buchenwald. A soul useless in that place, and one he seemed to want to give back. But, he gave it up, not to the God of his fathers, but rather to the impostor, cruel and insatiable, to the enemy God. They had killed his God, they had exchanged him for another.[14]

And so on the day of his father's death, the young boy, now doubly orphaned—bereft of his father and of his father's God—did not follow tradition and recite the *kaddish.* He abstained, he later recalled, because he "felt empty, barren: a useless object, a thing without imagination." And because to say *kaddish* "in that stifling barracks, in the very heart of the kingdom of death, would have been the worst of blasphemies."[15]

In Buchenwald, as in all the other regions of hell, life's equation was negated: "*not* to breathe" was "*not* to be" was "*not* to speak." An anti-God acting in behalf of anti-Man literally stifled human life, choking it off in the throat. The ghettos were so crowded and so constricted as to be almost asphyxiating. "I do not exaggerate when I say we have reached a state of lack of breath," Chaim Kaplan writes; "there simply is no air" (p. 362). As for the camps, day after day the poison gases showered down—one hears them in the hallucinatory refrain of Paul Celan's "Todesfuge": "Black milk of morning we drink it at dusk / we drink it at noon and at dawn we drink it at night / we drink and we drink."[16] No wonder, then, as Celan wrote in another of his poems, that the condemned "invented no song," "devised no kind of language." How could they?

And yet it is not altogether true that they left behind no testimony, for they did. To witness it, gaze at the finger-clawed messages that mark the ceilings and walls of the "bathhouses" of Auschwitz and try to imagine what occurred as those iconic signatures were placed. *They* compose the language of life at its end point, the last utterances of those whose lungs and breath and speech all collapsed under the assault of the gas. For safety's sake, and for sanity's, it is best to keep some distance from testimony so direct and unembellished as this, for if we were to truly hear the accumulated silence that followed the victims' screams, as Elie Wiesel has warned, it would deafen the world.

Is it not our privilege to have that danger mediated for us by the poets, those who come just before silence and keep us from knowing too well the terror that lies on its other side?

CHAPTER 5

Contending with a Silent God

Elias Canetti, in a notebook entry of 1942, sought to describe freedom in its most elementary sense, this at a time when throughout Europe freedom of every kind was being extinguished. This is what he wrote: "The origin of freedom lies in *breathing*. Anyone can draw breath from any air, and the freedom to breathe is the only one that has not really been destroyed to this day."[1]

Events were to prove him wrong, drastically so. A year later, in an entry of 1943, Canetti jotted into his notebook the following: "How odd. Only the Bible is strong enough for what is happening today, and its dreadfulness is what comforts us" (p. 41). He does not mention just which books of the Bible he was reading, but, given the violent death that was spreading across Europe, he could have stopped with the story of Cain and Abel in Genesis. One of the root meanings of the Hebrew name Abel ("hevel") is "breath," indicating already in the story of the first fratricide that the most basic of human freedoms—the freedom to draw life from breath—was brutally suppressed. The European war intensified this brutality a millionfold, especially in the violence it directed against the Jews, bringing Canetti to brood in explicitly biblical terms about the intertwinings of man's fate and God's: "One cannot say 'God' anymore, He is marked forever, He has war's Mark of Cain on his brow . . ." (p. 52). Why this branding of God? The question is answered by another question recorded in the same notebook entry: "Do we not see them, people, being sent to death by the trainload?" Could God be detached altogether from that mass destruction? The implication that he could not has raised for many in the post-Holocaust period theological questions of the most troubling kind.

In the essay that he contributed to *Commentary*'s "Symposium on

Jewish Belief" (August 1966), for example, Richard Rubenstein wrote as follows: "When I say we live in the time of the death of God, I mean that the thread uniting God and man, heaven and earth, has been broken. We stand in a cold, silent, unfeeling cosmos, unaided by any purposeful power beyond our own resources. After Auschwitz, what else can a Jew say about God?"[2]

The question with which Rubenstein concludes—*After Auschwitz, what else can a Jew say about God?*—is, among other things, a poet's question, and in an attempt to answer it, it will prove useful to look at some more of the work of Paul Celan and Nelly Sachs. In doing so it must be stressed that, as in the case of Canetti's notebook jottings, the writing to be examined here is not in any sense of the term formal theology. It is poetry, yet poetry of a kind that is seriously preoccupied with theological questions, the most basic of which, though framed differently by each poet, is some variation of the query cited above. An examination of the ways in which the two poets ask and answer the question will reveal something of the range of possibilities still seemingly available to the poetic imagination "after Auschwitz."

I

The distances that separate the world of Paul Celan's poetry from that of most of his readers today are formidable enough to require a brief introduction to the poet's life. Celan was born in Czernowitz, the capital of Bukovina, in 1920. This city, also the home of the Yiddish writers Eliezer Steinberg and Itzik Manger and the Hebrew writer Aharon Appelfeld, had a large and thriving Jewish community, which numbered almost forty percent of the total population. When one includes the Jews in the neighboring communities elsewhere in Bukovina—in particular, Sadagora, to the north, the seat of the Ruzhiner Rebbe, and Vizhnitz, in the foothills of the Carpathians, the home of an equally famous Hasidic court—the total Jewish population of this area probably exceeded one hundred and twenty thousand before the war. Nationally, Czernowitz belonged to Romania (today it is part of the Soviet Union), but culturally it remained in many ways part of the Hapsburg Empire, and most of the Jews there looked to Vienna as their cultural capital and spoke German as their first language. Celan (whose name at birth was Paul Antschel) was not a notably devout Jew as a young man, but in later years, when Czernowitz as he knew it had been destroyed and the poet was living in exile, he took it upon himself in some of his poems to re-create imaginatively strains of the Jewish legacy that he had received from his native region. This is how he described his homeland in the text of a speech made in Bremen in 1958:

> The landscape from which I come to you—by way of what detours! but are there even such things as detours?—this landscape may be unknown to most of you. It is the landscape that was the home for a not inconsiderable part of those Hasidic tales that Martin Buber recounted to us all in German. If I may be permitted to enlarge this topographic sketch, which now reappears before my eyes from such a distance, this region was one in which men and books lived.[3]

Celan shared with Buber not only this intimate dialogue between books and men but also the German language and the larger idea of language as the fragile yet indestructible basis for any meaningful existence. When all else had been taken from Paul Celan, when his homeland had been occupied by the Nazis and his parents deported to one of the death camps, his language alone remained as a link to the past. The poet lived in it as permanently and as securely as he ever did again in any physical landscape. Celan was a man of several languages—he translated from the Russian, French, English, Italian, Portuguese, and Hebrew—but, although he spent most of his adult life in Paris, German remained for him the closest form of living speech, and he rendered it in his poetry in some startling ways. Language was not only the medium of his poet's art: it was its constant challenge, its primary subject matter, its most authentic world. Language was both origin and destination for Celan, and he was acutely sensitive to its proximities to silence, madness, and death. The pressures that threatened to push life over its thin borders into these destructive realms were real to him and, in his later years, constant. Poetry, as a consequence, was almost one with ontology and for Celan formed a basic point of orientation for a life of perception, volition, and personally articulated speech. "Go with art into your own most narrow place," he remarks in *Der Meridian*, "and you will set yourself free."[4] Like Rilke, who affirmed that *Gesang ist Dasein,* that poetry is existence, Celan attempted to build a home for himself in words.

But first and always there were the "detours," the fluctuations of a busy life that moved the poet continually between the shifting poles of exile and home-seeking. These include periods of study and work in Paris, Czernowitz, Bucharest, and Vienna. In 1941, when his native city was occupied, Celan and his family were removed to the ghetto. In 1942 his parents were taken away to an extermination camp and the poet himself sent to a forced-labor camp, from which he escaped. He married in 1950 and spent the rest of his life in Paris, travelling occasionally to Germany for poetry readings and to receive literary prizes (journeys that were always difficult for him). In the year before he died he visited Israel, where he presented readings from his poetry to audiences that included some of his former countrymen from Bukovina. Then in the spring of 1970, shortly before he would have been fifty years old, the final detour: the body of Paul Celan was discovered in the Seine, apparently a suicide—a shocking denial of the world of books and men.

Celan's death occurred at about the same time as Nelly Sachs's, and with the passing of these two important poets, that distinguished line of Jewish authors who have written in German comes closer to its end. This fact in itself adds a special poignancy to Celan's suicide, for as long as he lived and wrote there remained some strong living connection of Jews to German-speaking culture, a culture that was significantly enlarged and enriched by the contributions of its Jewish writers over the past two centuries. Celan helped extend that line in a major way, and the particularly desperate manner in which he helped bring it to a close strikes resonances that travel all the way back to Heine.

As an inscription to one of his poems Celan quotes from the Russian poet Marina Tsvetayeva to the effect that "All poets are Jews." The meaning of this startling inscription, as I understand it, is that all poets write out of a harried condition, and none so much as those Jewish writers—Heine, Kafka, Else Lasker-Schüler, Gertrud Kolmar, Nelly Sachs, and Paul Celan, among many more—who have written in German. The duality of that enterprise has always been exceptionally difficult, and the torments of alienation, exile, and a forlorn or violent death have all too frequently been the lot of so many of these writers. If it is the fate of all poets to be Jews, then what can one say more particularly about the extremities of fate that have marked the lives and deaths of the German-Jewish poets?

The poems themselves begin to tell us clearly enough. In looking at them I begin with "Zürich, Zum Storchen" ("Zurich, at the Stork Inn"), from Celan's fourth collection of poetry, *Die Niemandsrose* (1963). Significantly, the poem carries a dedication to Nelly Sachs, who might be taken as the second speaker in the poem.

> We talked about too much, about
> too little, About You
> and Pseudo-You, about

clouding through brightness, about
Jewishness, about
your God.

About
that.
On the day of an ascension, the
cathedral stood on the other side, it came
across the water with some gold.

We talked about your God, I spoke
against him, I
let the heart that I had
hope:
for
his highest, his death-rattled, his
wrangling word—

Your eye looked at me, looked away,
your mouth
spoke to your eye,
I heard:

But
we don't know, you know,
we
really don't know
what
counts.[5]

This poem is notable for several reasons. In its openness and
directness, it is far more explicit than most of Celan's poetry, which is
typically characterized by hermetic qualities of language. Here, the
poet is striving for a clarity altogether unimpeded by original syntax
or difficult turns of speech—in two lines (3 and 4) the phrasing is
unusual, but otherwise the diction of the poem is not in any way ambiguous or obscure. In terms of its major stylistic elements, in fact, the
poem should be readily accessible to most readers.

Nevertheless, this is not an "easy" poem, and one does not quickly
relax into a confident understanding of it. Despite the general cleanness
of line and phrase, there is a clarity here that troubles, or, to cite the
poem's own words, a "clouding through brightness." What is it in the
poem that clouds the light and complicates understanding? The day itself is a clear one, and the gold of the cathedral across the water seems
to sail in its bright reflection toward the speakers, as if to impose its
presence upon them. The day is also a holiday, honored by Christians

as Ascension Day, and its special character is not lost on the two companions. Just the opposite is true: as the cathedral sends its gold across the water to them, they are distracted from their conversation and momentarily held by the splendor of its gliding presence, which may mirror in the water below the heavenly flight above. This is the one magical moment in the poem, a moment of high color, liquid movement, and rare experience. Here the poem relaxes for a brief respite from the tension that otherwise grips it, and the imagination is allowed to indulge itself in a shimmering reflection of transcendence. But it does not rest here very long, for this is not to be a poem of rich sensuous apprehension or sustained imaginative pleasure. The golden spectacle is glimpsed but not really entertained. And while there is an insistent emphasis on transcendent truth in the poem, it is not to be of the kind that is joyously celebrated on the day when the risen Christ is said to have ascended into the heavens. Rather, the nature of the day and the ornate symbol that crowns it stand in sharp contrast to the conversation that preoccupies the two speakers.

They are talking about weightier matters, about Jewishness and the Jewish God; no wonder, then, that the talk was of "too much" and "too little." They also make reference to "Aber-Du," an ambiguous phrase that has been understood and translated elsewhere as "You-Again" but which can also mean "Pseudo-You," or that which is *not* "You." This second reading was the poet's own preference, in fact, and it may help suggest what it is that troubles the light and dims clarity: paradoxically, it may be the cathedral that beckons with its golden brightness, the single carrier of light in the poem, lifting the imagination heavenward but simultaneously obscuring the understanding, at least the Jewish way of understanding. And here it must be remarked that, above all, this is a poem about Jewish understanding, more specifically, about the state of such understanding after the Holocaust, which is nowhere mentioned in the poem, but which is nonetheless felt throughout.

How is this so? For one, "Zürich, Zum Storchen," although set in a restaurant, is not in any way analogous to such café pieces as T. S. Eliot's "Dans le Restaurant" or "Conversation Galante," poems of artifice in which dramatic "characters" inhabit "fictional" settings and engage in highly mannered conversation. The speakers in this poem are known to us by name and by fate, and from the start we know as well exactly what it is they are discussing: as in Celan's prose sketch "Gespräch in Gebirg" ("Conversation in the Mountains"), they are discussing what two Jews from different places almost always will be drawn to discuss when they meet, namely the troubled state of Jewishness and the place and special feeling of God amidst that trouble. The two are Nelly Sachs and Paul Celan, and they come together in Zurich, which seems an appropriate setting for two German-speaking Jewish poets who live altogether outside of their natural language environments: Nelly Sachs, who managed to flee her native Berlin with her elderly mother and to reach safety, if never again truly another home, in Sweden; and Paul Celan, who fled to a new, if continually tormented life, in Paris. They do not quite sit down and weep for their exile, as Eliot did in *The Waste Land,* but they do feel the tense incongruity of their situation.

For they are in Zurich on a day that is celebrated by almost everyone else in the city as one marking triumph over death and hope for all mankind, yet to them, who do not assent to this conception of divine transcendence and do not embrace its hope, it is not Ascension Day at all but, more distantly and neutrally, "the day of an ascension." It has been their fate to learn and write the poetry of another kind of ascension, that of "Israel's body, dissolved in smoke" and curled upward in the air through "the chimneys / on the dwellings of death so cleverly conceived," as Nelly Sachs formulated it in one of her most famous poems. The two ways of ascension clash and cannot be reconciled, and although only one is made explicit in the poem, both can be felt.

As the two talk of Jewishness and of God, then, it can only be against their own heavy experiences of each, which is to say, of the cruelly diminished state of each after the Holocaust, which has marked their lives and thrust upon them their special vocation as elegiac poets. The Holocaust registers throughout their poetry, and it is felt in "Zürich, Zum Storchen" as well.

Where is it felt? In the questions that are raised and the answers that are given about God. Celan speaks of him in terms of angry defiance, speaks *against* him, yet his heart opens in hope for his "word," described here as "his highest, his death-rattled, his / wrangling word." The terms are confused, but purposely so, for this conception of God is a troubled one: his "highest" word we take to be Creation, his "death-rattled" word the final choked gasp before death, his "wrangling" word perhaps with reference to Abraham's quarrel with God over the lives of the doomed men of Sodom. His "word" moves between life and death, then, with the opportunity for mediation between the two kept open. The poet, in a state of emotional turbulence, feels all three together, and almost as one. No wonder, then, that he does not claim this God as his own, but twice refers to him as "your God." The rejection is emphatic, yet so too is the expression of hope: "I / let the heart that I had, / hope."

The unusual phrasing calls attention to itself here: the wording is not "I hoped" or "I let my heart hope," but "I let the heart that I had hope," which is to say, the only heart still left to me. Left to me after what? That the poem does not say, at least does not say explicitly, but if we are attuned to the silences of Celan's poetry and know how to read them as well as the words, we know how to answer. The void is always the same for this poet, and although his proximity to it may differ from poem to poem, his awareness of its causes and composition does not: silence and ashes form the compound of suffering in Celan's world and shape the stuttered music of his *Todesfuge*. Here, from "Es war Erde in ihnen" ("There was earth in them"), is the sound, the origin, and the fate of that emptiness:

> They dug and dug, and thus their day
> passed on, and their night. And they did not praise God
> who, they heard, wanted all this,
> who, they heard, knew all this.
>
> They dug and heard nothing more;
> they did not grow wise, invented no song,
> devised no kind of language.
> They dug.

The poet's companion in "Zürich, Zum Storchen," herself possessed of this same dark knowledge, likewise is unable to "praise God," but neither can she assent to the embittered view of him expressed earlier. She does not speak against him, does not speak for him, and hardly speaks at all to the poet but, turning within, replies in bafflement and quiet resignation, "We don't know, you know, / we / really don't know / what / counts." And there the poem ends, in sadness and close to the very edge of silence, from which so much of the poetry of Paul Celan and Nelly Sachs comes and back into which it frequently fades.

There are analogies between this silence and that felt by Hölderlin at the beginning of the nineteenth century and by Nietzsche toward its close, yet it must be emphasized that Hölderlin's felt sense of living in a time of spiritual dearth and Nietzsche's proclamation, in the words of the madman of *Die fröhliche Wissenschaft,* that "God is dead," stand in extreme contrast to the historical and metaphysical dimensions within which Paul Celan and Nelly Sachs wrote their poetry. When Hölderlin asks, in the memorable seventh stanza of "Brod und Wein," "und wozu

Dichter in dürftiger Zeit?" ("and what are poets for in a time of dearth?"), he raises a question about the vocation of poetry that is so fundamentally aggrieved as to be almost unanswerable. Yet he does answer it, in terms that stress the lingering values of the Christian and Classical world views and that assign to the poet something of the Dionysian function of the earlier priests of the wine-god. When, however, Celan asks the same kind of question in such a poem as "Tübingen, Jänner" ("Tübingen, January"), one that directly evokes Hölderlin, the answer given is in such fractured speech as to be almost unintelligible:

> If
> a man came,
> came into the world, today, with
> the light-beard of
> the patriarchs: he would,
> were he to speak of this
> time, he
> would only be able
> to babble and babble,
> perpe-, perpet-
> uallyally.
>
> ("Pallaksch. Pallaksch.")

The nonsense words that close this poem are also part of the language of Hölderlin, albeit Hölderlin in his madness, a state that Celan obviously sees as closer to the condition of the post-Holocaust poet. The historical distance between the two poets is measurable: if, in the early nineteenth century, the poet labored to maintain his language in a time of general impoverishment and need, by the middle of the twentieth century he was far more strenuously tested and by forces actively threatening and carrying out devastation. Hölderlin's trial, which tested him severely and ultimately broke him, was to live as a poet of intense religious sensibility in an age when the gods had already fled and holy names were lacking; the challenge to Celan was of another kind, for while it incorporated the problems that troubled Hölderlin, it also went beyond them. The following lines from Celan's poem "Engführung" ("Stretto"), for instance, could not have been written by a poet of the nineteenth century:

> Came, came,
> Came a word, came,
> came through the night,
> wanted to shine, to shine.

Ash.
Ash, ash.
Night.
Night-and-night.

How is one to understand such poetry as this, poetry whose compulsive stuttering brings language frighteningly close to Hölderlin's
helpless "Pallaksch, Pallaksch"? It will not do to try to explicate it in
terms of the speechlessness of an existential angst, for with Celan we
are well beyond that. The night of Hölderlin and even of Nietzsche was
precipitated by that radical transvaluation of values that abandoned each
of them to extreme states of ontological loneliness and terror, finally
trapping the poet and philosopher in madness. The night that Celan
knew was darker and more terrible still, for this time history determined it literally, not metaphorically, and swept away innocent millions, including the poet's own family, into empty spaces in the sky:
"The place where they lay, it has / a name—it has / none. They did not
lie there" ("Engführung").

The poet is left alone in this night, with the responsibility to remember and record those who went into it, but is almost without recourse, in language or in act, to carry out his function. His word comes
stuttering through the night, wanting to illuminate it, but discovers
only its own dumbness before the void. And entering *that,* the poet
finds his legacy and his charge: "All the names, all the / cremated
names. / So many / ashes to bless" ("Chymisch").

Yet how does one utter the blessing over smoke and ash? There are
poems in which Celan manages to stutter "Ho, ho- / sannah," "Ho- /
sannah." There are others, written out of rancor and cynicism, in which
he is quicker to curse than to bless. And still others, such as "Stehen"
("To Stand"), in which the poet is altogether without words and can
only hold his ground in dumb witness, himself a silent psalm:

To stand, in the shadow
of the scar up in the air.

To stand-for-no-one-and-nothing.
Unrecognized,
for you
alone.

With all that has room in there,
even without
language.

This is a remarkable poem and, in its rare way, a strangely affirmative one, for although it carries the poet to the very limits of language, it is not nihilistic. To the contrary: in the face of an overwhelming nihilism, the poem maintains its ground in being. Stripped of speech, it nonetheless refuses to be cancelled out and establishes itself with firm, even if silent, resolve. The degree of autism here is frightening, but the moral stance—the insistence on surviving and, in the very act of surviving, on *serving*—thrills as well as humbles us.

The parallel with Hölderlin is again instructive. The earlier poet's behest, in "Wie wenn am Feiertage . . . ," was that his fellow poets venture to stand bareheaded under the thundering God and, grasping the divine charge in their hands, wrap it in song as an offering to the people. Hölderlin was fully aware of the danger involved in such intense and unmediated experience, but he urged the poets on, all the same, "for if only we are pure in heart, / Like children, and our hands are guiltless, / The father's pure ray will not sear our hearts." The highest poetry is born, in Hölderlin's ennobled view of the art, when the poet is ignited in song by the "far-flung down-rushing storms of / The God."[6]

But in Celan's day the storms were not of the God; they raged against Him. The poet may have remained fully as pure and as guiltless as before, but now his heart was seared all the same, even if there was no heavenly fire for him to drink. Instead, there was that relentless flow of poison gas, the "Schwarze Milch der Frühe," which poured through the gas chambers and, in so pouring, emptied the sky of its God. In place of the heavenly throne, a deep scar in the air attested to the cosmic rupture. Still, it remained incumbent upon the poet to take up his place below, even if this time he was conscious of "standing-for-no-one-and-nothing." The danger was not the one Hölderlin had foreseen, namely, that of being too frail a vessel to hold the divine charge; rather it was to stand in readiness and open expectation for a power that no longer streamed, for the word that no longer spoke. "Unrecognized" and unaided by any force, the poet nonetheless would persist in his vocation as poet and offer up his silent song "for you / alone."

The quality of dedication in Celan's poem is hardly to be equalled in recent literature and nowhere to be surpassed. Its degree of faith before the void, its pure *standing* as a fundamental ontological truth, finds its equivalent in the Psalms, of which Paul Celan was as close as we have come to having a modern master. Kant's criterion for the highest art, that it exhibit a purposiveness without purpose, is not only satisfied in such a poem as "Stehen" but given a moral dimension as well, for to hold one's ground before the groundless, to maintain one's silent breath before "the word [that] died past here," is to enter, but to refuse to succumb to, the nothingness of night. In theological terms, the parallel is with Habakkuk, a more vocal contender with the silent God, but one whose stance is strikingly similar to the one we notice here:

> How long, O Lord, shall I cry,
> And not be heard?
> . . . .
> I will stand at my post,
> I will take up my position on the watch-tower
> And look to see what He will say to me,
> And what He will reply to my complaint.
>
> (Hab. 1:1, 11:2)

From time to time, but only seldom in our time, one confronts a poem that one admires not only as a language-act but also as an act of exceptional moral courage. "Stehen" is such a poem, a retrieval out of the night, an utterable silent prayer.

Celan wrote others of this kind, including the following: "Psalm," "Die Schleuse" ("The Sluice"), and "Benedicta," from *Die Niemandsrose* (1963); "Weggebeizt" ("Cauterized"), "Schlickende" ("Mud-choked"), and "Einmal" ("Once"), from *Atemwende* (1967); and "Wirk nicht Voraus" ("Don't Act Ahead"), from *Lichtzwang* (1970). In each of these poems the proximity to silence, that is to say, to poetic expiration, is nearly absolute, yet in each of them there is as well an intimation that some absolute meaning may reside within, or on the other side of, silence. To reach it, the poet risks everything native to him as poet and sets out to navigate "a tiny / unnavigable silence" and arrive on the other end.

What awaits him there? Some of these poems extend consciousness far enough to allow us to begin to know, but our knowledge can only be formulated in the language of paradox, which belongs to either the highest or lowest perception, to rare religious insight or its opposite, yet uneasily related form, madness. "Psalm," a poem of deep devotional yearning, addresses and affirms God as "No one," yet a "No one" whose presiding Absence seems to embody the fullness and majesty of omnipotent Presence. In "Die Schleuse" the poet risks passage through the final sluice in an effort to rescue and retrieve "back into, / and across, and beyond the brine" a single word that had been lost to him: the Hebrew word *Yiskor,* which announces the Jewish memorial prayer for the dead. In "Benedicta" Hebrew again mingles with German but this time also with Yiddish to articulate a form of blessing that might serve the poet after his voice had otherwise already exhausted itself: the word *gebentsht* ends this poem, as *Yiskor* ended the previous one, on a note of traditional Jewish piety. The linguistic process, which is clearly meant to reflect and express a spiritual progress, is a strange yet characteristic one for Celan: as its first step, it involves a journey through the German language to reach Hebrew and Yiddish as the deeper and more fitting languages of prayer; as its second step, the abandonment of language altogether for the privilege of standing in some eerily silent, yet possibly luminous, devotion. It is as if the price exacted for entering the Holy of Holies had to be a purity so absolute as to exclude even speech, without which or beyond which, in mute presence, one might begin to properly address Him-whose-Name-Is-No-one.

There is ample precedent for such experience in the literature of mysticism, and more than one scholar has searched through Jewish and Christian mystical writings for sources that might help explain some of the problematic features of Celan's poetry. The following quotation, taken from I. L. Peretz's story "Cabalists" and offered as analogy and not as source, may serve as well as any to illuminate the qualities of silence in some of these poems and clarify their special dimensions of prayer. The words are those of an elderly Kabbalistic master to his young pupil, and they begin to approximate the workings of the poetic process in the poems we have been examining:

"There is melody that requires words: this is of low degree. Then there is a higher degree—a melody that sings of itself, without words, a pure melody! But even this melody requires voicing, lips that should shape it, and lips, as you realize, are matter. Even the sound itself is a refined form of matter.

"Let us say that sound is on the borderline between matter and spirit. But in any case, that melody which is heard by means of a voice that depends on lips is still not pure, not entirely pure, not genuine spirit. The true melody sings without voice, it sings within, in the heart and bowels.

"This is the secret meaning of King David's words: 'All my bones shall recite. . . . ' The very marrow of the bones should sing. That's where the melody should reside, the highest adoration of God, blessed be He. This is not the melody of man! This is not a composed melody! This is part of the melody with which God created the world. . . ."[7]

In reading such poems as "Stehen," "Psalm," and "Einmal," one begins to feel that something close to this kind of secret knowledge must have been accessible to Paul Celan, although one shudders to think what it must have cost him to acquire it. "Night rode him," as he wrote in one of his late poems, and he was not reluctant to let it take him all the way "over / the human-hurdles." There, his mortal voice hushed or perhaps attuned to a higher music, he found whatever song may have awaited him beyond the night:

Thread suns
over the gray-black wasteland.
A tree-
high thought
strikes the tone of light: there are
still songs to sing beyond
mankind.

II

To read Nelly Sachs after Paul Celan is inevitably to experience something of a letdown, for while in terms of her major concerns she is a cognate poet, she did not possess a poetic idiom comparable to Celan's, and her writings, valuable as they are, do not make so decisive and lasting an impact. When she received the Nobel Prize in 1966, Nelly Sachs remarked that she sought throughout her poetry to "represent the tragedy of the Jewish people," and her several books succeed overall in that intention, yet she left behind no single poem so powerful as any of Celan's best. To describe her in this way is not to deny the interest or worth of Nelly Sachs's writings, but to point out that her poetry amasses its greatest strength not so much in separate pieces as in larger blocks. The accumulative effect of her collected work, rather than the more concentrated effect of single poems, is what moves us and makes persuasive her achievement.[8]

The one overriding task of Nelly Sachs's poetry is to make intelligible, and hence in some manner more bearable, a "landscape of screams" (C, p. 127). In her earlier books this landscape is palpably that of the Holocaust; in her later books it is more abstract, a landscape of sheer pain that no longer shows its precise origins in history. As it recedes from the phenomenal world, the range of Nelly Sachs's poetic voice lowers but also intensifies, particularly in the late poems, where it hovers close to its inevitable end in silence. Yet unlike the silence of Celan's major poems, which hints at some deeply recessed and possibly numinous power within or beyond, that which we feel in Nelly Sachs's poems most often seems empty and without any saving echo. The poet slips off into the voiceless, leaving us little trace of where she has gone except to her end.

This sense of the ultimate dumbness and finality of life can be traced throughout the poetry of Nelly Sachs, although in her earlier books it is more often likely to be found together with poems that indicate some sense of more transcendent possibilities, of "a mystery that *begins* with night" (S, p. 57). Just what this mystery is, however, and how one passes successfully through the terrors of night to reach it, is never disclosed. There are numerous poems that point to a lost lover waiting beyond, and others that hint at some vague kind of resurrection. A group of poems on "The Land of Israel" affirms renewal of the Jewish people in the rebirth of the national state (although they also caution against the excesses of nationalism). And one ecstatic poem, "Chassidim Tanzen" ("Hasidim Dancing"), makes emphatic the transformative powers inherent in mystical prayer. Otherwise, the poet's means of coping with the horrors that overwhelmed her time are chiefly limited to two: a stoical endurance in the face of gross suffering, and a maternal desire to soothe and quiet an excess of worldly pain by enfolding it into herself.

Each of these two attitudes enabled Nelly Sachs to write some strong poems, but neither one was sufficient to help her interpret or push back the night, whose legacy continued to weigh heavily upon her. In particular, the survivors of that night, who, like the poet, remained haunted by those who perished in it, pressed darkly on her imagination, as shown all too clearly in such a poem as the following one:

> Here
> in the folds of this star,
> covered with a rag called Night,
> they stand and wait for God.
> Their lips have been sealed by a thorn,
> their language lost to their eyes,
> they speak like fountains
> in which a corpse has drowned.
> Oh the old men,

who carry their charred descendents in their eyes
as their only possession.[9]

> ("Greise," "Old Men")

There are many others like it, poems that express the emptiness
and torment of a bleak and generally meaningless survival, a death-in-
life existence whose "every minute [is tinged] with a different darkness." The poet, possessed by heavy sorrow, weeps like the biblical
Rachel for her lost children. *Klagen,* or lamentation, is in fact one of the
two defining emotions in Nelly Sachs's poetry, the other being
Sehnsucht, or yearning. The first is expressive of the poet's pervasive
grief over those lost in the Nazi Holocaust; the second expresses the
pathos of reaching forward to a future that still might be born. Between
the two, in present time, there is little except pain and the numbness of
loss. Reality, as defined by life activities measurable in time and space,
is hardly to be felt, and anything external to the poet's grief and yearning is altogether thin and evanescent. When the landscape of the poems
is not that of screams, it is composed of air, stars, sand, stone, seeds,
dust, breath, and shadows, fading and ephemeral things that tend rarely
to be quickened by life. They are of the stuff of night and carry the
poet's language increasingly toward silence. Little else remains but the
embrace of the void, "a circling ring / which has lost its finger" (S. p.
333).

It was Nelly Sachs's fate to become the poet of that emptiness, a
poet of almost unrelieved grief and unanswered yearnings. "I am to go
out and search horror" (C, p. 247), she writes in one of her late poems,
and, in another, "This can be put on paper only / with one eye ripped
out" (S, 387). The declarations are self-conscious but not inaccurate to
the emotions of the poetry. When their language is not that of naked
pain—"recurring rhymes cut out of night's blackness"—it tends either
to become enigmatic or to fall off into dumbness and long for death:

I journeyed so far down
beyond my birth
till I met early death
who cast me back
into this singing pyramid
to measure out the inflamed
realm of silence
and whitely I yearn for you
death—be no longer stepfather to me—

From the very start, it was characteristic of Nelly Sachs's language to begin and end in exclamation, not so much resolving as exhausting itself. "Oh the chimneys," "Oh the night of the weeping children," "Oh the hills of dust"—such constructions as these, opening the mouth in shocked wonder before experience too horror-ridden to be grasped by speech, typify much of the early poetry. By the time of the last two books, however, the use of exclamation and apostrophe becomes very sparing, and a sense of general and final exhaustion tends to prevail: "O-A-O-A / a rocking sea of vowels / the words have all crashed down—" (C. p. 281).

As here, many of these late poems are reflections on the poet's own approaching end, and in their depiction of diminishment and decline, of creative crumbling, they can be very moving. Her later work, often written out in the form of fragments and small enigmatic parables, sometimes just barely finds its way into expression at all. Here, for example, is a poem quoted in its entirety: "Mystery on the border of death / 'Lay a finger upon your lips: / Silence Silence Silence—'" (C, p. 305). Why this reverence before silence? A one-line poem tells us: "But silence is where the victims dwell—" (C, p. 297).

This silence, and her heavy awareness of what caused it, made and unmade Nelly Sachs as a poet. As with Paul Celan, it was her burden and her privilege to write "the Psalm of Night," but unlike him she could rarely find in the night any hidden source of meaning that might clarify her suffering and direct her poetry. One of her late poetic fragments reveals the poignancy but also the incompleteness of her search: "If now you desperately call the one name / out of the darkness—" (C, p. 249). The line recalls the opening of Rilke's first *Duino Elegy*, but Nelly Sachs did not possess the rare powers of a Rilke, and no answering angel appears in her poetry. This is what does:

Who calls?
One's own voice!
Who answers?
Death!

Does friendship end
in the camp of sleep?
Yes!
Why does no cock crow?
It waits until the rosemary kiss
swims on the water!

What's this?

The moment of abandonment
from which time fell away
slain by eternity!

What's this?

Sleep and death are without traits

To her credit, Nelly Sachs persisted in her important work for as long as her strength and craft held out. Her last extended effort was called "Die Suchende" ("The Seeker"), and the title accurately sums up a major part of her quest. She was a seeker and, like Celan, became a student of Jewish religious writings. She sought particularly in the Kabbalah to discover some means to enable her "to make legible the wound" that scarred her time. Her readings in the *Zohar* confirmed her own intuitive sense that "in the unknown gold is hidden" (S, p. 377), and she did not shrink from dropping beneath the normal levels of consciousness to "labor for God in the depth" (S, p. 345). Yet there is little evidence in the poetry that she found anything there that might have allowed her to arise again, renewed by some fuller understanding of *das Leiden Israels* or her own anguished survival. Rather, the results of her brave but difficult plunges into the dark waters of her time brought her only closer to that extreme measure of solitariness that marks her poetry: "In the well with no one— / lost—" (S, p. 363).

Nelly Sachs was the poet of such abandonment, the recorder but also the victim of her tragic times, which inflicted upon her an almost impossible vocation: to transcribe, without ever being able to comprehend fully, the hieroglyphs of suffering. Toward the end, when it was apparent that language itself was giving way, her only recourse was to the raw expression of naked pain: "Vowels and consonants / cry out in every language: / *Help!*" (S, p. 393).

With that final, helpless cry we are already beyond poetry and back into the landscape of screams. A final submergence there, not into but out of a world of significant meaning, is what we are left with. The only termination for so much torment was termination itself, which is where Nelly Sachs's poetry begins and also ends: "Oh time, that only points to dying, / How easy death will be / having practiced for so long."

III

The finality of silence in the poetry of Nelly Sachs has its counterpart in post-Holocaust theology, as we noted earlier with the example of Richard Rubenstein. Yet, as indicated by some of the theological poems of Celan, there are other options as well, including those that belong to defiance. In this latter connection, it is fitting to recall the way that Emil Fackenheim ended his own contribution to the *Commentary* symposium: "Is not . . . the Jew of the generation of Auschwitz required to do what, since Abraham, Jeremiah, and Job, Jews have always done in times of darkness—contend with the silent God, and bear witness to Him by this very contention?"[10]

Fackenheim's position seems closer than Rubenstein's to that of the poets of the Holocaust, particularly when one includes among them some of the best of the Yiddish poets (discussed in the next chapter), who are especially strong contenders with God. His position is also closer to that of classical Judaism, which has long been familiar with national tragedy and which acknowledges the self-concealing as well as the self-revealing aspects of God. "Who is like unto Thee among the speechless, O God, / Who can be compared with Thee in Thy silence?" as a medieval Hebrew poet expressed the dilemma. The problem for poetry after Auschwitz—and it is one with the broadest problems of the religious life—is one of living with this concealment, that is to say, of reaching some difficult balance between contention and submission, of finding a way between the necessities of language and an imposed silence. The strain on poetry, just as the strain on faith, has been extreme, to the point where both poet and believer must frequently find ways to maintain themselves altogether outside of the means that define their existence and authenticity. Yet, paradoxically, it is within this tension and, in our day, perhaps *only* within it, where a true power of perception resides, producing at rare moments a coalescence of poetic and theological insight. Bereft of language, silence itself occasionally functions as an expressive means of faith, even as a form of prayer, but only if it is a committed silence, turned toward the Voice, even in its own Silence.

CHAPTER 6

The Poetry of Survival

> After gazing at the death of human beings, I was confronted . . .
> by the death of stones. . . . Ten or a dozen rickety marionettes were
> jerking sledge hammers about—not to mention their bones. Another
> group was hauling wheelbarrows. The party was demolishing some
> old tombstones. The blind, deafening hammer blows were scattering
> the sacred characters from inscriptions half a millennium old. . . . An
> *aleph* would go flying off to the left, while a *he* carved on another
> piece of stone dropped to the right. A *gimel* would bite the dust and a
> *nun* follow in its wake. . . . Several examples of *shin*, a letter
> symbolizing the miraculous intervention of God, had just been
> smashed and trampled on by the hammers and feet of these
> moribund workers.
>
> —PIOTR RAWICZ

> The deader the language, the more alive is the ghost. Ghosts
> love Yiddish, and, as far as I know, they all speak it. . . . I not only
> believe in ghosts but in resurrection. I am sure that millions of
> Yiddish-speaking corpses will rise from their graves one day, and
> their first question will be: Is there any new book in Yiddish read?
>
> —ISAAC BASHEVIS SINGER

As I have tried to show in the previous chapters, for the Jewish writer genocide carried with it specific threats of linguicide, the extirpation of a distinctive code of expression as part of the total destruction of European Jewish life. This was particularly true for the Yiddish writers of the Holocaust. While the Nazis sought to implement their Final Solution throughout Europe, they concentrated the most destructive phases of their terror in the countries of Eastern Europe, where

Yiddish had taken root centuries before and, despite weakening by as-similation and emigration, had continued vigorously as the popular folk language of the Jewish masses. Poland, Russia, and Lithuania were major centers for Yiddish, as were parts of Hungary, Romania, and Czechoslovakia. Commerce was conducted in Yiddish and a Yiddish press, Yiddish schools, theaters, fraternal orders, and political group-ings all flourished throughout this large region. The immolation of lit-erally hundreds of Jewish communities in Eastern Europe meant, then, the end of Yiddish culture, a distinctive phase of Jewish civilization al-most a thousand years old. The densest and richest sources of Jewish creativity, biological as well as cultural, were suddenly and ruthlessly eliminated. Yitzhak Katznelson, who had already established himself as a Hebrew poet, returned to Yiddish to pour out his lament for this destruction in his "Song of the Slaughtered Jewish People," a long, epic-like poem written in classical hexameters:

> The sun rising over Poland and Lithuania will no longer
>   find a Jew
> Sitting by a light in the window saying Psalms, or at dawn
>   on his way
> To synagogue. Peasants with their carts will come to
>   the town
> But there will be no Jews there to deal with them on
>   market day. . . . [1]

No Yiddish poet writing in the war years or after has been able to free himself entirely of this tragic sense. Almost by definition now, the work of such poets is bound to be at some point inherently mournful and elegiac, darkened by the consciousness of a double loss: that of the immediate past, which has been largely decimated and, as a conse-quence, that of an irrecoverable or unrealizable future. For who will be left to read the Yiddish authors? Their displacement has been all but total, a fact that must turn any poet disconsolate. It may turn him as well to a panicked search for a translator, a poor substitute for native readers, it is true, but perhaps the only means remaining to reach any readers at all.

This search, in its anguish, desperation, and sometimes even frenzy, forms the base for a memorable story ("Envy; or, Yiddish in America") by Cynthia Ozick, which can serve to introduce one of the major Yiddish poets of the Holocaust, Jacob Glatstein. Here is Edelshtein, the hard-working but untranslated—hence unknown—Yiddish poet, in one of his many attempts to enlist the help of a translator:

> Hannah, youth itself is nothing unless it keeps its promise to grow old. Grow old in Yiddish, Hannah, and carry fathers and uncles into the future with you. Do this. You, one in ten thousand maybe, who were born with the gift of Yiddish in your mouth, the alphabet of Yiddish in your palm, don't make ash of these! A little while ago there were twelve million people—not including babies—who lived inside this tongue, and now what is left? . . . Yiddish, I call on you to choose! Yiddish! . . . Hannah, you have a strong mouth, made to carry the future—[2]

Poor Edelshtein. Try as he may, he does not find the translator he needs, and as a result his poems remain hidden away in the carefully tended crypts of his all but unread Yiddish. As a writer who does his work in a language that history has cruelly diminished, Edelshtein knows that "whoever uses Yiddish to keep himself alive is already dead" (p. 67). Yet Yiddish is more than his literary medium—it is his life's companion, its commitment, his inheritance from the past and his legacy to the future—and for moral as well as artistic reasons he cannot abandon it, for he also knows that "whoever forgets Yiddish courts amnesia of history" (p. 61). Yiddish is his memory, and he can no more easily step out of it than he can forego his own origins, yet in remaining true to these, he runs the risk of being abandoned by the very history that he has dedicated himself to preserving. Edelshtein does not find a translator, which is to say that he does not find a major audience for his life's work, and in the end he is almost driven out of his mind by the frustrations of an enforced solitude.

"Envy; or, Yiddish in America" is a funny story as Ms. Ozick tells it, but it is also painful in the extreme, for there is too much of recent truth here: "And the language was lost, murdered. The language—a museum. Of what other language can it be said that it died a sudden and definite death, in a given decade, on a given piece of soil?" (p. 42).

Is there a reply to this question, a poet's reply? The general dilemma of the modern poet, as Robert Frost conceived of it in one of his own best poems, is "what to make of a diminished thing?" The modern Yiddish poet encounters the question in much harsher terms, for to him Frost's troubling line has precise historical associations and refers inescapably to his language, his people, his culture. The Holocaust struck at all three so forcefully as to have not only diminished them but nearly destroyed them. The Yiddish poet, then, hears the whimper of diminution but, more terribly, also the bang of chaotic destruction, and the question that he must frame is not just what to make of diminishment but what—if anything—to make of the near obliteration of his essential world.

The response of postwar Yiddish poets to this dilemma has been nothing short of astonishing, for as is manifest in the work of such writers as Jacob Glatstein, Chaim Grade, Itzik Manger, Aaron Zeitlin, and Abraham Sutzkever, among others, Yiddish poetry reached some of its highest levels of achievement in the decades since the end of the Second World War. As Eliezer Greenberg and Irving Howe have stated in the introduction to their valuable anthology, *A Treasury of Yiddish Poetry,*

> It is a time for silence, but silence is impossible; nothing can be said, but everything must be spoken; and from the impermissibility of words comes powerful speech. . . . For the Yiddish novelists and short story writers, the destruction of European Jewry has brought difficulties almost beyond overcoming. . . . For the poets, however, precisely this constriction of subject matter has been a major, and in a tragically perverse way, fruitful theme.[3]

Among the poets, Jacob Glatstein stands out as a writer of strength and sustained accomplishment. His dedication to memorializing and, in some measure, preserving and continuing Yiddish culture was resolute, and on the basis of it alone he would have won an honored place in modern Yiddish poetry. The fact is that he deserves a place in modern poetry in general, for to the major commitment that he brought to a powerful subject he added as well the qualities and accomplishment of a serious and thoroughly practiced craftsman.

Glatstein came to America in 1914 from Lublin, where he was born in 1896. For most of his life he earned his living as a writer and editor on several of New York's Yiddish newspapers, most notably *Der Tog* ("The Day"), for which he wrote a column twice a week. He also edited various Yiddish periodicals, served as director of Yiddish public relations for the American Jewish Congress, and was a member of the national executive board of the Farband, the Labor Zionist fraternal order. All of this activity was carried out within the context of an essentially Yiddish-oriented world, which was the defining frame of the poet's life and work. "The joy of the Yiddish word," as he expressed it, was genuine to him and maintained itself as a vital source of personal strength and artistic energy.

While still a youth in Eastern Europe Glatstein began to write in Russian, and during his first years in the United States he also attempted to write poetry in English. His early associations with some of the Yiddish poets in New York soon brought him around to Yiddish, however, and the many volumes of poetry, fiction, and essays that he later published were all to be in Yiddish.[4] During the fifty years between his first and his last volumes, Glatstein matured to become a master of the Yiddish language and one of the most challenging poets of Jewish experience in this century. It is largely the nature of this experience and what it did to both the Yiddish language and the people who spoke it that gave Glatstein his direction as a writer and kept him going through several difficult turns in his career.

The history of modern Yiddish literature is still to be written with the kind of authority the subject deserves,[5] but when such a study comes to be made it will reveal Jacob Glatstein's central involvements with the major currents of Yiddish poetry, and particularly with that of the *Inzikhistn,* or Introspectivist movement. Glatstein came after both the early poets of the labor movement and social protest (principally Joseph Bovshover, David Edelstadt, Morris Rosenfeld, and Morris Winchevsky) and that colorful and energetic group of younger writers, *Die Yunge,* who established themselves in opposition to the didactic, sentimental, and social trends in Yiddish poetry (Moishe Leib Halpern, Reuben Iceland, David Ignatow, Zisha Landau, Berl Lapin, Mani Leib, Joseph Opatashu, Joseph Rolnick). It is in the nature of literary movements to generate reactions against themselves, and it fell to Jacob Glatstein, A. Glanz-Leyeles, and N. B. Minkoff, the major figures of the *Inzikhist* movement, to establish themselves against *Die Yunge* and, in so doing, to help win a place for Yiddish poetry in the larger movement of literary modernism.

The poets of the Introspectivist group were interested in writing a firmly disciplined and intellectual poetry, one that would overleap the sentimental or ideological bounds of Yiddish writing defined by their predecessors and establish the Yiddish poet more squarely in the modern world. In terms of their time period, the early 1920s, the "modern world" meant the assertive and sometimes self-indulgent world of the "I," and it is one of the contributions of the *Inzikhistn* that they established a place for the personal pronoun in Yiddish poetry.

Far more than any of their predecessors, they were concerned with experimental forms and with exploiting the natural rhythms of Yiddish speech, and they found free verse, which they perfected, to be their best medium. They were fully alert to new developments in literature outside of Yiddish, read the latest American poets, and were resolved to accommodate in their own language the best of what was being done in English. In *In Zikh* ("Within Oneself," 1920), the anthology in which they made their debut (and also the title of their literary journal), they expressed their full confidence that Yiddish was "fine and rich enough for the deepest poetry," and they spoke of their determination to write a universally meaningful, solid, and precise Yiddish poetry. In their own terms, "All the high achievements of poetry, indeed the highest, are possible in Yiddish."

As for the specifically Jewish element and the role it was to play in their new program, the *In Zikh* manifesto faced the issue directly:

> In regard to our Yiddishkeit, we would point out that we are Yiddish poets by virtue of the fact that we are Jews and write in Yiddish. Whatever a Yiddish poet may write about is, ipso facto, Jewish. One does not need specifically Jewish themes. . . . It is not the task of the poet to prove his Yiddishkeit. Only in two ways are we definitely Jewish—in our affection for Yiddish as a language and in our respect for Yiddish as a poetic instrument.[6]

Had history not interfered, the *Inzikhistn* might have had more of a chance to carry out this aspect of their manifesto, but it is doubtful even then that they would have gone very far in their universalizing direction. As Max Weinreich, Maurice Samuel, and others have pointed out, Yiddish is genuinely a folk language and reflects the values of a specific national history.[7] It is rich and poor in direct proportion to the ways in which the Jews of Eastern Europe were rich and poor, and as a result it is ideally suited to express certain kinds of experience and less well suited to express others. The natural sources for the Yiddish poet, as they come through the language itself, are folk sources: folk sayings, folk legends, folk humor, folk songs, the jokes and lyrics of the *badkhonim*, the Hasidic tales, etc. When one adds to these folk elements the source that is at the very heart of Jewish civilization, the Hebrew Bible, one sees that the major lines of Jewish history do not mix in equal measure "the Yiddish shul and the cross, the mayoralty elections and a decree against our language."

As Chana Faerstein pointed out in an appreciative essay on Jacob Glatstein, it was well and good for the Yiddish poet to say that his imaginative associations might lead him "to the banks of the Ganges, or to Japan," but "after the Nazis crossed the Rhine, it may be said that [Glatstein] retreated from the banks of the Ganges."[8] Given the mood of the times, it is understandable that in 1920 the poet could be moved to say that "for us there does not exist the sterile question as to whether the poet should write about national or social or personal problems. We make no distinction between poetry of the heart and poetry of the mind"; but by 1938, enraged by what was taking place in his native Europe, the same poet was to write, "Good night, wide world, / big stinking world, / Not you but I slam shut the gate." By this later date the poet had resolved to return to his basic origins in Yiddishkeit, and he could genuinely put to rest "the sterile question" concerning the proper and most vital subject matter for Yiddish poets. History itself was defining it for him: "Damn your dirty culture, world . . . I'm going back to the ghetto."[9] After the late 1930s, Glatstein's poetry is more intense in purpose, alternately angrier and more reflective in tone, and recognizably more Jewish than the earlier poetry. Glatstein strengthened rather than weakened as a poet during this period, perfected his idiom, and, writing with insight and authority, evolved his major subject: the survival, after terrible trials, of the Jewish people, and the survival as well, even if precariously so, of the Yiddish language.

In reading him, one is struck in particular by two recurring concerns: the nature and role of the Jewish God during this last, and also worst, stage of Jewish history; and the newly complicated role of the Yiddish poet in its aftermath. Both relate to the ancient bond of covenant, established in the revelation at Sinai and, as suggested by one of Glatstein's most famous poems, perhaps broken in the counterrevelation of our own time:

> We received the Torah on Sinai
> and in Lublin we gave it back.
> Dead men don't praise God,
> the Torah was given to the living.
> And just as we all stood together
> at the giving of the Torah,
> so did we all die together at Lublin.

This poem is a radical rewriting of lines in Psalm 115—"It is not the dead who praise the Lord, / not those who go down into silence"—just as it is a shattering extension of verses in Exodus and Deuteronomy that stress the ongoing response of the Jews through the

generations to the Sinaitic theophany. That corporate or collective in-
volvement in revelation occurred in the Holocaust as well, where at
Lublin and countless other places like it the generations were levelled.
Was there implicit in their destruction a recantation of the Torah and a
drastic fall of its author into reduction and displacement? Those are the
questions raised in lines from such a poem as "My Brother Refugee":

> I love my sad God,
> my brother refugee.
> I love to sit down on a stone with him
> and tell him everything wordlessly
> because when we sit like this, both perplexed,
> our thoughts flow together
> in silence.
> A star lights up, a fiery letter.
> His body longs for sleep.
> The night leans like a sheep against our feet.
> . . . .
> My God sleeps while I keep watch,
> my tired brother dreams the dream of my people.
> He's small as a child
> and I rock him into the dream.
> Sleep, my God, my brother refugee,
> sleep, and vanish into our dream.

(Pp. 71–72)

God is not gone from Glatstein's Holocaust poems, but, as here, he
is gravely demoted and translated into humbler, sadder terms. Like the
wandering Shechinah (divine manifestation) mentioned in numerous
midrashim, he is more the victim than the master of his people's fate and
has become, like another displaced and weary Jew, worn down and
almost exhausted by the burdens of a difficult history. One feels a pity-
ing affection for him rather than any awe. And far from looking to him
for consolation, one is moved to comfort him. "How I love my un-
happy God," Glatstein exclaims with tender irony, "now that he's
human and unjust" (p. 71). This is not said in mocking tones but with a
genuinely felt pathos, that which belongs to family feeling at its most
intimate and compassionate. One detects it again in "God of My
Forefathers":

> For us you weren't such
> a sophisticated God.
> We didn't have to bone up for you.

A Jew would wake up in the morning,
open his eyes,
say something Jewish—
and immediately hear you sigh.
It was happier with that sigh.
Now—a Jew sighs, his God sighs,
the morning sighs,
heaven sighs hymns to God.
. . . .
This is as far as it's given us to know—
up to the sigh.
Further than that all effort is useless.

(P. 101)

With God diminished to the point of a barely locatable sigh, Jewish life is brought low and undergoes a dislocating transformation: " . . . without our God / we have a funny look: / When they shaved you off from us / we walked around looking like boy-Jews, / cheap vaude-villians" (p. 100).

God himself is not impervious to this fate, for in Glatstein's understanding of the covenantal bond, the destiny of God is as much tied to that of his people as the other way around. Not only is a common fidelity wanted but a common history is shared, one whose brutal side disfigures and diminishes the divinity through the violence done to the Jews. As one of Glatstein's most moving poems presents this sense of tragic parity and interdependence,

Without Jews there is no Jewish God.
If we leave this world,
The light will go out in your tent.
Since Abraham knew you in a cloud,
You have burned in every Jewish face,
You have glowed in every Jewish eye. . . .
A broken Jewish head
Is a fragment of divinity.
We, your radiant vessel,
A palpable sign of your miracle.[10]

With the violent breaking of those vessels—an historical disaster with suprahistorical implications—the miracle-maker is almost undone, himself the victim of an overpowering terror. The reduction of the creature reduces the creator as well, and both seem to begin to "die together." The vision is one of guttering and waning, the snuffing out of light and the sources of light. Understood against its sources in Jewish esoteric thought, this is a radical, anti-Lurianic poem, a "dekabbalization," one might even call it, for in its portrayal of a broken people and its fragmented God, it represents a reversal of the kabbalistic account of origins, according to which reintegration or restoration succeeds an initial cataclysmic shattering. In Glatstein's post-Holocaust rewriting, though, there is no *tikkun,* or healing of the cosmic rupture, but only the shards of the disaster piled up to evidence the extinction rather than the effulgence of the creative fire:

> Now the lifeless skulls
> Add up into millions.
> The stars are going out around you.
> The memory of you is dimming,
> Your kingdom will soon be over. . . .
> The Jewish dream and reality are ravished. . . .
> Jewish God!
> You are almost gone.[11]

Following the shock of so profound a reduction, we return to Robert Frost's disturbing question: what to make of a diminished thing? As Jacob Glatstein's own poems seem to pick up and rephrase this, the question becomes: how to survive as a Yiddish poet when the greater part of the Jewish world that one has known has been "silenced in Maidanek woods, / finished off with a few shots" (p. 103)? Or, in yet another rephrasing of the same problem, how can one hold up as a Yiddish poet—which is one way of saying, how can one survive as a conscious and articulate Jew—when all the years of one's childhood have been "walled up / and frozen / in an isolated inconsolable / deleted silence" (p. 90)? The need, as Glatstein knew, was for "durable words" (p. 94), but as he also knew, "words have never sickened so young" (p. 117), and "it's as hard to return to / old-fashioned words / as to sad synagogues" (p. 109). One knows exactly where they are but can no longer bring himself to enter them. To do so—to use the old words as if the old life had maintained itself unchanged—would mean to be the poet of a merely nostalgic Yiddishkeit. Where, then, were the new words to come from, words that might lead one beyond a nostalgic Jewishness and out of "a cave of silence"?

Glatstein's response to this dilemma was nothing short of magnificent, and the poems that issued from this period of his work can stand with the most challenging poetry that has been given us over the last three decades. From the poet's resolve to enter the deep night of wordlessness and, from that perilous position, to "grasp and take in /

these destroyed millions" (p. 73), there came a poetry of profound
affirmative return, a lyricism of homecoming and survival. "Marks on
the Snow" and "The Joy of the Yiddish Word" are two poems that
signal this high achievement, but the poem that embodies it most fully
and presents most vividly the progress of a deep retrieval out of the
night is "In a Ghetto":

> In a days-and-nights ghetto
> our rescued life is lying,
> everything that happens,
> fated and accomplished,
> is Jewish through and through.
> We haggle away our days,
> borrowing and lending,
> then we turn off
> the frightened nighttime lamps
> of our lone burdens.
> Too bad, Yiddish poet,
> you're not fated to become
> a fortress of quotations.
> The Old Testament that they threw back at you
> over the fence
> was already converted when I picked it up long ago.
> Now you're alone again.
>
> Alone.

The poem turns at this point, on the recognition of total solitude, and
finds a sudden power with an awareness of the poet's special sense of
mission:

> Poet, take the faintest Yiddish speech,
> fill it with faith, make it holy again.
> All your virtuous deeds huddle at your feet
> like trusting kittens;
> they look in your eyes
> so you'll stroke them and fulfill them.
> You don't realize everything's at stake.
>
> So you'll fulfill them.
>
> Be on guard. The wasteland calls again.
> A wild plow grinds a great surfeit to dust
> and finds a skeleton's heart.
> And if you can talk yourself into believing
> that a skeleton has no heart,

then you must know, sick boy,
that the whole glowing
incandescent life
on the other side of the fence
can't strengthen you, can't exalt you
because it's a skeleton-heart
with all its joy,
pity and chimes of faith.

Poet, what of the night?
Our liberation is tiny,
unguarded, unprotected.
Become the watchman; guard,
preserve—
this believing-hoping happily-ever-after song
of a next year
is forever
bitten into your believing bones.

                                        (Pp. 110–11)

Jacob Glatstein's resolute sense of the Yiddish poet's power and purpose—to become the watchman, to guard and preserve—brings a sublime close to this poem and helps carry the poet beyond the terror and negations of silence. What to make of a diminished thing? Nothing less than a thing of beauty, to be fulfilled and cared for, watched over and preserved in its sacredness. Such an answer, as Glatstein was privileged to discover, took him back into life and restored him to the poet's task of joyfully reconstructing language:

Sing into the valley of bony words
rise up, letter by letter,
I love you, dead world of my youth,
I command you, rise up, let your joy revive,
come close, letter by letter, warm, pulsing,
meaning nothing,
but dancing towards the world,
blotting out the clouds like bright birds.

                                        (P. 118)

With this kind of affirmation we return to the wisdom of Edelshtein, the fictional poet with whom we began, for despite all his problems, and they are many, there are certain basic truths that he has not lost. Here is one of them: "In Talmud, if you save a single life it's as if you saved the world. And if you save a language? Worlds maybe. Galaxies. The whole universe" (p. 83).

III. Deceptions and Corruptions

CHAPTER 7

The Immolation
of the Word

If God is, it is because He is in the book. If sages, saints, and
prophets exist . . . , it is because their names are found in the book.
The world exists because the book does.

—EDMOND JABES

On the evening of May 10, 1933, some four and a half months after
Hitler became Chancellor, there occurred in Berlin a scene which had
not been witnessed in the Western world since the late Middle Ages. At
about midnight a torchlight parade of thousands of students ended at a
square on Unter den Linden opposite the University of Berlin. Torches
were put to a huge pile of books that had been gathered there, and as the
flames enveloped them more books were thrown on the fire until some
twenty thousand had been consumed. Similar scenes took place in several other cities. The book burning had begun.[1]

It was Heine, prescient of most things German, who foresaw the outcome of all this. One begins by burning books, he wrote, and ends by
burning men.[2] Less than a decade after the first Nazi bonfires were lit,
the crematoria were in operation, their flames, rising as high as
seventy-five feet above the chimneys, visible for miles around. "These
flames not only illuminate the final end of an old era; they also light up
the new," Joseph Goebbels told the 40,000 students of Berlin University
who had gathered to watch the burning of the books.[3] The Propaganda
Minister's words could as readily have been spoken at Auschwitz or
Treblinka, for the logic of auto-da-fé links the literary and human
holocausts in a direct and unbroken line of malevolent will and
causation.

There were some who thought otherwise, who considered the Nazis mere hooligans who soon enough would be brought back to civilized ways. André Schwarz-Bart portrays this benign attitude through the character of Herr Kremer, the "delicate humanist" and kind-hearted teacher who judged German fascism to be a temporary phenomenon, the rule of the tavern that somehow had managed to break through into government. Like all such aberrations, it would be recognized for what it was and put in its place: "Soon they will all be sent back to their bars or prisons," Herr Kremer considered; "soon the old Germany will punish her bad boys." The old Germany, and particularly the Germany of Schiller, "whose slightest verses radiated civic consciousness," was a nation based in a culture of humane values, not the likely site for a return of the terrors of the Inquisition. Such a nation, instructed in civics and poetry, would stand as "an eternal dike against barbarity." Herr Kremer confidently rested his case in a belief in the humanizing values of poetry: "The day when Schiller was known to the entire population of the world would be a fine day" (pp. 205–208).

The bonfires were to prove him wrong. Tons of books were put to the torch, including more than a few espousing a civic consciousness as noble as that of Schiller himself. The aim, as Goebbels stated it, was to rid German life of all foreign elements, foremost among them "Jewish intellectualism." And much more than books were to be burned. On a single night—that of November 9, 1938—191 synagogues were sent up in flames across Germany. Shortly thereafter the human burnings began, some of them in killing centers located only a short distance from the major centers of German culture (such as Buchenwald, near Weimar, which carefully preserved as its prized centerpiece the famous "Goethe Oak").

George Steiner, who has written unusually well about the proximity of political barbarism to Western traditions of learning, draws the most challenging kinds of attention to the fact that mass murder had little trouble flourishing side by side with activities previously regarded as guarantees of humane conduct:

> We know now that a man can read Goethe or Rilke in the evening, that he can play Bach and Schubert, and go to his day's work at Auschwitz in the morning. . . . Moreover, it is not only the case that the established media of civilization—the universities, the arts, the book world—failed to offer adequate resistance to political bestiality; they often rose to welcome it and to give it ceremony and apologia. Why?

What are the links, as yet scarcely understood, between the mental, psychological habits of high literacy and the temptations of the inhuman?[4]

While we are not in a position to answer Steiner's questions, their challenge remains a continuing one, for documents of all kinds survive in abundance to attest to the proximity of high culture to the grossest forms of bestiality. Nazi poster and magazine art provide popular illustrations of the ways in which the disciplines of learning, religion, and artistic effort could be put to the service of brutal power. Martin Heidegger's inaugural address as rector of Freiburg University, aligning the labors of the scholar with those of the soldier, is a muted and more "refined" example of this complicity. Professor Heidegger's denial of scholarship funds to Jewish students at the university and, contrastingly, the preference he gave to those who fought in the SA or SS is a more active and unsettling example of the same thing.[5] Yet Heidegger was hardly alone, nor was his the most blatant example of such participation. The fact of the matter is that thousands of such actions can be cited, directly implicating intellectuals, artists, scientists, jurists, and churchmen in the day-to-day program of the Nazi movement. Corruption ran deep and spread through the ranks of German culture.[6] Nowhere does it show up so well as in the German language itself.

According to Victor Klemperer, one of the earliest and most incisive students of the language of the Third Reich, Nazi-Deutsch found its deepest and most characteristic expression not in the propaganda speeches of Hitler or Goebbels against "international Jewry" and "Bolshevism" but in the common usage of the people, which had absorbed and been corrupted by the habits of totalitarian thought:

> The strongest effect was not executed by individual speeches, articles, or leaflets, posters or flags; it was not the result of anything that had to be taken in by conscious thoughts or feelings.
>
> Rather, Nazism penetrated the flesh and blood of the masses by means of single words, turns of phrase, and sentence structures that were all forced upon them by endless repetition and thus were absorbed mechanically and unconsciously. We are used to regarding the Schiller distich—"a cultivated language that poetizes and thinks for you" [*eine gebildete Sprache, die für dich dichtet und denkt*]—in a purely aesthetic and harmless way. . . .
>
> But language not only poetizes and thinks for a person; it also guides his feelings and his whole inner being, the more so as he gives himself over to it unconsciously. What, then, if this cultivated language

is the carrier of poison? Words can be tiny doses of arsenic—swallowed unnoticed in little doses they apparently have no effect, but after a while there is a process of poisoning that sets in. If one equates heroism and virtue with "fanaticism" long enough, one may after a time truly believe that to be a fanatic is to be a hero and that one could not be a hero without being a fanatic. The words "fanatic" and "fanaticism" were not invented by the Third Reich, but their value was changed by it, and they came to be used more on a single day than previously was the case over years. . . . Nazi language changes the value of words and the frequency with which they are used. . . . It saturates words, phrases, and sentences with its poison, making language a slave for the terrible system. . . . [7]

Klemperer presents dozens of examples of words that were "fanaticized" or otherwise deformed, seriously handicapping the language as a code of individualized expression and preparing the way for the work of propaganda. Similar studies by other scholars have further shown the extent of linguistic manipulation and distortion during the Third Reich.[8] One result of this corruption was the substitution of the slogan for more logical or rational forms of speech, emphasizing ponderous, abstract nouns and voiding the predicate. Thus the enormous popularity of such senseless but popular rallying cries as "Ein Reich, ein Volk, ein Führer" or "Das Reich ist der Führer." One can grow impassioned in such language but not think in it. Even better suited for emotive purposes, and hence for winning the uncritical political allegiance of the masses, was the antiphonal "Deutschland erwache, Juda verrecke," which magically and almost liturgically blessed and damned in the short space of a four-word formula. Formulaic thinking was, in fact, basic to Nazi-Deutsch, as was a preference for vague but elevated rhetoric, of the kind we find in the prose of Heidegger during this period. Michael Hamburger, in looking at the Freiburg University address, points out some of the resemblances it shows to contemporary political usage:

> The word which I have rendered as "students" is *Studentenschaft*— "studentry," as it were—and its function is to telescope a great number of individuals into a corporate abstraction. Elsewhere these individuals become "*the* German student" and all the universities become "*the* German university." Heidegger's vocabulary alone accomplishes a *Gleichschaltung* which excludes the very possibility that any one student might have a will of his own. . . . [Heidegger] adds his own existential halo . . . to such established phantom words as *Geist, Schicksal,* and *We-*

sen; and the whole performance serves to convince the young scholars of Germany that their freedom consists in conformity, their will in obeying the new laws. What Heidegger was providing here is not philosophy, as we understand it, but secularized theology; and the religion it expounds is the religion of nationalism.[9]

That National Socialism theologized politics and secularized theology in order to politicize it cannot be overstressed by anyone wanting to understand the success of the Nazi movement. Language played a disingenuous but decisive role in these transformations, for in the appropriation of sacred terminology Hitler, Goebbels, Rosenberg, and others seemed to be extending quite naturally the prerogatives and pieties of Christian faith to their own political practice. The use of terms like *Offenbarung* ("revelation"), *Glaube* ("faith"), *Unsterblichkeit* ("immortality"), and *Gnade* ("grace") was constant and heavy. The intention was clear: to effect, almost invisibly, a transference of popular Christian loyalties and allegiances to the new centers of power. The purpose was to encourage the German masses to "believe in the Führer" and to honor his authority in much the same way that religious practice over the centuries had directed faith and guided principles of conduct. Once it became established as dogma that "the Führer is always right," as prescribed by one of the commandments of the Nazi party, everything else would follow in undiscriminating patterns of respect and reverent obedience.

Gleichschaltung—the flattening out of all separate and individual features in favor of a loyal and obedient uniformity—was precisely the intention, and the temporary success, of Nazi-Deutsch. Molded to serve the will of the total state, Nazi-Deutsch proved itself most effective in the bureaucratic and military language of the party and in the artistic, social, religious, and political programs that were in their employ. Its rhetoric, at once obscure and elevated, abstract and bombastic, was hardly a precise instrument of communication, but then it was not supposed to be. Its function was to conceal more than to impart, to restrict and regulate thinking and hence to order conduct along desired lines. In furthering this process of cultural *Gleichschaltung,* academicians of stature were often as complicitous, even if at times naïvely so, as the functionaries who worked for Goebbels and Rosenberg. All contributed to the reduction and exploitation of German as a living language.

Among writers living during the early years of the Nazi period,

none was better equipped to gauge what was happening than the
Viennese-Jewish author Karl Kraus. As journalist, satirist, polemicist,
dramatist, and poet, Kraus occupied a singular place in Viennese literary
culture, which he reviewed, reviled, and in a sense dominated through
Die Fackel ("The Torch"), the journal that he first edited and then wrote
for exclusively over a period of thirty-seven years. For nine months
after the Nazis came to power, in January, 1933, *Die Fackel* did not
appear; when finally it did, in October of that year, it consisted of only
four pages, including a brief untitled poem by Kraus with these lines:
"Don't ask what I've been doing all this time. / I remain silent; / and
don't say, why. / [. . .] The word fell into a sleep, when that world
awoke." That world was the world of Hitler, before which Kraus initially fell dumb. His first reaction to Hitler was in fact something close
to incomprehension and dismay: "Is that which was perpetrated here
upon the spirit still a matter for the spirit?" His answer, not long in
coming forth, was *Die Dritte Walpurgisnacht* ("The Third Walpurgis
Night"), "a work of language about language . . . in [which] Kraus
came to grips with Hitler in a manner that was uniquely his: he passed
judgement on the Nazis by exposing the depravity of their language,"
as Sidney Rosenfeld writes.[10] Throughout his career, Kraus had dedicated himself absolutely to language, "the universal whore whom I turn
into a virgin." In reaction to the destruction wrought by the First World
War, he had written an immense drama, *Die letzten Tage Der Menschheit*
("The Last Days of Mankind," 1922), which is, among other things, a
sustained exposé and indictment of the role of language, through daily
misuse, in inuring people to the horrors of warfare. *Die Dritte Walpurgisnacht* was written out of a similar dedication, for it quickly became
evident to Kraus that under the heel of Nazism the metaphorical richness of language was being ground into a state of brutal literalness. This
Untergang der Sprache, or deterioration and decline of language, was the
measure by which human decline revealed itself, especially so in the
betrayal of old metaphors through the new reality:

> When these power politicians still talk of "holding a knife to the
> throat of their opponent," of "shutting his mouth for him," of "shaking
> a fist at him"; when they threaten constantly to take action "hard-
> handedly," there remains but one surprise: that they are still employing
> figures of speech but no longer metaphorically. The government that
> wants to "brutally beat down anyone who opposes it"—does so. . . .
> And the rejection of the figurative is complete in this promise by a re-

gional governor: "We don't say: an eye for an eye and a tooth for a tooth. No, if anyone puts out one of our eyes, we will break off his head, and if anyone knocks out one of our teeth, we will smash his jaws."

Such violence, Kraus goes on to say, is carried out without any preconditions and is born less in reprisal for deeds misdone than as a means of originally executing them apart from any provocation. His analysis of the linguistic contributions to Nazi violence and to linguistic transformation under it is acute:

> . . . this restoration of the content to the empty phrase is occurring with every turn of speech in which an originally gory or physical content long since had been refined to fit the sense of an intellectual attack. Not even the most subtle variety is able to escape this process—not even the frightful expression: "To pour salt into open wounds." Once it must have happened, but we had forgotten so to the point of rejecting any notion of a real act, to the point [even] where it was completely impossible to be aware of one. [The metaphor] was used to indicate the terrible reminder of a loss, the stirring from without of an inner pain. That we still have; the act from which it was derived was forgotten.

Nazism, in closing the space that formerly mediated between violent words and violent deeds, transmuted this "inner pain" into reality of the harshest sort. To illustrate, Kraus goes on to quote a report from a concentration camp that relates how a group of Nazis, acting out of "fun," forced an inmate to hold his bleeding hand, cut while peeling potatoes, into a sack of salt. The screams of the poor man filled his persecutors with mirth. Such a thing "remains inconceivable," Kraus continues, "but because it happened, the expression is no longer usable. . . . The metaphor comes to life and dies."[11]

In such instances—and Kraus offers numerous others—it is as if "a bloody dew clings to the flower of speech." It would be a happy occurrence, Kraus considered, if this blood were only metaphorical, but he knew that under the new conditions of German life this was not to be so. Under the dominant faith of National Socialism, in fact, a destructive transubstantiation was taking place, which returned figurative language to its unholy origins so that blood flowed out of the enveloping crusts of words. The new literal sense that metaphorical expression was made to take effectively invalidated language and made it forfeit its usefulness as the primary means of social and cultural discourse.

One result was that German hardly lived as a literary language during the years of the Third Reich. The exodus of German authors was something unprecedented: according to some estimates as many as 2,500 writers went into exile, including Thomas and Heinrich Mann, Bertolt Brecht, Stefan George, Robert Musil, Erich Maria Remarque, Franz Werfel, and others of equal prominence. Suicide was to carry away others—Stefan Zweig, Walter Hasenclever, Ernst Toller, Kurt Tucholsky, and Walter Benjamin among the best known. Of those who remained, most chose the option of a silent "inner exile" or compromised and wrote inferior work. One of the distinctions of the Third Reich was, in fact, that it produced within its own borders almost no works of literary merit. This was not for lack of trying, for Goebbel's Ministry of Propaganda and Enlightenment mobilized the literary resources of the nation in ambitious ways, supervising some 2,500 publishing houses, 23,000 bookshops, 3,000 authors, 50 national literary prizes, and 20,000 new books annually. Libraries increased from 6,000 in 1933 to 25,000 at the height of the war, and over 43 million books were donated to the *Wehrmacht* by civilians. These are staggering figures, yet the dominant text by far, with more than 6 million copies sold, was Hitler's *Mein Kampf*.[12] Literature stole out of Germany shortly after Hitler came into power and was not to return in substantial, uncompromised terms until he was dead and the war was over.

One of the tasks it necessarily had to assume in the postwar period was to face up to the spoliation of the language, a task that some— again, George Steiner most provocatively among them—have thought beyond easy repair. "The German language was not innocent of the horrors of Nazism," Steiner insists, but was used "to give hell a native tongue":

> The unspeakable being said, over and over, for twelve years. The unthinkable being written down, indexed, filed for reference. . . . A language being used to run hell, getting the habits of hell into its syntax. Being used to destroy what there is in man of man and to restore to governance what there is of beast. Gradually, words lost their original meaning and acquired nightmarish definitions. *Jude, Pole, Russe* came to mean two-legged lice, putrid vermin which good Aryans must squash, as a party manual said, "like roaches on a dirty wall." "Final solution," *endgültige Lösung,* came to signify the death of six million human beings in gas ovens. (Pp. 99–100)

While Steiner's charge that the German language was almost irreparably polluted under Hitler is a controversial one, the fact is that those who faced the "hell" he refers to and managed to survive and to write about it refer frequently to the prevalence of a benighted and all but incomprehensible tongue. Upon entering Buchenwald, Eugen Kogon attests, the new inmate was asked by a recording clerk "the name of the whore that shat you into the world," to which vulgarism the astonished prisoner was supposed to offer up the name of his mother.[13] Kogon also reports the question that camp guards often would ask one another when new transports arrived: "Wie viele Stücke" (How many "pieces")? Such phrases were common, for Jews were considered and spoken of as "stuff" or "material," not as people. A memorable account of this tendency toward extreme linguistic dehumanization comes in *The Last of the Just* when Schwarz-Bart portrays what happened to a woman who tripped on the arrival platform at Auschwitz: "Immediately a German stepped forward with one of those savage animals baying on his leash, and obviously addressing himself to the animal, he shouted . . . , *'Man, destroy that dog!'*" (p. 368). After an inversion that extreme, what is there left to say? The common tongue, based as it is on maintaining at least a minimal adherence to some human norm, no longer serves in situations such as those where the social inflections of language are willfully forgotten or unabashedly destroyed. Wiesel reports that his father was knocked to the ground by an older camp inmate whom he addressed with his accustomed politeness, as if the retention of such expressions as "please" or "excuse me" were offenses sufficient to bring on blows. "The only word which had any real meaning here," Wiesel writes, was "'furnace,' [for] it floated on the air, mingled with the smoke."[14] Otherwise, words lost any previous civilizing function they had once had and either dropped out of the camp vocabulary or were turned into barks:

> The language of night was not human; it was primitive, almost animal—hoarse shouting, screams, muffled moaning, savage howling, the sound of beating. . . . A brute striking wildly, a body falling; an officer raises his arm and a whole community walks toward a common grave; a soldier shrugs his shoulders, and a thousand families are torn apart. . . . This is the concentration camp language. It negated all other language and took its place.[15]

The speech of free men, Primo Levi stresses, is so far removed in connotative value from that known in the camps as to make it almost inapplicable as an interpretive code. *Selekcja, Kapo, Muselmann*—these are virtually untranslatable terms. But even the less specialized vocabu-

lary—"hunger," "tiredness," "fear," "pain," "winter," "work"—
misses the mark, Levi insists, for these words, used in their everyday or
normative sense, imply an order of experience that did not exist for the
camp inmates, who commonly felt themselves to be living either in an
absurd world or in hell. Whatever it was, the Holocaust universe was
not a place that could easily be reached or expressed by the common
vocabulary. Had the camps lasted longer, Levi asserts, "a new, harsh
language would have been born," and only this language could possibly
begin to depict the extremities of living and dying that millions had
suffered.[16]

Part of the difficulty that German writers have faced in the post-
Holocaust period derives from the inescapable connection their lan-
guage makes with this "new, harsh language." For the fact is that this
other language was not only born but it was put into usage on a daily
basis. German was "infected" with the falsehoods and bestialities of
Nazi practice, as Klemperer and Steiner and other students of Nazi-
Deutsch agree, and would not quickly be rid of such contamination.
Steiner is particularly firm:

> Languages have great reserves of life. They can absorb masses of
> hysteria, illiteracy, and cheapness. . . . But there comes a breaking
> point. Use a language to conceive, organize, and justify Belsen; use it to
> make out specifications for gas ovens; use it to dehumanize man during
> twelve years of calculated bestiality. Something will happen to it. . . .
> Something will happen to the words. Something of the lies and sadism
> will settle in the marrow of the language. (P. 101)

Günter Grass managed to carry over into the prose of *Hundejahre
(Dog Years)* something of the special accents and diction of the dehumanized speech we have been noting. He was also able to reproduce
Heidegger's own peculiar version of the same in some parodic moments
of his novel (Walter Abish more recently has attempted something similar in "The English Garden," the opening story of *In the Future Perfect*).
More than the fiction writers, though, it is the playwrights who have
had to contend with these massive linguistic disturbances, for their re-
liance on the spoken word is crucial and forms much of the basis for
dramatic dialogue. For none has the problem been more acute than for
those dramatists who have attempted to stage Auschwitz. For our concerns, the preeminent example is Rolf Hochhuth, who has admitted,
implicitly and explicitly, that in the end such staging cannot be done.

Hochhuth makes that point emphatic in his notes to act five of *The Deputy* as well as in his postscript to the play, "Sidelights on History":[17]

> The question of whether and how Auschwitz might be visualized in this play occupied me for a long time. Documentary naturalism no longer serves as a stylistic principle. . . . No attempt was made to strive for an imitation of reality—nor should the stage set strive for it. On the other hand, it seemed perilous, for the drama, to employ an approach such as was so effectively used by Paul Celan in his masterly poem Todesfuge, in which the gassing of the Jews is entirely translated into metaphors, . . . for metaphors still screen the infernal cynicism of what really took place—a reality so enormous and grotesque that even today . . . the impression of unreality it produces conspires with our natural strong tendency to treat the matter as a legend, as an incredible apocalyptic fable. No matter how closely we adhere to historical facts, the speech, scene and events on the stage will be altogether surrealistic. (Pp. 222–23)

Because, as the playwright concludes, "we lack the imaginative faculties to be able to envision Auschwitz," other means had to be found in an effort to avoid the limitations of both naturalism and surrealism. The first might be managed by intentionally playing down or otherwise understating the "almost incredible events of Hitler's war and the number of its victims"; the second, by "palliat[ing] and adjust[ing] events to fit the human capacity for imagination" (p. 293). Such at least were Hochhuth's declared intentions, sensible ones given the problems before him, which called for solutions of imaginative restraint rather than extension. The latter could only lead to theatrical hyperbole, something on the order of trying to stage chaos itself, or its cosmological equivalent, hell. Actually, as we shall soon see, there is more than a suggestion of hell in the play, a suggestion that Hochhuth cannot always successfully restrain. That fact sets him problems of historical understanding as well as of dramaturgy, for to follow the lead of allegorical or mythical representation is to move away from history toward apocalyptic thinking, a tendency that does not suit Hochhuth's moral cast of mind.

Precisely because he is so overwhelmingly a moralist, the playwright has shifted much of the primary focus of *The Deputy* away from Auschwitz and its tortures to those who allowed the torturers free rein to create a hell on earth and administer it virtually within the public eye. To be sure, the driving questions behind this play are all generated by the fact of Auschwitz, but there are a host of supporting facts behind this fact—most especially the scandal of huge social and institutional forces that cooperated with the Nazis and, by so doing, helped them implement their program. Foremost among these institutions, as far as Hochhuth is concerned, was the Church, whose silence in the face of Hitler's *Endlösung* not only undermined the office of "the highest spiritual authority of the century" but, as a consequence, fundamentally undermined the major moral support structures of European civilization.

Given these concerns, in addition to those already noted about the impossibility of credibly staging Auschwitz, it is understandable that the central conflicts in *The Deputy* should be largely rhetorical ones, as represented by the strongly contrasting speeches of the major antagonists. In this play about the criminality of reticence, language takes precedence over dramatic action and might even be understood as its trigger, the flash point for conflict not only of opposing characters but also of conflicting world systems and metaphysical attitudes. *The Deputy* is, unabashedly, an extended polemical statement, a dramatization of historical, political, and theological argument, and its power throughout is largely that of words in conflict with one another and with the moral evasions of silence.

While *The Deputy* is written chiefly in a modified form of blank verse,[18] Hochhuth employs as well a diverse range of vocabularies and a variety of styles to enrich and complicate his language. Even a casual attention to his German shows a selective and at times heavy use of dialect, military argot, the business or "shop" talk of industry and commerce, diplomatic and ecclesiastical jargon, and theological argumentation. These differentiated styles are significant, for they allow the playwright to range across professional and class lines to explore and expose the hierarchy of guilt from top to bottom. At its lowest level are such minor SS functionaries as Witzel, whom Hochhuth describes in his stage notes as using "a rude, obscene, blustering tone . . . [a] brutal loquacity picked up from his superiors" (p. 132). His speech, "not marked by any dialect, [but] merely sloppy to the extreme," reveals its vulgar nature more readily in German than in English translation:

> "Einpacken hier . . .
> Los—pack deinen Dram zusammen . . .
> Fuffzich Pfund Gepäck pro Judennase—
> und nur Wäsche und Fressalien.

Alles annere wird ausgebackt, 'n bisschen
plötzlich—los—avanti!
. . . .

Mir haam viel Familiensinn, verstehnse.
Die beiden Kinner komm och mit . . .
Wer nich arbeiten kann, wird extra—
wird sonderbehandelt.[19]

"Pack up! . . .
Get busy—pack up your stuff . . .
Fifty pounds of baggage per Yid—
and nothing but clothes and eats.
Everything else left behind—and
hurry up about it—get moving—avanti!
. . . .

We don't like to break up families, see?
The two kids are coming along . . .
Those who can't work are given extra—
given special treatment.

(Pp. 133–35)

The crudity of this speech is barely suggested by the English, which simply cannot convey the brute ugliness of Witzel's barking commands. He speaks in the lowest registers of Nazi-Deutsch, for which there is no easy English equivalent, and as a result the demeaning tones of his orders and the savage innuendo of his open threats about *Sonderbehandlung* are not adequately transmitted to English readers. English serves better for much of the dialogue involving Salzer, the SS police chief of act three, and for most of the officers' banter in the bowling alley scene of act one, but the specifically crude and obscene nature of the German used in these instances belongs to a language all its own. Hochhuth remarks in his lengthy postscript that he based the dialogue in the officers' club on documents that were used in the Krupp trial or reprinted in scholarly collections of Nazi source material (p. 344). In these respects, then, he is clearly striving for a naturalism on stage, an effect that he reinforces through the use of Nazi song lyrics in the third scene of act one and through several references in act three to Himmler's famous speech before the SS in Posen (cited in chapter 2 of the present study). Hirt's talk about gathering human "specimens" and "material" and Eichmann's about "processing" eight million European Jews (pp. 51, 53, 61) likewise belong to the perverse language-world of the Third Reich. When, at the end of the play, the Doctor points to

Carlotta, a young Italian woman he has just shot, and orders a guard to "get *that* cleared away too," (p. 2840), we know we have reached the end of depravity. Background sound effects provided by the grating noise of a cement mixer and a buzz saw add to the violence of this raw argot and help to reinforce its mechanistic and sinister aspects.

The coarse, brutal side of Nazi-Deutsch contrasts sharply with the more elevated rhetorical styles used elsewhere throughout *The Deputy*. Riccardo, the young priest and intended tragic hero of the play, speaks in the impassioned tones of the idealist-martyr that he is to become, an imploringly didactic and exhortative style that he learns from Gerstein and later assumes as his own. His speeches—declamatory and contentious as they become—are intentionally aimed to provoke, and their polemical thrusts, especially in act four, raise the argumentative nature of the play to some of its most anguished levels.

Riccardo's adversaries, the Pope and the Doctor, round out (with Gerstein) the principal actors of the play. They are set off from one another by the separate offices they hold, by their sharply contrasting costumes, and by the distinctive styles of speech they employ, but at the same time they are joined in shockingly close alliance and seem almost to constitute two sides of the same personage. To determine who they are and what roles they assume in Hochhuth's imagination, one need only recall that the playwright subtitled his play "A Christian Tragedy."

How does such a conception reconcile with Hochhuth's clear intentions to write an historical drama, and one moreover based on documentary sources? *The Deputy* first began to take shape, the author has stated, when, upon reading about the Nazi period, he discovered the figure of Kurt Gerstein, a member of the Protestant Confessing Church, who early went into opposition against Hitler and joined the SS in an effort to subvert it from within. As a chemical engineer Gerstein was employed at Belzec and Treblinka and personally witnessed the mass murder of the Jews at those camps. His description of what took place in the gas chambers constitutes one of the rare eyewitness accounts we have of the extermination process.[20] Hochhuth was overwhelmed by this account of atrocity, as he was by the agony of the man who reported it, considering Gerstein "more like a fictional creation than an historical personage, . . . so 'modern' a Christian that we can scarcely understand him without considerable background in Kierkegaard" (pp. 14–15).

Hochhuth was strongly moved as well by two other Christian martyrs, Father Maximilian Kolbe, a Polish priest incarcerated in Auschwitz who gave up his life to save another prisoner, and Provost Bernhard Lichtenberg of Berlin's St. Hedwig's Cathedral, who publicly declared himself on the side of the persecuted Jews and even asked to accompany a transport of them to Dachau. *The Deputy* is dedicated to these two Christian opponents of Nazism, and they, together with Gerstein, stand behind Riccardo, in other respects a fictional or invented character, and account for much of his moral drive.

Flanking Riccardo on either side are the Doctor and the Pope, who, as the classical embodiments of evil and virtue respectively, ought to be in radical disequilibrium but, in fact, prove to be almost in league. That is a shocking alliance, which, of course, helped make *The Deputy* so controversial a play, provoking a debate that Eric Bentley has called the "largest storm ever raised by a play in the whole history of the drama." Since the Doctor is at least partly modeled on the notorious Dr. Mengele of Auschwitz, Hochhuth could have stood on firm historical ground in re-creating him for the drama, but, as he notes, he "deliberately deviated from historical portrayals of this mysterious 'master,'" whom he regarded as an "uncanny visitant from another world." The Doctor is Hochhuth's devil figure, someone to whom he awards "the stature of Absolute Evil—far more unequivocally so than Hitler. . . ." An allegorical figure, the Doctor is, in the playwright's conception of him, a personage apart "from all human beings and . . . to anything that has been learned about human beings . . . [;] with this character, an ancient figure in the theater and in Christian mystery plays is once more appearing upon the stage" (pp. 31–32). Gerstein describes him to Riccardo as "not a man at all, not human, / [but] . . . the Auschwitz angel of death" (p. 77).

Far from being a fallen angel, however, the Doctor is in command throughout the play and, as the personification of evil, wields an immense power, including an immense rhetorical power. A charmer and corrupter of women, he has little difficulty talking his way into sexual adventure; among his fellow SS officers, who respect him even while they fear him, he is a vaunting presence, who one moment may be gallant and the next break into the bawdiest and most loathsome of beerhall songs; among the frightened children and women on the platforms of Auschwitz, he can be deceptively calming and reassuring, even as he prepares to send his victims to their deaths. His greatest pleasure, though, is neither with his women, whom he perverts, nor with the men of the SS, whom he generally despises, but with God, whom he delights in challenging, and with Riccardo, a priest of God, whom he taunts in mean-spirited theological argument and forcefully seeks to reduce to unbelief. Alternately charming, ironic, cynical, brilliant, and deadly, the Doctor overwhelms everyone in his path through his eloquence and cunning, and to the end of the play he remains unvanquished, an absolute nihilist who is undisputed Lord in the kingdom of death.

The Doctor's role, then, in Hochhuth's specifically Christian conception of *The Deputy,* is clear: he is "the principle of evil in the flesh" (p. 72), the anti–Christ who stands as a dramatic foil to the principle of good. By entitlement, the latter is incarnate in the Pope, who, as Vicar of Christ, is designated to speak for the sanctity of life but whose silence before Hitler actually makes him an "accessory to murder" (p. 80). *The Deputy* exists by right of that accusation, which is the energizing source of the play's polemical thrust and gathers into a single focus every one of its historical, political, moral, and theological arguments. Although the Pope is on stage for only a relatively brief time and does not even make his appearance until act four, his presence is felt throughout, for the charge of guilt against him is the initiating and sustaining force for the entire play, and the source as well for the worldwide debate that started with the play and has continued well after productions have ceased.

This ongoing debate underscores the epic conception of Hochhuth's drama—epic understood here as argument involving history. Erwin Piscator, who gave *The Deputy* its world premiere in Berlin, stressed in his production the specifically political dimension of history, but that is not Hochhuth's primary understanding or concern. Rather, the playwright has placed the accent on the moral and spiritual aspects of history and has given us not so much a political play as a religious one; or perhaps it is more accurate to say that he has situated his play at that point of history where politics, morality, and religion intersect— and collapse. The focal point for that epic influence—and epic failure—is the Pope.

"History," Hochhuth has said, "is such a wide-open area, and such a devastating phenomenon, that human demeanor can, presumably, be interpreted only from those extreme, those polar situations, into which history places us" (*Storm,* p. 56). The Doctor, as we have already seen, is an allegorical representation of one of these extremes. The Pope is intended to represent the other extreme. The question is: is the latter an historical representation or, once more, a mythical one? There is no doubt at all that Hochhuth modeled his Pope on Pius XII; the greatest part of his "Sidelights on History" is given over to citing his documentary sources on Pacelli, the Concordat, and Vatican policy during the war. And, of course, it was the identification with Pacelli that brought forth such heated denunciations of the play, frequently from people in the highest levels of the church hierarchy who admitted they had neither seen it nor read it. In an open letter to an English periodical, Cardinal Montini attacked the play publicly for its slander of the Pope, as Cardinal Spellman did in a letter to the *New York Herald Tribune.* Any number of others responded similarly. All such protests were prompted by what was specifically, and not incorrectly, understood to be serious accusations against Pius XII. Nor is there any denying that Hochhuth's documentary intention is to indict Pacelli.

The Deputy, though, far from being a tract, is situated somewhere between documentation and art, as all imaginative representation of the Holocaust must be. This middle ground is difficult to occupy, for it must accommodate the claims of both history and interpretation. Hochhuth was fully aware of the problems involved in mining historical materials for the theater and addressed himself to them explicitly in the opening paragraphs of his postscript:

> . . . as far as possible I adhered to the facts. I allowed my imagination free play only to the extent that I had to transform the existing raw material of history into drama. Reality was respected throughout, but much of its slag had to be removed.
>
> Anyone who retraces the roads of historical events, littered as they are with ruins and corpses; anyone who reviews the contradictory, complacent or wildly distracted statements of the victors and victims; anyone who makes even the most modest effort to pick his way through the rubble and incidental circumstances of so-called historical events in order to reach the truth, the symbolic meaning—will find that the dramatist "cannot use a single element of reality as he finds it; his work must be idealized in *all* its parts if he is to comprehend reality as a whole." (Pp. 287–88)

We have already seen how, following such principles, Hochhuth is moved to reconceive character away from historical definition toward myth, and specifically toward Christian mythology. Whatever the historical Kurt Gerstein may have been like—his was such an uncanny personality that to this day scholars are unable to agree on his character—the Gerstein of *The Deputy* is an actor in a Christian drama, "more like a fictional creation than an historical personage," as Hochhuth has said. The Doctor likewise is not to be grasped primarily against the historical model of Josef Mengele but, more to the point of his presence in the play, against a Mephistophelian or Luciferian model. This same freedom for imaginative interpretation is exercised in the case of the Pope as well, whose extension out of history and into what Hochhuth calls the truth of "symbolic meaning" necessitates from time to time a certain amount of distance from the documentary sources. I do not suggest a complete divorce from historical understanding, of course, but rather a perception of how, in dramatizing history, the playwright necessarily adapts Pacelli to the larger imaginative purposes of his drama. As he himself puts it, "To me, Pius is a symbol, not only for all leaders, but for all men . . . who are passive when their brother is deported to death" (*Storm*, p. 43).

Following this lead, it is not difficult to see what role the Pope assumes in Hochhuth's symbolic religious drama: he is Cain, who silently looked away from his brother's death and refused all responsibility for it.[21] This is a damning accusation but the play makes it nonetheless—and continually so, locating it always in the same way: in the Pope's refusal to answer the summons set before him by history. History, understood in moral terms—the dominant terms of this play—centers in responsibility, the acknowledgment that men are accountable for their deeds. That is why to the fratricide history is to be avoided at all costs, as illustrated so vividly in the speech by Himmler noted in chapter 2 and prominently cited by Hochhuth toward the end of act three. Himmler's denial of the liquidation of European Jewry was, as the playwright stresses, categorical: it was to be "a *never written* and *never to be written* page of glory . . ." (p. 183). This silence echoes in the silence of the Pope, which "imposes," as Riccardo says, "a guilt upon the Church for which we must atone" (p. 156). To maximize the severity of this judgment, Riccardo makes the ultimate accusation against the Pope, linking him still more closely to a covering up of the crime of fratricide:

A deputy of Christ
who sees these things and nonetheless

permits reasons of state to seal his lips—
who wastes even one day in thought,
hesitates even for an hour
to lift his anguished voice
in one anathema to chill the blood
of every last man on earth—
that Pope is . . . a criminal.

(P. 102)

Ironically, among the characters in *The Deputy* it is one of the church's ranking members who comes to develop this line of thinking to its end point and to name the criminal, although he does so unwittingly and in more apologetic tones. It is the Cardinal who introduces Cain into the play, and by name, although, of course, not with direct reference to the Pope. This happens in scene two of act three when the Cardinal is told that the Jews of Rome are being seized by the Nazis and carried off under the Pope's very windows. "Now," says the Cardinal to Gerstein, "even the Pope / must condemn you before the whole world! . . . / You're forcing the Pope publicly / to take note of those crimes . . ." (p. 147). As matters transpire, the Cardinal is proven wrong, for the Pope is to say nothing, or next to nothing. Yet the Cardinal cannot know this and he continues his speech, arguing against Gerstein's insistence that "God / would not be God if he made use of a Hitler. . . .":

Oh yes, oh yes, most certainly, my friend!
Was not even Cain, who killed his brother,
the instrument of God? Cain said to the Lord:
my sin is too great ever to be forgiven.
And still, you know, God set a mark on Cain
so that no one who came upon him would ever kill him.
What is it your Luther says:
secular rule derives from Cain, you know. . . .
What can we know
of the terrible detours of the Lord!

(P. 148)

In what follows, *The Deputy* takes one of the boldest detours in religious dramaturgy, for the only character in the play to incur a physical mark of guilt is the Pope, who stains himself with ink in act four, a clearly symbolic branding that ties him directly to Cain and later to Pontius Pilate. The Pope's identification with Cain is further reinforced through his position as chief resident of the Eternal City (Cain, it will be recalled, is remembered as the founder of cities) and through his assumption of the commercial and diplomatic obligations of secular rule to the extent of compromising the responsibilities of his spiritual office: "Reasons of state," he declares, "forbid our pillorying Herr Hitler as a bandit" (p. 206). Primarily, though, it is the Pope's abdication of his moral duty to speak out directly and forcefully in behalf of the Jews— an abdication reflected in the absolute evasiveness of his imperious, ornate, and altogether empty language—that ultimately incriminates him. Following upon a symbolic washing of his hands, the Pope, in an almost liturgical chant, declares himself:

> We are—God knows it—blameless of the blood
> now being spilled. As the flowers
> in the countryside wait beneath winter's mantle of snow
> for the warm breezes of spring,
> so the *Jews* must wait, praying and trusting
> that the hour of heavenly comfort will come.
> (*He has dried his hands; now he rises.*)
> We who are here assembled in Christ's Name
> will pray. . . .
>
> (Pp. 220–21)

About such speech, Hochhuth writes in his stage notes to this scene: "Words, words, a rhetoric totally corrupted into a classic device for sounding well and saying nothing" (p. 212). Language is always revelatory, as any good playwright knows, and the Pope's language, marked as it is by high-sounding generalities and decorative but meaningless turns of phrase, shows him to be at once unfeeling and uncaring. These rhetorical tendencies are so pronounced in the speech just cited as to make it seem fabricated, yet in writing it Hochhuth is on firm ground, for he relies here upon objective documentation, transcribing from the *Osservatore Romano* of October 25, 1943, a speech by Pius, which he reproduces verbatim save for a single change: where the Pope used the word *Poles,* Hochhuth substituted *Jews* (p. 350; *Storm,* p. 62). Otherwise, the playwright was in this instance obeying a strictly naturalistic fidelity, supporting his charge that in the face of Hitler's crimes to say nothing and to do nothing are equally reprehensible and are tantamount to recapitulating the crime of Cain.

The central didactic point of *The Deputy,* then, is ringingly clear:

far from being "blameless of the blood being spilled," the bystanders to
genocide, and especially those in positions of authority, are as guilty as
the perpetrators. In Hochhuth's moral reading of history, the Pope's
professed "neutrality" implicated him directly in the *Endlösung,* for to
remain silent before that event was effectively to condone it. On the
spiritual plane, in the playwright's typological or allegorical reading,
the silence of the Vicar of Christ meant that Christendom's highest
spiritual authority was abdicating its power over human affairs and
transferring that power to the anti-Christ—in effect, placing "the devil
on the throne of fire and smoke." The Doctor, as we have seen, is
portrayed in just these terms at Auschwitz, which, with "its pall of
smoke and glow of fires" (p. 227), is Hochhuth's modern version of
hell. What is most shocking, but at the same time entirely consistent
with the religious indictment this play makes, is that Hochhuth, searching history for antecedent influences, makes the spiritual architect of
Auschwitz not Heinrich Himmler but Ignatius Loyola, whose *Spiritual
Exercises* are cited in act five as the natural text for "crematorium reading" and quoted as a kind of prototype of the extermination camps:

> "I see with the eyes
> of imagination the tremendous glow of flame
> and the souls locked in the *burning* bodies.
> I smell with the sense of smell smoke, sulphur,
> excrement and rotting things. . . ."
>
> (P. 280)

Among all Hochhuth's documentary sources, this last may be the
most damning, for it links the church to the Holocaust not only
through the person of the Pope but through one of its great saints,
whose powerful imaginings of auto-da-fé implicate Christian practice
over the centuries and make it appear the forerunner of the crimes of
the Nazis.[22] The Doctor's speech joins the issue head-on:

> What gives priests the right to look down on the SS?
> We are the Dominicans of the technological age.
> It is no accident that so many of my kind,
> the leaders, come from good Catholic homes. . . .
> Hitler, Goebbels, Bormann, Kaltenbrunner. . . .
> Höss, our commandant, studied for the priesthood.
> And Himmler's uncle, who stood godfather to him,
> is nothing less than Suffragan Bishop in Bamberg! . . .

A civilization that commits
its children's souls into the safeguard
of a Church responsible for the Inquisition
comes to the end that it deserves
when for its funeral pyres it plucks
the brands from our furnaces for human bodies. . . .
Your Church was the first to show
that you can burn men just like coke.
In Spain alone, without the benefit of crematoria,
you turned to ashes three hundred and fifty thousand
human beings, most of them while alive, mind you.
Such an achievement surely needs the help of Christ.

(Pp. 248–49)

Riccardo's reply to this is little more than a helpless admission of the Church's past guilt and the desperate idea that if "the devil exists, God also exists." "Otherwise," he says turning to the Doctor, "*you* would have won a long time ago" (p. 253). But as *The Deputy* represents the contest between Christian faith and its ancient adversary—and what is this play if not a severe testing of Christian beliefs in the time after Auschwitz?—the devil does win. By the end of act five, Riccardo is dead, Gerstein is being led away to his death by an SS guard, and the Pope has long since retreated into an empty spirituality. The last person seen on stage is the Doctor, who walks off, smiling, with the text of Loyola's *Spiritual Exercises* tucked under his arm.

The lives of men and the lives of books are always powerfully linked, but rarely has there been a linkage as perverse as the one on which Hochhuth ends his play. His basis for doing so is elaborated upon in "Sidelights on History," where, quoting Schellenberg, Himmler's closest confidant, the author once more appeals to the authority of his documentary sources to reinforce what otherwise would be one of the most improbable points of his play:

"Himmler owned an extremely large and excellent library on the Jesuit Order and for years would sit up late studying the extensive literature. Thus he built up the SS organization according to the principles of the Jesuits. The *Spiritual Exercises* of Ignatius of Loyola served as the foundation; the supreme law was absolute obedience, the execution of any order whatsoever without question. Himmler himself, as *Reichsführer* of the SS, was the general of the order. The structure of leadership was borrowed from the hierarchical order of the Catholic Church." (P. 309)

One would want to know a good deal more about Himmler and also have some way of testing the cause and effect relationship of reading and acting before accepting so bold a thesis as this, yet the fact that Hochhuth accepts it is powerfully relevant to his play, which exposes in extreme revisionist fashion the relationship between a high degree of religious literacy and the lowest levels of antireligious behavior. The Doctor boasts of having "a theological mind" and of once having studied in seminary (p. 247). His black uniform is an exact stage parallel to the black soutane of Riccardo, whom he accepts, he says, as his "partner." And much of the Doctor's dialogue is couched in terms of religious categories, albeit ones that he inverts, parodies, and looks to destroy. These are all instances once more of *Widerruf,* or extreme symbolic renunciation, a dramatic principle that works throughout *The Deputy.* Moreover, such principles of inversion operate in history as well and are a key part of the linguistic history of the Third Reich, as we saw earlier in this chapter, and as Pius XI, Pacelli's predecessor, took note of in his encyclical of March 1937 ("Mit Brennender Sorge"), when he spoke out against the Nazi practice of adopting the vocabulary of Christian dogma for a political program that was pervasively anti-Christian. Although this Pope did not mention Hitler by name, he surely had the latter in mind when he protested that "if he did not wish to be a Christian, he must refrain at least from enriching the vocabulary of his heresy from out of Christian terminology."[23] That observation was acute, and although it had little practical effect it knowingly registered the truth that National Socialism in its German strain was as much a rival religious movement as it was a political one, an insight that informs *The Deputy* from beginning to end. Had the Nazis ever been able to complete their thrust against the Jews, in fact, it is likely that they would have turned next against the churches. Hochhuth makes that point clear when he notes in his postscript that Himmler, schooled though he was in Christian religious literature, boasted that, "We shall not rest until we have rooted out Christianity" (p. 305). Jorge Luis Borges offers a lucid judgment upon this complex eventuality of religious self-destruction in his "Deutsches Requiem," a brilliant little story whose central insight may serve to bring the matter to a close for us: "The history of nations . . . registers a secret continuity. . . . Luther, translator of the Bible, could not suspect that his goal was to forge a people destined to destroy the Bible for all time."[24]

It is not yet clear whether Nazism effected so total a destruction, but it is certain, as *The Deputy* powerfully argues, that when the supreme leaders of the Church allow the moral teachings of biblical faith to be silenced, destruction is probably not far off.

For the Jews, originators of the Bible and history's most continuous link with it, destruction began, as we observed earlier, with the burning of the books. The fires of the Inquisition had consumed other than just the Jewish religious writings, as did the Nazi bonfires, but at the heart of Europe's religiously inspired autos-da-fé there is always the Hebrew Bible and its commentaries. Borges glimpses that fact for us in the quotation above, as does Jabès in the prefatory inscription to this chapter. We can conclude with citations of a more extended sort, which show how in Jewish fate the lives of books and the lives of men and women are mutually determined.

Readers of *The Last of the Just* will recall a scene of a pogrom in Stillenstadt, a sleepy German town in the Rhenish provinces, but a scene hardly localized to that place, for throughout Germany on the night of November 10, 1938, hundreds of Jewish synagogues and libraries were put to the torch. In Schwarz-Bart's imaginative retelling of *Kristallnacht,* the Levy family, huddled together behind locked doors in the upper floors of their dwelling, await their fate. What is it the mob below wants from them? A "friendly" German offers a "saving" piece of advice: "Give them some prayer books for the fire in the street. . . . They're all worked up. At least you have to give them that." Contemplating the sacrifice of books as a possible way out, Benjamin Levy replies, "Just the books?" "The books first," answers his aged father mockingly, and then, wielding an iron bar, delivers himself unflinchingly of the traditional Jewish reply to barbarism: "For a thousand years the Christians have been trying to kill us every day. And we have been trying to live every day. And every day we manage it somehow. Do you know why? Because we never give up our books. Never, never, never!" (pp. 269–70).

Schwarz-Bart romanticizes the episode somewhat, no doubt, but his point is no less compelling: in the fate of the Jews, books are a shield against savagery, a front line of defense against the coming on of night, and they are to be fought for with the same strength and determination we apply to life itself. Without them, as Chaim Kaplan wrote in his diary, the Jews were condemned to a state of double darkness, "physical darkness because the electricity has been shut off . . . , but worse than that, mental darkness" (p. 43). More fully and perceptively than anyone else of his generation, Kaplan saw the absolute terror of the Nazis and under it the inevitable spoliation of Polish Jewry: "This is not the eve of destruction, . . . but destruction itself. . . . Just as darkness rules the streets of Warsaw, so does it dominate our minds. The conqueror depletes the spirit along with more material things. Every spark of light is a potential breach in the kingdom of darkness of bestial Nazism" (pp. 67–68).

For that very reason, every such spark was systematically extinguished by the agents of darkness, and as he watched the shutdown of the schools and synagogues, the end of the newspapers and the radio stations, the pillage and padlocking of the Tlomackie and Sejm Libraries, Kaplan knew all he needed to know about the will of the enemy. It broke his heart to realize that the Jews, stripped of their culture, would be virtually defenseless against such an antagonist: "I fear such people! Where plunder is based on an ideology, on a world outlook which in essence is spiritual, it cannot be equalled in strength and durability. . . . The Nazi has robbed us not only of material possessions, but also of our good name as 'the people of the book . . .'" (p. 91).

Yet in one crucial respect Kaplan was wrong: he felt certain that a nation possessed of both the book and the sword "will not perish" (p. 91). The Thousand Year Reich, which grew out of a people of high culture, nonetheless crumbled into ruin after a mere twelve years. Because it had an inferior sword or an inferior book? The author of *Mein Kampf* wreaked havoc upon Europe and then went to his suicide. His book may be read today as part of the literature of infamy, but otherwise it is without interest. Heine, who was spared the fate of having to read it, nevertheless was intimate enough with what Borges calls the secret continuity of nations to see what was coming: "German thunder is truly German; it takes its time. But it will come, and when it crashes it will crash as nothing in history crashed before. The hour will come. . . . A drama will be performed which will make the French Revolution seem like a pretty idyll. . . . Never doubt it; the hour will come."[25]

CHAPTER 8

Exploiting Atrocity

No stage drama can possibly register the magnitude of the historical crash that Heine foresaw and that Hitler was later to bring on. Nevertheless, literature can at its best help contain some of the resulting shock waves and begin to make them audible. In order to do that, though, one must be able to listen well, in ways unobstructed by self-interest of one kind or another. To do otherwise is to exploit atrocity by misappropriating it for private or political ends. All such efforts at "adapting" the Holocaust are bound to fail—artistically, for reasons of conceptual distortion, and morally, for misusing the sufferings of others. Each of the works to be considered in this chapter shows the effects of such misappropriation, although not all have been universally understood and valued as exploitative.

The most prominent dramatic work in this vein is Peter Weiss's *The Investigation,* a play that purports to "contain nothing but facts" but that shapes facts, and on occasion misshapes them, to serve a specific ideological vision of history.[1] Even more so than *The Deputy, The Investigation* is an example of documentary theater, a mode that Weiss sees as particularly well suited for political expression—a view that he elaborates in "The Material and the Models: Notes toward a Definition of Documentary Theatre": "Documentary Theatre takes sides. . . . [It] is valueless if it is afraid of definitions, if it shows only the conditions and not the causes underlying them, and if it does not reveal the need to eliminate these conditions and the possibilities of doing so. . . ."[2]

Despite this declaration of political intentions, Weiss claims a strict objectivity for documentary theater, stating with considerable emphasis that he wanted to pursue "a scientific investigation of the reality of

Auschwitz, to show the audience, in the greatest detail, exactly what happened."[3] Such an aim is admirable, but it is not easily reconciled with the need to "take sides." Otto Best sums up the inevitable difficulties that arise from these divided intentions:

> The material is changed in one way or another by the operation of the conceptualizing intention. The role of the author becomes all the more important because it is his attitude that determines the preservation of the values of documentation and argumentation. . . .
>
> The objectivity inherent in the concept of documentation is negated and makes nonsense of the purpose of documentation to the extent that the author, who is striving to achieve stage reality, no longer serves the material but makes use of the material and deprives it of autonomy. When a court case becomes a show trial, the spectator is not enlightened; he is subjected to propaganda, he is reduced.[4]

The specific court case behind *The Investigation* was the Auschwitz War Crimes Trial held in Frankfurt am Main in 1963–65. Weiss attended a number of the trial sessions and also read Bernd Naumann's reports about them in the *Frankfurter Allgemeine Zeitung*.[5] From these, as well as from the courtroom testimony that he heard, he distilled the material for his play—necessarily a selective and highly concentrated version of the trial proceedings. The result is a play in eleven cantos, or "songs," each devoted to a particular aspect of torture at Auschwitz. Thus "The Song of the Platform," "The Song of the Camp," "The Song of the Swing," etc. These wind down in Dantesque fashion to reach finally "The Song of Cyclon B" and "The Song of the Fire Ovens," a descent that retraces, in gruesome and revolting detail, the fate of millions. Terror of the worst sort accompanied those who were forced to undergo the agony of any one of these several stations, and Weiss is unsparing in chronicling their ordeal. He does so in trial fashion by bringing on to his stage a judge, a prosecuting attorney, a counsel for the defense, nine witnesses (the actual trial at Frankfurt am Main included 359 witnesses), and eighteen defendants (out of an actual twenty-three). These constitute the list of characters in the play; those in the last grouping bear individual names; the others do not. This general anonymity is preserved throughout, in keeping with the author's desire to have the witnesses appear less as persons than as "mere speaking tubes" ("Note"). Even the named accused are presented by and large without notable distinction of individual character, and the final impression they leave is that of a vaguely sinister chorus of criminals, all foreswearing responsibility for their crimes, for almost all claim that they were "only following orders" and "doing their duty." Although they may be called "Mulka" and "Kaduk" and "Boger," the accused are presented less as persons acting out of individual motives than as nondescript and almost anonymous victims themselves— "symbols," as Weiss calls them, "of a system that implicated in its guilt many others who never appeared in court" ("Note").

What is really on trial in *The Investigation,* in fact, is this "system," itself unnamed in the play but the true center of the author's attention. For apart from endlessly cataloguing atrocity, which he does in a spare, unemotional language that conveys an austere detachment, Weiss is intent on exposing what he considers to be "the causes underlying" atrocity—the "system" that built and ran Auschwitz. This is how he infers it:

> Many of those who were destined
> to play the part of prisoners
> had grown up with the same ideas
> the same way of looking at things
> as those
> who found themselves acting as guards
> They were all equally dedicated
> to the same nation
> to its prosperity
> and its rewards
> And if they had not been designated
> prisoners
> they could equally well have been guards
> We must drop the lofty view
> that the camp world
> is incomprehensible to us
> We all knew the society
> that produced a government
> capable of creating such camps
> The order that prevailed there
> was an order whose basic nature
> we were familiar with

(P. 107)

While most of *The Investigation* is a stylized but otherwise faithful transcription of testimony at the Auschwitz trials, the speech just given is the author's interpolation—an instance of the playwright's "taking sides." He does not do that often, but when he does his intentions are clear: the aim of documentary theater, he has written, is to show "that reality, however opaque it may appear, can be explained in every detail."[6] Weiss's comprehensive explanation is that Nazism reduces to capitalism, an ideological position that the author has held to firmly and explicitly in comments made outside of the play. "I want to brand Capitalism,"[7] Weiss has said, seeing in it the origins of the system that created the camps in order to reap large profits from them.

Just how inadequate an explanation for Auschwitz that is immediately becomes clear to anyone who has read the literature about the camps—or, indeed, to anyone who listened carefully to what was said at the War Crimes Trial in Frankfurt. Far from exposing a profit motive for Auschwitz, the evidence all points the other way: to gratuitous waste and needless elimination of human resources. The camps, far from existing for the primary purpose of exploiting slave labor for cheap production, murdered their slaves en masse and produced little more than corpses. Yet as an ideological socialist Weiss needs a motive more in line with the dictates of dialectical materialism and finds his "explanation" in capitalism, under which system, he maintains, the prisoners and the guards could be virtually interchangeable.

Such a conception begins to account for the peculiarly lifeless quality of all the characters in this play, who are portrayed less as persons than as stand-ins for the nondescript and almost hypothetical "rulers" and "victims" of the "system." Otto Best, who entitles his study of *The Investigation* "Making the World Aware of the (Capitalist) Inferno as the Condition for the (Socialist) Paradiso," draws the only conclusions possible from this development:

> The frantic attempt to place the blame for the existence of the extermination camps not upon Nazi Germany alone, but upon the capitalist system as a whole must be understood as the intention of an author who sees a common denominator for fascism and capitalism. . . .
> The information conveyed by this oratorio is certainly that Auschwitz was hell, a hell made by men for men. But the quest for the explanation of this truth is not touched upon; it is swallowed up by the cliché that the phenomenon of an Auschwitz is the inevitable consequence of capitalist exploitation. The connections between Auschwitz and the conglomerate of National Socialist ideology is nowhere brought to light, the historical references are lacking. An "objective" case history would certainly have better served the cause of consciousness raising.[8]

The historical references are lacking because Weiss's reading of history in *The Investigation* is disinterested in the actual perpetrators and victims of Auschwitz. With few exceptions, his verse is toneless and undifferentiated, a language by and large disassociated from feeling and incapable of expressing character. Some of the stock jargon of Nazi-Deutsch is employed, but otherwise the German of *The Investigation* is pervasively dispassionate, flat, and empty—an instrument for mechanically recording the witnesses' testimony, registering the defendants' predictable evasions and denials, and little more. Such a language stands in striking contrast to that actually used at the Auschwitz trials that served Weiss as his intended model, for there, as the playwright himself notes, the confrontations between the witnesses and the accused, as between the prosecuting and defense attorneys, were "overcharged with emotion" ("Note"). Weiss discharged the speeches of their emotional qualities, which is to say he reduced them from the level of actual human discourse to a code of raw data that would accommodate his political design. In doing so he transposed pain away from the persons who had to suffer it to a place within the abstract frame of ideology. This extension out of history and into the blank spaces of politically determined schema was carried to such an extreme in the play that the word "Jew" nowhere appears in it. Instead, one hears only of "the 9 million 600 thousand persecuted / who lived in the regions / ruled by their persecutors / 6 million have disappeared" (p. 266). The playwright is altogether indifferent to the specific identities of the "persecuted" and their "persecutors" and seems to regard them as little more than ciphers in his political arithmetic—and interchangeable ciphers at that, as he explained in an interview:

> The Nazis did kill six million Jews, yes, but they killed millions of others. The word "Jew" is in fact never used in the play. . . . I do not identify myself any more with the Jews than I do with the people of Vietnam or the blacks in South Africa. I simply identify myself with the oppressed of the world. . . . *The Investigation* is about the extreme abuse of power that alienates people from their own actions. It happens to be German power, but that again is unimportant. I see Auschwitz as a scientific instrument that could have been used by anyone to exterminate anyone. For that matter, given a different deal, the Jews could have been on the side of the Nazis. They too could have been the exterminators. *The Investigation* is a universal human problem.[9]

To see Auschwitz in such terms is, of course, not to want to see it at all—a failure of both artistic and moral vision that characterizes

Weiss's play in any final analysis of it that is not bound by the author's own doctrinaire reading of history. Hochhuth has one of his characters say at the beginning of *The Deputy:* "Investigation! What's there to investigate? Ashes?" (p. 40). The answer to this question can only be, "Yes, ashes, and who made them, and what they were before they were turned into ash." Weiss, for all that he dwells on beatings and phenol injections into the heart, is in fact less interested in investigating the specific location of such cruelty in history than he is in appropriating it for political ends. The recitation of pain in *The Investigation* is awesome, and one comes away from the play numbed by the realization of just how much punishment the author exposed himself to in writing it, but at the same time unconvinced that he ever once envisioned the dead as having been alive.[10] To him the ashes are so much data, the residue of a burnt-out system. The people, victims and executioners both, are brought back as little more than the depersonalized "speaking tubes" of a political morality play.

Sophie's Choice, William Styron's best-selling novel of the Holocaust, is another prominent example of the tendency to universalize Auschwitz as a murderous thrust against "mankind." As such, it has the effect, and no doubt also the intention, of removing the Holocaust from its place within Jewish and Christian history and placing it within a generalized history of evil, for which no one in particular need be held accountable. Auschwitz may have been a great horror, "a supreme horror," as Styron calls it, but one "on the part of the human race." "I do not believe it is true," he says "that you can damn a whole nation, Germany, in this case, for the concentration camps." It is as if Auschwitz achieved itself, helped along by modern methods of technology, to be sure, but otherwise, to quote the kind of elevated language that Styron loves to use, the apotheosis "of the titanic and sinister forces at work in history and in modern life that threaten *all* men, not only Jews."[11]

The Holocaust may have been an enactment of "absolute evil," but it was so as the result of particular crimes against particular people. Hitler was never hesitant to indict that people by name, nor was Himmler any less precise in setting up the camps where they were to be murdered. Why, then, a generation after the bloody deed, is a writer like Styron so evasive in discussing it? What brings him to favor the kind of "philosophical and historical *spaciousness,*" to quote him once more, that abstracts the crime against the Jews as "a menace to the entire human family"?

As Styron sees it, "it minimizes the evil of the Nazi organization and desecration of life to see it only as a fulfillment of Nazi anti-Semitism. . . . To say that only Jews suffered, is simply to tell a historical lie." "I intend no disrespect to Jewish sensibilities," he remarks, as he recalls that "vast numbers of Gentiles shared in the same perdition visited upon the Jews." To be sure they did, but the crime of the Holocaust did not spread out neatly and evenly among the Jews and Gentiles alike. Most of European Jewry was murdered, and the murderers were European Gentiles, some of whom also died. The extent of the dying and the motives behind the deaths were not equivalent, though, and it simply makes no sense to add up all the corpses without distinction and pile them on to some abstract slaughter heap called "mankind." To generalize or universalize the victims of the Holocaust is not only to profane their memories but to exonerate their executioners, who by the same line of thinking pursued above also disappear into the mist of a faceless mankind.

Not surprisingly, that is where Styron prefers to see them, for he holds strongly to the view, set forth in *Sophie's Choice* and elsewhere, that it is "inexcusable to condemn any single *people* for *anything*," as he has one of his characters say, "and that goes for *any* people . . . even the Germans!"[12] In one of his interviews, Styron has even gone so far as to say that "if you examine Nazi Germany, one of the remarkable things about the whole story, one of the most moving parts of the story, is the number of Germans who stood up and became martyrs because of their opposition to Nazism." Such a view of Nazi Germany goes beyond apology and enters fiction as a new and extravagant mythology, for the facts of the Holocaust, as any credible history of the period will bear out, simply do not support Styron's praise for the German citizenry under Hitler. Some genuine heroes and martyrs there doubtless were, but the vast numbers of Germans, far from opposing Nazism, either remained conspicuously quiet or ardently threw Hitler their support.

Fiction, or "story," as he twice refers to it in the quotation above, gets a bad name when it confronts history in so fanciful a manner, yet it is probably the case that, owing to its affective powers and its ability to satisfy certain mythological cravings we all have, fiction can achieve a more immediate and pervasive impact than history. For this very reason, fictional representations of the Holocaust need to be judged against a particularly careful standard of truth, for we are in a period right now when it is still far from certain that most people are willing to pay

credence to the historicity of the Holocaust and, indeed, when some are
actively intent on subverting it.[13] The lines that separate fact from fiction need to be scrupulously observed, therefore, lest the tendency to
reject the Holocaust, already strong, be encouraged by reducing it altogether to the realm of the fictive.

It is not possible here to separate out the many comminglings of
fact and fiction in *Sophie's Choice,* but a few prominent examples need
to be looked at. One involves Styron's identification of Hans Frank, the
Nazi Governor General of a large part of occupied Poland, as a Jew (p.
249). None of the histories consulted bears out this identification, although it is possible that Styron has had access to sources that the historians do not know; if so, he should declare them. Otherwise, to reinvent Frank fictively as a Jew is unpardonable and of a piece with such
earlier malicious allegations by others that Hitler was a Jew, Heydrich
was a Jew, Eichmann was a Jew, etc. By this line of reasoning, the most
powerful persecutors of the Jews were other Jews, and the whole awful
business can be passed off as an internal affair, of no concern to anyone
else and without implication for them.

History, of course, sees it otherwise and tells us the precise names
of the victimizers. One was Rudolf Höss, the Commandant of Auschwitz, whom Styron carries over, by name, into his narrative. In doing
so he has relied heavily, and unwisely, on Höss's autobiography, a
self-exonerating piece of writing that Höss did in a Polish prison while
awaiting execution. It is true, as Samuel Johnson said, that in the
shadow of the gallows a man's mind is powerfully concentrated, but it
is also likely to take a pious and self-serving turn. Höss's memoirs,
generally accurate about the deeds of others, portray the author, in his
own words, as being "unknowingly a cog in the wheel of the great
extermination machine created by the Third Reich."[14] In their typically
formal and understated way, Höss's reflections on the making of a Nazi
cry out for posterity to recognize that the commander of Auschwitz
"had a heart and that he was not evil."[15] These are Höss's own words,
among the last he wrote. Styron responded to them charitably and at
considerable length and has given us a fictionalized portrait of Höss that
would have satisfied many of the latter's own wishes, showing us that
he was a mass murderer, yes, but not an intentionally cruel one. Be-
sides, as the novel goes on to show, he was capable of the tenderest
feelings for animals, loved his horse, and could approach loving a
woman. Could such a man have been all bad?

The most troublesome of Styron's Nazi portraits, though, is neither Hans Frank, who is mentioned only in passing, nor Rudolf Höss, but someone called "Hauptsturmführer Fritz Jemand von Niemand," an SS doctor at Auschwitz. Dr. Jemand von Niemand is assigned to the platforms of the camp, where, like his infamous historical prototype, Dr. Mengele, he could decide on the spot and with the merest wave of a hand who might live and who would die. A drunken, degenerate, sadistic type, he toys with Sophie and forces her to choose between her two children: one will go immediately to the furnaces, the other will live awhile longer. "Which one will you keep?" (p. 483), he taunts her. Such things happened at Auschwitz, and, repellent though they may be, it is imperative that they be recorded and remembered. To fictionalize them as the handiwork of a Nobody, though—which is more or less how "Jemand von Niemand" translates—is, through the workings of abstraction, to all but dismiss them. As Auschwitz has painfully shown, inhuman crimes are committed by human criminals, particular men and women destroying other men and women. To see it differently, as part of some modern mystery play about a vast and undifferentiated evil, is not to want to see it at all. A certain strain of Christian universalism, exemplified by Styron at his most pious, prefers not to see it at all, or, if such evil must be witnessed, to see it in "spiritual" terms. As evidence, consider what the novelist makes of his SS doctor:

> The doctor must have waited a long time to come face to face with Sophie and her children, hoping to perpetrate his ingenious deed. And what, in the private misery of his heart, I think he most intensely lusted to do was to inflict upon Sophie, or someone like her—some tender and perishable Christian—a totally unpardonable sin. It is precisely because he had yearned with such passion to commit this terrible sin that I believe that the doctor was exceptional, perhaps unique, among his fellow SS automata: if he was not a good man or a bad man, he still retained a potential capacity for goodness, as well as evil, and his strivings were essentially religious. (P. 484)

Dr. Jemand von Niemand, this murderous abstraction, "was reaching out for spiritual salvation" (p. 485), and, although he may have sent thousands upon thousands of people to die, "his soul thirsted for beatitude" (p. 486). The doctor, undergoing "the crisis of his life" (p. 485), would have *preferred* "to pursue more normal medical activities" but instead conducted the hordes of the condemned to the crematories. Nevertheless—and here Styron's charity surpasses itself—"It may be hard to believe, but the vastness and complexity of Auschwitz permitted some benign medical work as well as the unspeakable experiments which—given the assumption that Dr. von Niemand was a man of some sensibility—he would have shunned" (p. 486). In this liberal manner—taking the large-hearted, spacious, spiritual view—Styron unfolds his novel of the Holocaust as an extended parable of all men's travail.

"All men" in *Sophie's Choice* are represented chiefly by a woman—Sophie Zawistowska, a Polish Catholic survivor of Auschwitz. Why choose Sophie as the representative victim of the camps? "Although she was not Jewish," the narrator says, "she had suffered as much as any Jew who had survived the same afflictions, and . . . had in certain profound ways suffered more than most" (p. 219). To make that point graphic, poor Sophie has to be put through hell, not only in Auschwitz, where, as expected, the Nazis cruelly mistreat her, but, after her liberation, in New York, where, in "the Kingdom of the Jews" (by which Styron means Flatbush), others can abuse her as well. Chief among Sophie's postwar oppressors is Nathan, her Jewish lover, a brilliant but mad fellow who strikes one as an inspired cross between Othello and Svengali. In Nathan all the white man's fears about black potency come together with the Christian's fears about an imagined Jewish diabolism. Nathan is everything extreme—extremely caring and extremely cruel, extremely talented and extremely erratic and crazy. In the end, after alternately loving Sophie lavishly and beating her mercilessly, he will drive her to her most extreme choice—to become a partner with him in a romantic suicide pact. This she will do (stylishly, with the record player on providing background music), but before her exquisite Liebestod can arrive, poor Sophie is made to endure a whole series of physical, sexual, and psychological attacks, being victimized in turn by her domineering and racist father, Rudolf Höss, his lesbian house maid, a New York subway digital rapist, a strapped-out Polish assassin, her frigid husband, another lesbian comrade-in-arms, and mad Nathan. Her twenty months' imprisonment in Auschwitz (she is sent there for stealing a ham!) results in the loss of her two children and her teeth; her brief period of wished-for rehabilitation in Jewish New York will deprive her of the remnants of her faith, at least part of her mind, and, ultimately, any will to live that may have been left her. On the slopes of her decline, though, she can nevertheless ride to sexual ecstasy time and again with her crazy, hopped-up Jewish lover, parade the streets and beaches of New York with him dressed in expensive,

custom-made period outfits, hold down an office job with a Jewish
doctor, devote endless hours listening to classical music, narrate the
story of her brief, tormented life, and even bring to sexual and artistic
maturity a young aspiring Southern writer who, in the summer of
1947, wandered into "the Kingdom of the Jews" just in time to catch all
of this going on and help push it along.

Now what, it might be asked, does this mighty erotic struggle
have to do with Auschwitz? By and large, nothing at all. The Old
South, though, which brought up its young on the "tall tales and be-
guiling horrors of the Protestant/Jewish Bible" (p. 39), twisted the erotic imagination of Stingo, the novel's protagonist, badly out of shape, so
that he ended up years later "an ineffective and horny Calvinist among
all these Jews" (p. 37). More than anything else, *Sophie's Choice* is given
over to exorcising Stingo's sexual demon, a feat constantly sought,
forever delayed, and finally achieved at the expense, once more, of suffering Sophie.

Here it needs to be noted that Sophie represents a new and singu-
larly perverse type of sex object that is beginning to emerge in the writings of certain authors drawn to the most unseemly side of the
Holocaust—namely, she represents, in her abused and broken body,
the desirability of the Mutilated Woman. In the camps themselves, as
virtually all survivor accounts indicate, the central, most frustrated, and
hence most abiding appetite was for food. Other passions were
secondary and, it seems, for most were held in abeyance. As a result,
one of the characteristics of Holocaust writings at their most authentic
is that they are peculiarly and predominantly sexless. This is doubtless
one reason why latter-day authors who have had no direct, firsthand
experience of the camps have such a hard time writing about them: the
contemporary imagination, inflamed as it is by hyped-up sexual fantasies, can hardly understand an order of experience where eros is so
deprived and the sexual drive so stunted. Nevertheless, the improbable
presents its own stimulus and challenge, and, as *Sophie's Choice* shows,
we now are witnessing the emergence of a literature dedicated to developing an Erotics of Auschwitz. What begins as a flow of sympathy for
the utterly victimized camp survivor ends as a great surge of almost
cannibalistic desire:

> She stretched out her hand. . . . As she did so I saw for the first
> time the number tattooed on the suntanned, lightly freckled skin of her

forearm—a purple number of at least five digits. . . . To the melting love in my stomach was added a sudden ache. . . .

As she went slowly up the stairs I took a good look at her beautiful body, with all the right prominences, curves, continuities and symmetries, there was something a little strange about it—nothing visibly missing and not so much deficient as reassembled. And that was precisely *it*, I could see. The off quality proclaimed itself through the skin. It possessed the sickish plasticity (at the back of her arms it was especially noticeable) of one who has suffered severe emaciation and whose flesh is even now in the last stages of being restored. Also, I felt that underneath that healthy suntan there lingered the sallowness of a body not wholly rescued from a terrible crisis. But none of these at all diminished a kind of wonderfully negligent sexuality having to do at that moment, at least, with the casual but forthright way her pelvis moved and with her truly sumptuous rear end. Despite past famine, her behind was as perfectly formed as some fantastic prize-winning pear; it vibrated with magical eloquence, and from this angle it so stirred my depths that I mentally pledged to the Presbyterian orphanages of Virginia a quarter of my future earnings as a writer in exchange for that bare ass's brief lodging—thirty seconds would do—within the compass of my cupped, supplicant palms. (Pp. 51–52)

Much of *Sophie's Choice* is given over to descriptions of this kind and seesaws back and forth between accounts of Sophie's highly charged, on-again-off-again affair with Nathan and Stingo's desire to supplant the Jew and exercise his own sexual rights with his woman. The language that Stingo uses to describe their noisy lovemaking tells a good deal about his own imagined role in the affair: "I felt another nail amplify my crucifixion: they were going at it again upstairs on the accursed mattress. 'Stop it!' I roared at the ceiling, and with my forefingers plugged up my ears. *Sophie and Nathan!* I thought. Fucking Jewish rabbits!" (p. 45).

If this book tells us anything at all about the Holocaust, it is that more is needed to penetrate so extreme a history than a transposition of erotic and aesthetic motives onto a landscape of slaughter. In relating his story of the Polish girl who stole a ham and forever after suffered sexual, moral, and psychological abuse, Styron has written not so much a novel of the Holocaust as an unwitting spoof of the same. By reducing the war against the Jews to sexual combat, he has misappropriated Auschwitz and used it as little more than the erotic centerpiece of a new Southern Gothic Novel.

As *Sophie's Choice* reveals all too clearly, the literary imagination can be easily seduced by the erotic underside of totalitarian terror and can readily accept it as a metaphor for what exists just beneath the normal life of social and sexual behavior. If grasped by a discriminating mind, such an insight might go far toward an understanding of one side of the Nazi appeal, for there is no denying that the promise of absolute lordship and absolute submission projected by the political program of the Third Reich speaks to sexual yearnings of a powerful and, it would seem, pervasive kind. Lina Wertmüller glimpsed this equation in her *Seven Beauties* but then proceeded to turn it into a film that is hardly more than a cartoon.[16]

Wertmüller's preoccupations are serious ones, centering as they do in the sexual implications of politics and the political implications of sexuality. These connections can be powerful ones, and for that reason they are usually regulated by the social rules, religious beliefs, cultural norms, and legal mandates that make up a civilization. With the advent of Nazi rule, all such interdictions fell away, allowing political and sexual behavior of the most extreme sort to find expression. The result was a blatantly new model of government—the concentration camp—in which the freedoms of both political and sexual life were denied almost absolutely to the subject class and indulged in to the point of perversion by those who ruled. For the inmates, appetite reduced to the struggle for an extra piece of bread or thicker portion of soup; for their overlords it frequently was stimulated by the provocations of sadistic pleasure. The deprivations of the one and the indulgences of the other met in the common ground of terror and concluded in death—not, however, death as the natural equalizer of all men and women but as an ultimate power that belonged by right to the few who controlled it and would exercise it at will over those beneath them.

There doubtless are metaphorical possibilities in such an equation, but any artist attempting to actualize them must realize that history got there first. To recall Karl Kraus's insight, when the metaphor comes to life, it dies. As a result, all figurative imaginings of human exploitation and atrocity have to contend with the new standards so gruesomely established by events. The representation of these events, and especially their visual representation, is bound to call attention in the first place to their historical occasion, not their metaphorical implications. And until the first is assimilated fully into consciousness, it is almost impossible to advance to the second. One might be able to say that life is a madhouse or a whorehouse, if that is one's view of life, and get away with it, but if the standard for the mad- or whorehouse is set by the Nazi concentration camps, then the metaphorical leap into broader definition will fail. That is exactly what happens in *Seven Beauties,* a film whose political-sexual focus looks to embrace the world of the camps and the world beyond almost as if there were no distinctions between them.

Their common link, as Wertmüller projects it, is rape, as executed by and on Pasqualino, the film's hero. He is a thoroughly shabby and rather stupid hero, alternately pathetic and comic, and there is no clear indication at all on the filmmaker's part that he is to be admired; in fact, the converse is usually true, for the price he pays for his survival is an abominably high one, a point that Wertmüller makes emphatic enough. Inasmuch as the film is about survivorship, indeed, it suggests an indictment of Pasqualino's ways to freedom far more so than it does approval.

Survivorship, though, is a piece of a larger and more broadly encompassing theme in *Seven Beauties,* and that has to do with the pervasive political-sexual exploitation of men and women in general. Wertmüller's "metaphor" for that is the camp experience, which she projects as being paradigmatic of human cruelty at its most extreme. That it was, and for this reason it cannot be relegated to a secondary position as "background" for other social disturbances. As the paramount expression of political and sexual bestiality, the camps necessarily assume a foreground position, for they are less an "example of" or a "metaphor for" than the thing itself. John Simon, who received *Seven Beauties* with a long and admiring review,[17] sees it otherwise, claiming that an "artist has the right to use even the death camps as a metaphor, to reimagine or reinvent them to suit his or her vision."[18] Questions of artistic taste and decorum aside, the larger question becomes: a metaphor for what, a vision of what, a reimagining toward what ends? The death camps cannot be easily "used" symbolically to enlarge other subjects, for inevitably they reduce them all to triviality; nor can they be artistically reinvented on the stage or the screen without the effects appearing hopelessly synthetic, a result that Wertmüller is unable to avoid whenever her camera focuses on camp scenes. Knowing that she cannot possibly achieve verisimilitude, she generally bathes such scenes in a kind of soupy mist, as if to suggest that the camps had an underwater existence of some vague kind. She even puts a behemoth or leviathan in charge of these sordid depths—a monstrous female camp commandant who is referred to as "the Beast." But neither the camouflage nor the distortion works, and in the end Wertmüller manages to produce little more than what one reviewer called—approvingly—a "death-house comedy."[19]

Here is one example among several that might be cited—the film's first entrance into the world of the camps:

> Concentration camp—exterior—interior—daytime. Oppressive fog and dark skies over the camp. Wagner's "Die Valkyrie" still playing. Through the fog we see the naked multitudes waiting to be shorn, disinfected, and washed. Stacks of bodies, living skeletons walking aimlessly around. Forced labor. A prisoner hanging from a beam, swinging gently. Barbed wire surrounds everything. Hundreds of naked skeletal corpses. (P. 289)

Verbally, this description amounts to no more than a list of clichés; visually, to nothing more than a segment from a comic book horror magazine. Its naturalistic details reduce to a collection of screen dummies and props; its surreal qualities to the thinnest of Dantesque visions. To join the issue with Mr. Simon, then, the question becomes not so much one of the artist's "right" to reimagine the death camps but her ability to do so. If the second is lacking, then the first does not even come into question. The wiser course in such instances is the one taken by Hochhuth, who, acknowledging our incapacity to envision Auschwitz, backed off.

That is not the course chosen by Wertmüller, unfortunately, with the result that she has produced an antiromantic farce that exploits the terrors of the Nazi camps for grotesque effects—what another reviewer calls "death-house chic."[20] The political-sexual contest between Pasqualino, "the worm," and the commandant, "the Beast," is a confrontation that hardly needs the camp setting and is not enhanced by its foulness. The corpse "swinging gently" from a beam is not a metronome that can set the time for their lovemaking, such as it is, but literally a dead weight that the film cannot carry. If there is a metaphor in *Seven Beauties* that speaks to the truth of the film, it is that such conjunctions of the charnel house and the whorehouse are appropriations of atrocity that art at this stage cannot readily manage.

One cannot leave this film without reflecting a bit on its most extraordinary figure—not Pasqualino, who in his sentiments and actions is the quintessence of ordinariness, but his conqueror, "the Beast." An impossible cross between Ilse Koch, the wife of the commandant of

Buchenwald, and Marlene Dietrich, this female monster is Wertmüller's most original creation in *Seven Beauties* and its dominating symbolic presence. Since there never was nor could have been a woman commander of a Nazi concentration camp, the filmmaker is in this instance clearly inventing. The question is, what is she inventing? What fantasy is she serving by nominating a woman as the leading representative of Nazism in her film? Indeed, there could not have been a film—at least not this film—if Wertmüller had followed historical precedent and made the camp commander a man, for then the culminating scene of sexual confrontation would either not have been possible at all or would have appeared even more perverse than it already does. No, a woman was needed, although since the woman was to serve the double purpose of being a sexual combatant and the wielder of ultimate political power, she clearly would have to be a woman of a special symbolic character. What kind of woman is that?

Wertmüller answered this question in an interview when, speaking about her image of herself, she announced: "I'm the last ballbuster left."[21] Ernest Ferlita and John R. May, following this cue, comment at length on its implications for *Seven Beauties:*

> "They've broken my balls," the anarchist in *Seven Beauties* says. Now it appears to be Pasqualino's turn. The camera looks down at him from a high angle over the back and shoulder of the seated commandant. To Pasqualino, the commandant is a huge and forbidding mountain. Dare he attempt to climb her? . . . It is not the *size* of the ballbuster that intimidates so much as her *contempt*. Whether justified or not, contempt is her principal weapon. When the commandant orders Pasqualino to drop his pants and with a cold deliberation parts his shirt to inspect his penis, it is the gaze that withers, the gaze of a woman who, shapely or not, has over him the power of life and death. But even a ballbuster can have something of the victim about her. Pasqualino hardly knows what he says when he blurts out: "Maybe you're a victim of your sense of duty."[22]

In all the literature of the Holocaust, there is nothing that quite equals this reduction of Nazism to a sexual cartoon unless one turns to the pornography of Julius Streicher's *Der Stürmer*. There one will find such fantasies illustrated in abundance, although, of course, the sexual menace is there embodied in the Jew and not the Nazi. Lina Wertmüller inverts the equation but otherwise maintains and even heightens its pornographic qualities. By suggesting, however offhandedly, that the

monster may herself be a victim, she also introduces a note of apologet-
ics, for if "the Beast" is not a beast but, as Pasqualino suggests, "a poor
victim who is here killing people out of a sense of duty," the conclusion
becomes inevitable: "You're a victim! . . . Just like the rest of us . . ."
(p. 322). Sex and death, always the two great equalizers, coalesce in the
figure of the female commandant but are deflated by this sentimentality
before the fantasy dissolves in still another equalizer: excrement. Pedro,
the anarchist whose balls were broken, leaps to his suicide into the
camp latrine, shouting, "I'm going to dive into the shit!" (p. 329). In
the symbolic world of *Seven Beauties,* that descent into absolute foulness
can be taken as the film's culminating metaphor for its own imaginings.

The tendency to treat the Holocaust as entertainment continues
apace with Leslie Epstein's novel *King of the Jews.* The setting for most
of the novel is modeled loosely on the Lodz Ghetto, the first of the
ghettos to be established by the Nazis and the last one to fall. Lodz was
ruled by Mordechai Chaim Rumkowski, the leader of the Judenrat, or
Jewish Council, that governed the affairs of the ghetto. To say that
Rumkowski "ruled" Lodz is to say many contradictory things at once:
that he kept its industry going while collaborating with the Nazis in
feeding their factories of death; that he cared for the needs of numerous
orphans while countless numbers of their peers and their elders were
transported and destroyed; that he surrounded himself with the elaborate trappings of a prince while typhus and starvation daily reduced the
subjects of his princedom; that he was badly compromised—morally,
politically, religiously—but doubtless did save some Jews from the
Nazi conqueror, whose intent it was to destroy all. Rumkowski acted
out his impossible role as supreme ruler of the ghetto with a good deal
of flair and ostentatious pomp, having his picture printed on the stamps
and scrip of the ghetto, riding through its streets in a large carriage or
on a white horse, cutting a figure that crossed the neighborhood politi-
cian with the carnival showman and the messianic pretender. The
Polish writer Adolf Rudnicki wrote about Rumkowski in "The Mer-
chant of Lodz"; he is described in detail in Josef Zelkowicz's eyewitness
account of the Lodz Ghetto, "Days of Nightmare"; recorded in the
pages of Lucy Dawidowicz's history and Isaiah Trunk's study of the
Judenräte; photographed in Mendel Grossman's portfolio of pictures, *A
Camera in the Ghetto;* the subject of some passing reflection in
Ringelblum's journal; accounted for, in life and in death, by two interesting articles in *Commentary* magazine; a central figure in Leonard

Tushnet's *A Pavement in Hell,* which also carries his photograph; and more. Rumkowski, or "King Chaim," as he was popularly and derisively called, is not an unknown figure, then, just as the doomed city of Lodz is far from being unknown. Both, in fact, occupy prominent positions in the tragic history of Jewish fate under the Nazis.

What happens when this history is mined by the fiction writer depends, of course, on the ability of the imagination to cope with and comprehend some fearsome events. The mad, theatrical side of Rumkowski attracted Saul Bellow briefly in *Mr. Sammler's Planet,* but after turning him over for a page or two Bellow was wise enough to let Rumkowski go. Leslie Epstein, however, more indulgent of the zany and fantastical side of Rumkowski's megalomania, brings him back to life in caricature fashion and has him occupy the central place in a badly misconceived slapstick version of the Holocaust.

The issue at hand has less to do with the appropriateness of humor for this subject—Rachmil Bryks wrote some successful humorous tales about the Lodz Ghetto—than with how the comic mode is made to operate within a serious work of fiction. In its intended exploration of the wrenching moral dilemmas of the Judenrat, *King of the Jews* is a serious-minded novel, but it errs badly and continually in its reversion to farce as the principal mode of representing personal and historical tragedy. It is as if the play aspect of the novel can never be tamed or kept down: cows fall suddenly into graves, guns fire or misfire at the wrong moments, feet stumble and buttons pop, the mad go strolling the crooked streets, starving mothers become the butt of mistaken jokes about cannibalism, the apparent dead return to life in whimsical and improbable fashion, even the sun and moon perform their rotations in odd and attention-grabbing ways. There is hardly a character in *King of the Jews* who does not seem to be vying for some comic prize or other: sad-eyed orphan or wide-eyed buffoon, foolish pretender or arrogant rogue, madcap tummler or luckless schlemiel—they are all here. The style of the fantastical seems borrowed from Malamud, who has perfected it and usually knows just when to turn it on and off. As a means of examining the crises that daily beset the Jewish leaders of the ghettos, though, this style, especially when carried to comic excess, seems mischosen and a mistaken indulgence.

Epstein's odd choice of slapstick comedy as a prominent part of his narrative mode probably can be accounted for, at least in part, by his reading of Ringelblum's journal, in which Hitler is referred to as

"Horowitz," Mussolini as "Moshe Ber," etc. There is something funny
about these improbable switches, and something essentially Jewish
about them as well. Ringelblum's pages also record a sampling of the
Jewish jokes that circulated in the ghettos, several of which are quoted
verbatim in *King of the Jews*. These appear in Ringelblum's record side
by side with notations of a graver sort, providing in the historian's
shorthand the details of the ravagement of Jewish life by disease, torture, starvation, and despair and the community's efforts to hold out
against such impossible odds. Ringelblum, writing daily at the risk of
death, employed his code names as a safety precaution; it is doubtful
that he intended them to be seen as uproariously funny. As for the
many jokes he preserved, most of these *are* funny, in the grim and
unnerving way that gallows humor can be when it calls forth a desperate laugh. The desperation in Ringelblum is palpable and authenticates
the humor. In Epstein's book, the humor seems mostly gratuitous and
synthetic, a secondhand stab at fun swiped from someone else's grave.

This sense of secondhandedness points to an essential weakness in
King of the Jews. For this is a twice-derivative novel, taking its terms not
only from the recorded history of the Holocaust but as well from much
of the imaginative literature that has been written to represent aspects of
this history. In numerous instances, in fact, Epstein's novel anthologizes
and parodies some of the classic scenes and memorable statements of
Holocaust literature. An informed and attentive reader will recognize
snatches of Kosinski and Schwarz-Bart here, some hints of Lind and
Rawicz and Lustig, and repeated borrowings from Ringelblum and
Dawidowicz. Himmler's famous speech to his SS lieutenants is quoted,
as are some of Rumkowski's actual words. In themselves, there is nothing wrong with such borrowings, so long as they can be released from
their sources without too much textual disruption and integrated imaginatively into a new and coherent whole. In Epstein's novel the seams
show a good deal, though, and the result is, as stated above, a sense of
literary *déjà vu* or derivative representation.

One troubling implication of such a performance is that, in the
minds of some, the "Holocaust Novel" may now be seen as an available subgenre of contemporary fiction, to be written by anyone who is
on to and can master the "formula." One can hardly think of a more
disturbing turn of events, yet it may be upon us, one more by-product,
no doubt, of NBC's popular success with Gerald Green's "Holocaust."
Leslie Epstein's novel probably will not be received by the millions, but

the many who undoubtedly will read this "Novel of the Holocaust" will be drawn uncomfortably close to a cartoon version of life and death in the ghettos. They will be taken rather swiftly and effortlessly through the whole "pattern": the prewar normalcy and the coming of trouble; the beginnings of a propaganda campaign against the Jews and racial and religious incitement against them; the incipient threats at first against a few, and then openly against the many; the bureaucratization of terror and the growing "banality of evil"; the exploitation of slave labor and the emergence of the child smugglers; the omnipresent disease and hunger; the imposed quotas; the strikes and other temporary shows of resistance; the roundups and transports; the camps; the corpses; and a few survivors. None of this is "easy," but neither is it beyond the reach of a competent writer. To bring it all to life and give it the authority of imaginative conviction, though, takes more than facility and craftsmanship alone. The author of *King of the Jews* has plenty of the latter; he also has invention enough to call Rumkowski "Trumpelman" and his Nazis "Warriors" and "Death's-Headers." What he lacks is imagination enough to set his players within a solid and memorable context and have them appear as something more than stick-figures, or caricatures of the "types" they are meant to represent. The give-away comes time and again in the dialogue, much of which is written in the hyped-up form of rhetorical exclamation. Consider, as an example, Trumpelman, who, in what may be the novel's climactic scene, speaks the following lines:

> I, Trumpelman, came like a robber to rob you of your dearest ones. I, Trumpelman, took you by the hand and led you to death. It's Trumpelman who made you work until your hearts explode. No wonder you turn from him now! Abandon him! What a monster he is! Lock him up in a cage! Ha! Ha! That's your mistake, Jews! A big mistake! We are in the same cage together! There are no bars between you and me! And look! In this same cage with us there is a hungry lion! He wants to devour us all! He's ready to spring! And I? Trumpelman? I am the lion tamer. I stuff his mouth with meat! It's the flesh of my own brothers and sisters! The lion eats and eats! He roars! But he does not spring. Thus, with ten Jews, I save a hundred. With a hundred, I save a thousand. With a thousand, ten thousand more. My hands are bloody. My feet are bloody. My eyes are closed with blood. If your hands are clean, it's because mine are dirty! I have no conscience! That's why your conscience is clear! I am covered in blood completely![23]

What kind of a stage Jew is this one? With what kind of bravado does he speak? And in what kind of prose? His language is as artificial as his act is theatrical, yet in episode after episode one encounters this mixed mode of heroic melodrama and low farce. The model is that of the cabaret shtick, with everything either overstated or understated, and often both at the same time. In this particular instance Epstein was working from an historical model as well, for Trumpelman's speech is a reworking of an actual speech made by Jacob Gens, the Chief of the Vilna Ghetto:

> Many Jews regard me as a traitor and many of you wonder why I show myself at this literary gathering. I, Gens, lead you to death and I, Gens, want to rescue Jews from death. I, Gens . . . try to get more food and more work and more certificates for the ghetto. I cast my accounts with Jewish blood and not with Jewish respect. If they ask me for a thousand Jews, I give them because if the Germans themselves came, they would take with violence not a thousand but thousands and thousands and the whole ghetto would be finished. With a hundred I save a thousand; with a thousand I save ten thousand. You're people of spirituality and letters. You keep away from such dirty doings in our ghetto. You'll go out clean. And if you'll survive the ghetto, you'll say, "We came out with a clear conscience," but I, Jacob Gens, if I survive, I'll go out covered with filth and blood will run from my hands. Nevertheless, I'd be willing to stand at the bar of judgment before Jews. I'd say I did everything to rescue as many Jews as I could and I tried to lead them to freedom. And in order to save even a small part of the Jewish people, I alone had to lead others to their deaths. And in order to insure that you go out with clear consciences I have to forget mine and wallow in filth.[24]

Gens's words do not lack flamboyance but nonetheless were apparently too tame for Epstein, who felt compelled not only to appropriate them for his novel but to give them the flavor of a sideshow or circus setting, adding wild beasts and raw meat and the antic laughter of a carnival showman. The pathos of Gens's words is hardly without its theatrical side but at the same time is not merely ostentation. In Epstein's version, though, all is embellishment and flair—a rhetorical indulgence in the pleasures of self-aggrandizement. Novelistic appropriation of this kind is bound to result in misappropriation, for out of the pain of history it creates clowns.

The problems of metaphorical usage that we have been tracing find their fullest currency, as might be expected, in poetry, where the vocabulary of the ghettos and camps is often employed as a public refer-

ence not for the pain of history but for private pain.[25] The sufferings of
the Jews, denied specific acknowledgment in Peter Weiss's play, are less
likely to go unnoticed by the poets, but they tend to be taken up in
ways that have more to do with the amplification of personal anguish
than with the remembrance of historical atrocity. It is a characteristic, in
particular, of some of the more recent confessional poets to find images
for individual suffering in the extremity of the concentration camp experience, a tendency that can introduce an undeniable power into poetry
but at the same time one that may introduce a high degree of pathology
as well. In no writer are these elements so prominent and so mixed up
as in Sylvia Plath.

Reading Plath one is never far removed from a dominating sense of
laceration or infirmity, for much of her most memorable poetry opens
on to wounds. What is so strange about it, and so fetching, is that it
does so with pleasure. What normally frightens and deflates is expressed
by this poet with a disciplined gusto. "Cut" is an example:

> What a thrill—
> My thumb instead of an onion.
> The top quite gone
> except for a sort of a hinge
>
> Of skin,
> a flap like a hat,
> Dead white.
> Then that red plush.

The poem continues, in this same manner of controlled exuber-
ance, to dwell playfully on the bloodletting; it almost appears a lucky
accident, this cut, for out of it flows as much imaginative energy as
blood. "A celebration this is," reads one of the middle lines, and one
quickly learns to see in the sacrifice of flesh occasion for a sentiment
close to joy. Normally that would seem perverse, but in Sylvia Plath's
poetry the release of blood and the release of strong imaginings coin-
cide. Freedom and fluency both came in letting go, although the drift of
this freedom was to prove perilous.

The direction of the poet's surge is inward, but Plath sought another order of correspondences between her wounds and her words—
outer references that might register her inner pain. In "Cut" attention is
concentrated fancifully—no doubt too fancifully— in images of Indian
scalping, British battlefield charges, kamikaze suicide missions, and Ku

Klux Klan terror. That is a lot of violence for one small poem to carry—too much, indeed—and "Cut" is finally undermined by its own determined search for analogies. The poem shows too heady a rhetorical appetite for atrocity, and ultimately it is thrown off balance by a disproportion of public example to its private (and in this instance minor) occasion.

A desire to extend the circumference of the self outward into a larger world is characteristic of a kind of lyric poetry that typically favors a style far more open and declamatory than Plath's. Yevtushenko exemplifies it in his famous "Babi Yar," in which he traverses the centuries of Jewish suffering in order to indict antisemitism. Plath, while not a moralistic poet and certainly not a hortative one, occasionally gives her poetry a public dimension by trying to penetrate history by sensibility. Although she writes in highly disciplined and concentrated ways, she nevertheless may have discovered a thematic example, if not a formal one, in Yevtushenko, and she soon followed his celebrated reflections on Jewish fate with efforts of her own to match her private sufferings to those provided by an extreme history. This tendency becomes especially apparent in some of her late poems, in which, as she said, she tried to prove that "personal experience shouldn't be a kind of shut box and mirror-looking narcissistic experience. I believe that it should be generally relevant, to Hiroshima and Dachau, and so on."[26] Just how personal experience might ever be conceived as being "relevant" to Hiroshima and Dachau is unclear, but the effects of such thinking on her poetry soon became pronounced. In "Fever 103°" there are references to "Hiroshima ash," to "radiation," and to "pure acetylene." In "Lady Lazarus" the references are extended to include the camps as well:

> I have done it again.
> One year in every ten
> I manage it—
>
> A sort of walking miracle, my skin
> Bright as a Nazi lampshade,
> My right foot
> A paperweight,
> My face a featureless, fine
> Jew linen.

This is a poem about suicide, although suicide portrayed as a kind of big striptease. The imagery is loud and ostentatious, the rhythms pick up and begin to strut, the whole development of voice is toward a greater theatricality of manner not unlike that of a roadshow barker. The accent throughout is on the ghastly and the garish, on death as an extravaganza. The poem's tone is pitched high as a carnival come-on; its exhibits are freakish and ghoulish, meant both to entice and repel; and its final rhetorical turn is menacing, announcing to every amused voyeur that death as such a showy spectacular is not without its bite: "Beware / Beware. / Out of the ash / I rise with my red hair / And I eat men like air."

Such poetry presents a complex of problems to readers, ranging from matters of taste to matters of interpretation. One much-respected and much-used anthology sees fit to gloss lines four and five, explaining in a footnote that "the skins of some Jewish victims of the Nazis were used to make lampshades."[27] This note, while accurate to history, wisely does not attempt to show the correspondences between that history and Plath's own. How could it have? The first involves atrocity on a mass scale; the second, a willed effort at self-destruction. Are there any contact points between these two, a sufficient similarity to draw them into valid analogy? What order of imagination, if not of experience, must one first identify to allow passage from the private anguish of the suicide to the mass agony of destruction during the Holocaust? Such questions arise continually in reading "Lady Lazarus," for the poem indulges a fascination with extremity from beginning to end:

> And there is a charge, a very large charge
> For a word or a touch
> Or a bit of blood
>
> Or a piece of my hair or my clothes.
> So, so, Herr Doktor.
> So, Herr Enemy.
>
> I am your opus,
> I am your valuable,
> The pure gold baby
>
> That melts to a shriek.
> I turn and burn.
> Do not think I underestimate your great concern.
>
> Ash, ash—
> You poke and stir.
> Flesh, bone, there is nothing there—

A cake of soap,
A wedding ring,
A gold filling.

One knows where this language comes from but not what it's doing in such a poem. How did it get there? George Steiner continues this line of questioning in sharply pointed ways: "In what sense does anyone, himself uninvolved and long after the event, commit a subtle larceny when he invokes the echoes and trappings of Auschwitz and appropriates an enormity of ready emotion to his own private design? Was there latent in Sylvia Plath's sensibility . . . a fearful envy, a dim resentment at not having been there, of having missed the rendezvous with hell?" (p. 301). Steiner's answers are implied in the way he asks his questions: of course there is a larceny involved in such misappropriation, although in Plath's case it is a playful larceny, a dalliance with atrocity, which makes it all the more obvious and troublesome. For how in a poem that invokes Auschwitz can one have lines like these: "Dying / Is an art / like everything else, / I do it exceptionally well. / I do it so it feels like hell"? The jauntiness of rhythm and rhyme is finely handled here but introduces a tone that cannot help but mock the images of concentration camp horror that are so prominently featured. Despite the poet's intentions to bring into alignment the personal and the public sides of experience, the leap out of subjectivity seems merely willful in this instance and for that reason illegitimate. The theatrical and the historical jar one another discordantly, reducing the first to girlish play-acting and making the cruelty of the second appear too much a carnival display of assorted grisly contusions.

There are critics of Plath's poetry who see it otherwise—Arthur Oberg, for instance, who argues that "the public horrors of the Nazi concentration camps and the personal horrors of fragmented identities become interchangeable. . . . Belsen implies private man in the same way that the modern psychiatric-officed city implies historical Belsen."[28] A. Alvarez concurs, insisting that Plath "is not just talking about her own private suffering. . . . She assumes the suffering of all the modern victims. Above all, she becomes an imaginary Jew."[29] What is so terribly wrong with such criticism, as with the poetry that it offers easy sanction, is that its principal categories are not apposite: there is a radical imbalance between anyone's personal horrors of divided identity and the horrors brought on by the Nazis, an imbalance as fundamental as that between Belsen and Brooklyn. Not only are these things not

interchangeable—they simply do not compare, and no order of imagination can weld them into viable analogy. As to developing a poetic
posture that assumes all modern sufferings, that is to become an imaginary Christian, not an imaginary Jew.

Yet it is in terms of the latter that Sylvia Plath projected her sufferings, most famously in "Daddy," her boldest effort to manipulate the
language of the Holocaust for private ends and, for that reason, her
most problematic and distorted poem. Much of the distortion results,
again, from a skewed perspective, revealing itself in the tortured discrepancies between the poem's occasion and its mode of expression.
Here is how Plath herself described the poem: "The poem is spoken by
a girl with an Electra complex. Her father died while she thought he
was God. Her case is complicated by the fact that her father was also a
Nazi and her mother very possibly part Jewish. In the daughter the two
strains marry and paralyse each other—she has to act out the awful
little allegory once over before she is free of it."[30]

Plath's own father was Prussian-born but, as far as is known, was
not a Nazi; her mother was of Austrian descent and was not Jewish.
The daughter in the poem, then, entertains a revenge fantasy that is
strongly fictive. That is a commonplace of literature and does not by
itself enhance or detract from art. Plath's poetry, though, is so closely
linked to autobiography as to draw attention inevitably back and forth
between art and life. Both were to merge ultimately in her suicide, as in
those late poems that foreshadow it. "Daddy" was the most relentless
of these poems, a compulsive drive toward death that brings to a head
the poet's preoccupations with private and public violence.

Once more the question needs to be raised: is there symmetry—in
feeling if not in fact—between the sufferings of the girl with the Electra
complex and those endured by the victims of Hitler? Are there forms of
poetic language that can validate hyperbole so that the daughter's imagination of betrayal finds a legitimate comparison in the persecution of
the Jews? Alvarez thinks there are and goes so far as to propose that
"anyone whose subject is suffering has a ready-made modern example
of hell on earth in the concentration camps."[31] If it is "ready-made,"
though, it is by definition artificial, a type of composition that belongs
to facility rather than to art. And it is the facile elements in "Daddy"
that stand out and begin to cause the poem to slide into triteness:

> An engine, an engine
> Chuffing me off like a Jew.

A Jew to Dachau, Auschwitz, Belsen.
I began to talk like a Jew.
I think I may well be a Jew.

The snows of the Tyrol, the clear beer of Vienna
Are not very pure or true.
With my gypsy ancestress and my weird luck
And my Taroc pack and my Taroc pack
I may be a bit of a Jew.

What one observes in these lines, apart from their easy manner, is
the strong rhyme and the repetition compulsion, a deliberate part of the
poem's childishness, or its schizophrenia. The rhymes, here as
elsewhere, are all of a kind, reiterating constantly the emphasis on "do,"
"Jew," and "you." The repeated words and phrases generally center in
"I," or, to cite the poem's second language, in "Ich, ich, ich, ich." Since
in Plath's bilingual world "do" is also heard as "du," "Daddy" is at its
deepest level a poem about the difficulties of "Ich-und-du," or, more to
the point of its central aggression, about "what-I-do-to-you, you-Jew."
Moreover, the identity of the Jew remains fluid, embodied as it is
sometimes in the daughter-victim but also in the father-devil, causing
the Nazi-Jew dichotomy to break down. Ultimately, in fact, "Daddy"
does not divide along the lines of a persecution-victimization conflict
because both aspects of this violent pairing are assumed by the speaker
in the poem, who in her imaginary assault against her father enacts an
even greater violence against herself. A. R. Jones sees that extreme psychic damage as proper to the age, for "in a deranged world, a deranged
response is the only possible reaction of the sensitive mind":

> The poem is committed to the view that this ethos of love/brutality is
> the dominant historical ethos of the last thirty years. The tortured mind
> of the heroine reflects the tortured mind of our age. The heroine care-
> fully associates herself and her suffering with historical events. For in-
> stance, she identifies herself with the Jews and the atrocities of "Dachau,
> Auschwitz, Belsen" and her persecutors with Fascism and the cult of
> violence. The poem is more than a personal statement for by extending
> itself through historical images it defines the age as schizophrenic, torn
> between brutality and a love which in the end can only manifest itself,
> today, in images of violence. This love, tormented and perverse, is es-
> sentially life-denying: the only escape is into the purifying freedom of
> death.[32]

There are two replies to this: one formal, the other historical and ethical. The first, which would fault the poem for committing the imitative fallacy, should not be too much emphasized, for the urgencies and intensities of "Daddy" demonstrate beyond doubt that the poet was writing out of strong needs, and the violence of her rhetoric does seem an accurate register of her violent feelings. Plath's difficulty, like her critic's, lies elsewhere, namely, in supposing that sensibility, rent as it may be in "Daddy," can expose the atrocity of the age through exposing self-inflicted wounds. Suicide, the ultimate example of personally imposed violence, is still no metaphor for the destructions carried out at "Dachau, Auschwitz, Belsen"; to suppose that it is is to rend the psyche unnecessarily as well as to distort and diminish history. Moreover, to suggest that the only recourse beyond atrocity is to bring on still more of the same is simply perverse, most especially in a poem that invokes the concentration camps. If her critic has it right, the imaginary Jew in this instance imagined falsely, for nothing is further from Jewish imaginings than the desire to bring on more death or to escape into it in pursuit of some allegedly "purifying freedom."

The common element among the works reviewed in this chapter is imaginative misappropriation of atrocity. There is always a degree of illegitimacy or inauthenticity present in such imaginings, which usually expresses itself in either a deflation or inflation of language. In the first instance the appeal of art to the vocabulary of the Holocaust minimizes the terror of the camps by falsely generalizing or universalizing it; in the second instance, the effect is one of hyperbole or excessive strain, an invasion of history by hysteria. In both cases the result is a tendency to distort—on the one hand, by the error of reduction; on the other, by a faulty extension. Neither way seems capable of capturing the historical moment and carrying it over into art. Does there exist a language that might do that more successfully and, if so, what would it sound like? It is impossible to answer this question in ways that would apply uniformly or systematically to all Holocaust writings, but one can cite any number of touchstones that might indicate what is or is not authentic. Here is one, taken from a short story by Borowski ("The People Who Walked On"):

> Hunger had already started in this part of the camp. The redheaded Elder moved from bunk to bunk, talking to the women to distract them from their thoughts. She pulled out the singers and told them to sing,

the dancers—and told them to dance, the poets—and made them recite
poetry. . . .

"I can't stand it any longer! It's too disgusting!" [the Elder] whis-
pered. And suddenly she jumped up and rushed over to the table. "Get
down!" she screamed at the singer.

The women fell silent. She raised her arm. "Quiet!" she shouted,
though nobody spoke a word. "You've been asking me about your parents and your children. I haven't told you, I felt sorry for you. But now
I'll tell you, so that you know, because they'll do the same with you if
you get sick! Your children, your husbands, and your parents are not in
another camp at all. They've been stuffed into a room and gassed!
Gassed, do you understand? Like millions of others, like my own
mother and father. They're burning in deep pits and in ovens. . . . The
smoke which you see above the rooftops doesn't come from the brick
plant at all, as you're being told. It's smoke from your children! Now
go on and sing. . . ." (Pp. 91–92)

Song that comes after such knowledge, or despite it, is authentic
singing. Anything else runs the danger of seeming a pretense or an
exploitation of others' pain.

IV. Remembering the Holocaust

Epilogue

Inscribed on a plaque at one of the entrances to Yad Vashem, the Holocaust memorial and research center in Jerusalem, are these words, attributed to the Baal Shem Tov: "*Redemption Lies in Remembering.*" Although this is a piece of wisdom formulated some two centuries before the Holocaust, it has a direct application to it and to the kinds of problems we have been pursuing throughout this study. One's first reaction to extreme historical terror is typically one of stunned silence and almost breathless shock. In many cases, perhaps even in most, these are also one's last reactions. Nelly Sachs's line, "When the great terror came, / I fell dumb," is paradigmatic. For literature, as for all other expressive forms of post-Holocaust awareness, though, it is also terminal. To submit to the finality of silence is to confirm, however unwillingly, the triumphant nihilism of Nazism. To remind ourselves of its creed, formulated precisely and memorably by Rolf Hochhuth, we need only recall the counterrevelation announced in one of the Doctor's speeches in *The Deputy*: "The truth is, Auschwitz refutes / creator, creation, and the creature. / Life as an idea is dead."

Auschwitz, the largest and most destructive of the camps, was only one of the many killing centers in Europe where life and the idea of life were simultaneously extinguished. To do the Doctor full justice and add point to his doctrine of death, it is necessary to recall as well the ghettos and the other camps. André Schwarz-Bart names them for us at the ending of *The Last of the Just,* although curiously he does so within the matrix of a prayer:

> And praised. *Auschwitz*. Be. *Maidanek*. The Lord. *Treblinka*. And praised. *Buchenwald*. Be. *Mauthausen*. The Lord. *Belzec*. And praised. *Sobibor*. Be. *Chelmno*. The Lord. *Ponary*. And praised. *Theresienstadt*. Be. *Warsaw*. The Lord. *Vilna*. And praised. *Skarzysko*. Be. *Bergen-Belsen*. The Lord. *Janow*. And praised. *Dora*. Be. *Neuengamme*. The Lord. *Pustkow*. And praised . . . (P. 374)

Given the vast network of ghettos and concentration camps established by the Nazis and their allies throughout Europe, this litany could go on almost endlessly in this same discordant manner, its hallelujah savagely interrupted by, and almost overcome by, the recitation of these terrible names. Prayer at this point, like most other languages of the Holocaust, seems at best to be a halting and crippled thing, its chant of praise broken into disconnected fragments.

Or do the lines proceed in the opposite way, reasserting their affirmations in defiance of the death camps? Is the absolute nihilism of the latter strong enough to overpower an assertive faith in life and reduce it to mere stammering, or has the psalmic impulse been revitalized by oppression to the point where it can override and even incorporate the horror of mass human extermination?

Schwarz-Bart ends his novel in such a way as to leave the issue intentionally ambiguous and unresolved, reflecting what amounts to a struggle for primacy between the forces of life and the forces of death. At this point, all we can say is that we do not know which will prevail. Holocaust literature, which everywhere poses the question, is powerless to answer it at this stage of its development, for it is more an arena for conflicting and contesting claims than it is an assured record of some final knowledge. On the one hand it asserts the impossibility of ever truly knowing what took place in the ghettos and camps; on the other hand it charges us all with remembering and transmitting this same, hardly attainable knowledge. While this paradox never gets resolved, the effect of the literature taken as a whole is to leap beyond it and, by being itself a living record of remembrance, to guard against a total obliteration. The writing, everywhere embattled and often close to exhaustion or expiration, gives testimony to the dead, even as it declares that the places where they died are already receding from memory:

> . . . the forest is fast effacing all trace of that life . . . , of that already ancient death . . . the grass and the roots repossessing the place where the camp had stood. The first to collapse would be the wooden barracks, those of the main camp . . . , soon drowned by the invading tide of grass and shrubs, then later the two-story cement buildings, and then at last, surely long after all the other buildings, years later, remaining standing the longest, like the remembrance, or rather the evidence, the special symbol of that whole, the massive square chimney of the crematorium, till the day when the roots and brambles shall also overcome that tenacious resistance of brick and stone, that obstinate resistance of death rising among the waves of green covering over what was an extermination camp, and those shadows of dense black smoke, shot through with yellow, that perhaps still linger over this countryside, that smell of burning flesh still hovering over this countryside, when all the survivors, all of us, have long since disappeared, when there will no longer be any real memory of this, only the memory of memories related by those who will never really know (as one knows the acidity of a lemon, the feel of wool, the softness of a shoulder) what all this really was.[1]

It is in the face of this sense of natural and inevitable loss that Holocaust writing seems, at its best, to discover reflexes of assertiveness that produce the kinds of diaries, memoirs, novels, stories, poems, and plays that we have examined in these chapters. Taken singly, many seem records of despair; read collectively, as a diverse and multi-authored literature, they stand against the effacement of memory and reinforce the idea and integrity of history. "Is it necessary or good to retain any memory of this exceptional state?" Primo Levi asks at one point in his memoir.[2] Every writer of the Holocaust has answered this question positively and unequivocally, even if many of their answers have the effect of awakening only more questions. That is as it should be and must be, for given the history that has produced this literature in the first place, most answers would be facile or false or both. The reason for that is provided succinctly by Elias Canetti: "We have no standard any more for anything, ever since human life is no longer the standard."[3] The Holocaust effected that severe a levelling, and no easy reconstruction will be possible without first acknowledging the facts of human diminishment and the multitude of questions that arise in their aftermath. In order to do that, though, memory must be kept alive at all costs and the agents of memory preserved from further destruction:

The Jews are God's memory and the heart of mankind. We do not always know this, but the others do, and that is why they treat us with
suspicion and cruelty. Memory frightens them. Through us they are
linked to the beginning and the end. By eliminating us they hope to
gain immortality. But in truth, it is not given to us to die, not even if
we wanted to. Why? We cannot die, because we are the question.[4]

Even after the great destruction, that question stands, a victim but
also a refutation of the night.

Notes

Introduction

1. Stefan Kanfer, *The Eighth Sin* (New York: Random House, 1978), pp. 3–4.

2. Elie Wiesel, *Legends of Our Time,* trans. Steven Donadio (New York: Holt, Rinehart and Winston, 1968), p. 190.

3. Ibid., p. 182.

4. Erich Kahler, *The Disintegration of Form in the Arts* (New York: George Braziller, 1968), p. 3.

5. Abraham I. Katsh, ed., *The Warsaw Diary of Chaim A. Kaplan* (New York: Collier Books, 1973), pp. 85–86. All subsequent citations will be noted in the text within parentheses.

6. Edward Alexander, *The Resonance of Dust: Essays on Holocaust Literature and Jewish Fate* (Columbus: Ohio State University Press, 1979).

7. Samuel Beckett, "Three Dialogues with Georges Duthuit," *Transition* 49/5 (December 1949): 98.

8. George Steiner, *Language and Silence: Essays on Language, Literature, and the Inhuman* (New York: Atheneum, 1967), p. 168.

9. Edmond Jabès, *The Book of Questions,* trans. Rosmarie Waldrop (Middletown, Connecticut: Wesleyan University Press, 1976), p. 78.

1. The Problematics of Holocaust Literature

1. T.W. Adorno, "Engagement," in *Noten zur Literatur III* (Frankfurt am Main: Suhrkamp Verlag, 1965), pp. 109–35; but see also "Erziehung nach Auschwitz," in *Stichworte, Kritische Modelle 2* (Frankfurt am Main: Suhrkamp Verlag, 1969).

2. Reinhard Baumgart, "Unmenschlichkeit beschreiben," in *Literatur für Zeitgenossen: Essays* (Frankfurt am Main: Suhrkamp Verlag, 1966), pp. 12–36.

3. Michael Wyschogrod, "Some Theological Reflections on the Holocaust," *Response* 25 (Spring 1975): 68.

4. Elie Wiesel, "For Some Measure of Humility," *Sh'ma* 5/100 (October 31, 1975): 314; see also *A Jew Today,* trans. Marion Wiesel (New York: Random House, 1978), pp. 197–98.

5. Ernst Schnabel, *Anne Frank: A Portrait in Courage,* trans. Richard and Clara Winston (New York: Harbrace Paperback Library, 1958).

6. Emil Fackenheim, "Sachsenhausen 1938: Groundwork for Auschwitz," *Midstream* XXI (April 1975): 27–31.

7. See George Steiner, *Language and Silence* (New York: Atheneum, 1967), p. 67.

8. Two critical studies are in print: Irving Halperin's *Messengers from the Dead* (Philadelphia: Westminster Press, 1970) and Lawrence Langer's *The Holocaust and the Literary Imagination* (New Haven: Yale University Press, 1976); of related interest are Terrence des Pres's *The Survivor: An Anatomy of Life in the Death Camps* (New York: Oxford University Press, 1976) and Edward Alexander's *The Resonance of Dust: Essays on Holocaust Literature and Jewish Fate* (Columbus: Ohio State University Press, 1979).

9. A.J.P. Taylor, *The Second World War* (New York: G. P. Putnam's Sons, 1975), p. 149. By distinguishing "the war against the Jews" from the Second World War, I do not want to imply, of course, any approval of avoidance of the Holocaust in texts on the war period. My intention is quite the opposite: to see the Holocaust for what it was so as to afford it a greater emphasis in historical writings.

10. Elie Wiesel, *Night,* trans. Stella Rodway (New York: Avon, 1969), p. 44. All subsequent citations will be noted in the text within parentheses.

11. Elie Wiesel, "Snapshots," in *One Generation After,* trans. Lily Edelman (New York: Random House, 1970), pp. 46–47.

12. Uri Zvi Greenberg, "We Were Not Likened to Dogs among the Gentiles," in *Modern Hebrew Poetry,* ed. Ruth Finer Mintz (Berkeley: University of California Press, 1968), p. 126.

13. Elie Wiesel, "The Death of My Father," in *Legends of Our Time* (New York: Holt, Rinehart and Winston, 1968), p. 7.

14. Wiesel, "One Generation After," in *One Generation After,* p. 10.

15. Wiesel, *Night,* p. 42.

16. Jacob Glatstein, "Smoke," in *A Treasury of Yiddish Poetry,* ed. I. Howe and E. Greenberg (New York: Holt, Rinehart and Winston, 1969), p. 331; the translation is by Chana Faerstein.

17. Rolf Hochhuth, *The Deputy,* trans. Richard and Clara Winston (New York: Grove Press, Inc., 1974), p. 72. All subsequent citations will be noted in the text within parentheses.

18. Wiesel, "A Plea for the Dead," in *Legends of Our Time,* p. 8.

19. "My Teachers," in *Legends of Our Time,* p. 8.

20. Primo Levi, *Survival in Auschwitz,* trans. Stuart Woolf (New York: Collier Books, 1973), p. 94. All subsequent citations will be noted in the text within parentheses.

21. George Steiner, *In Bluebeard's Castle* (New Haven: Yale University Press, 1971), pp. 53–56. The landscape of hell is referred to repeatedly throughout the literature; the moral conditions that obtain, however, are altogether absent. My interest here is only in the endless tortures of the place, not at all in the ethical system that governs it in Christian religious writings.

22. *The Holocaust and the Literary Imagination,* pp. 82, 84.

23. Jerry Glenn, *Paul Celan* (New York: Twayne Publishers, Inc., 1973).

24. Götz Wienold, "Paul Celan's Hölderlin-Widerruf," *Poetica* 2 (1968): 216–28.

25. *The Warsaw Diary of Chaim Kaplan,* pp. 36, 209, 207, 213. As conditions in the ghetto changed, Kaplan vacillated between moments of religious despair and moments of faith; the attitude illustrated by the quotation cited in these passages, while prevalent, was not constant.

26. Nelly Sachs, *The Seeker and Other Poems* (New York: Farrar, Straus and Giroux, 1970), p. 387; the translation is by Michael Hamburger.

27. Yitzhak Katznelson, *Vittel Diary,* trans. Dr. Myer Cohen (Israel: Beit Lohamei Hagettaot and Hakibbutz Hameuchad Publishing House, 1972), pp. 59–60. All subsequent citations will be noted in the text within parentheses.

28. Saul Bellow, *Mr. Sammler's Planet* (New York: Viking Press, 1970), p. 211. All subsequent citations will be noted in the text within parentheses.

2. Holocaust and History

1. Alexander Donat, *The Holocaust Kingdom* (New York: Holt, Rinehart and Winston, 1965), p. 211.

2. Quoted in Lucy Dawidowicz, *A Holocaust Reader* (New York: Behrman House, 1976), pp. 130–34.

3. Emmanuel Ringelblum, *Notes from the Warsaw Ghetto,* trans. Jacob Sloan (New York: Schocken Books, 1974). All citations will be noted in the text within parentheses.

4. Mary Berg, *Warsaw Ghetto: A Diary,* trans. Norbert and Sylvia Glass (New York: L. B. Fisher, 1945).

5. Alexander Donat, *The Holocaust Kingdom;* Yitzhak Katznelson, *Vittel Diary;* Bernard Goldstein, *The Stars Bear Witness,* trans. Leonard Shatzkin (New York: Viking Press, 1949); Vladka Meed, *On Both Sides of the Wall* (Israel: Beit Lohamei Hagettaot and Hakibbutz Hameuchad Publishing House, 1973); Ber Mark, *Uprising in the Warsaw Ghetto,* trans. Gershon Freidlin (New York: Schocken Books, 1975).

6. Janusz Korczak, *Ghetto Diary* (New York: Holocaust Library, 1978). All citations will be noted in the text within parentheses.

7. Yitskhok Rudashevski, *The Diary of the Vilna Ghetto,* trans. Percy Matenko (Israel: Beit Lohamei Hagettaot and Hakibbutz Hameuchad Publishing House, 1973); *The Diary of Éva Heyman,* trans. Moshe M. Kohn (Jerusalem: Yad Vashem, 1974).

8. Anne Frank, *The Diary of A Young Girl,* trans. B. M. Mooyaart-Doubleday (New York: Pocket Books, 1953).

9. *Young Moshe's Diary: The Spiritual Torment of a Jewish Boy in Nazi Europe* (Jerusalem: Yad Vashem, 1971). All citations are noted in the text within parentheses.

10. See Terrence Des Pres, *The Survivor* (New York: Oxford University Press, 1976).

11. Joseph Katz, *One Who Came Back: The Diary of a Jewish Survivor,* trans. Hilda Reach (New York: Herzl Press, 1973); David Rousset, *The Other Kingdom,* trans. Ramon Guthrie (New York: Reynal and Hitchcock, 1947); Charlotte Delbo, *None of Us Will Return,* trans. John Githens (Boston: Beacon Press, 1978).

12. Bruno Bettelheim, *The Informed Heart* (Glencoe, Illinois: Free Press, 1960); Victor Frankl, *Man's Search for Meaning,* trans. Ilse Lasch (New York: Washington Square Press, 1963); Miklos Nyiszli, *Auschwitz: A Doctor's Eyewit-*

ness Account, trans. Tibere Kramer and Richard Seaver (New York: Fawcett Crest, 1960); Elie A. Cohen, *The Abyss: A Confession,* trans. James Brockway (New York: W. W. Norton & Company, 1973).

13. Alexander Donat, *The Holocaust Kingdom;* Eugene Heimler, *Night of the Mist,* trans. André Ungar (New York: Vanguard Press, 1949); Gerda Klein, *All But My Life* (New York: Hill and Wang, 1947); Seweryna Szmaglewska, *Smoke Over Birkenau,* trans. Jadwiga Rynas (New York: Henry Holt, 1947); Rudolf Vrba, *I Cannot Forgive* (New York: Grove Press, 1964); Leon Wells, *The Janowska Road.*

14. Lucy Dawidowicz, *A Holocaust Reader,* p. 1.

15. Ibid., pp. 131, 133, 134.

3. Imagination in Extremis

1. Isaac Rosenfeld, *An Age of Enormity* (New York: World Publishing Company, 1962), pp. 206, 208–209. All subsequent citations will be noted in the text within parentheses.

2. Wallace Stevens, "Adagia," in *Opus Posthumous* (New York: Alfred A. Knopf, 1957), p. 165.

3. Wallace Stevens, "The Noble Rider and The Sound of Words," in *The Necessary Angel* (New York: Vintage Books, 1965), p. 36.

4. John Hersey, *The Wall* (New York: Modern Library, 1967), pp. 5, 6, 11; Leon Uris, *Mila 18* (New York: Doubleday and Company, 1961).

5. Isaac Bashevis Singer, *The Slave* (New York: Farrar, Straus and Cudahy, 1962), pp. 13, 107; Bernard Malamud, *The Fixer* (New York: Farrar, Straus and Giroux, 1966), pp. 225–74.

6. André Schwarz-Bart, *The Last of the Just,* trans. Stephen Becker (New York: Atheneum, 1961), p. 3. All subsequent citations will be noted in the text within parentheses.

7. As is well known, Schwarz-Bart took some large liberties in reshaping the tradition of the *Lamed-Vov,* making it part of a family inheritance and a conscious act of vocation; for a more historical exposition, see Gershom Scholem, "The Tradition of the Hidden Just Men," in *The Messianic Idea in Judaism* (New York: Schocken Books, 1971), pp. 251–56; Scholem recognizes that as a novelist Schwarz-Bart "is not bound by scholarly conventions and can give free rein to his speculative fantasy" (p. 251).

8. Elie Wiesel, "Beyond Survival," *European Judaism* (Winter 1971/72): 8.

9. Jorge Semprun, *The Long Voyage,* trans. Richard Seaver (New York: Grove Press, 1964). For a detailed discussion of this novel, especially with reference to its handling of time, see Lawrence Langer, *The Holocaust and the Literary Imagination,* pp. 285–96.

10. Tadeusz Borowski, *This Way for the Gas, Ladies and Gentlemen,* trans. Barbara Vedder (New York: Penguin Books, 1976). Citations will be noted in the text within parentheses.

11. Czeslaw Milosz, *The Captive Mind,* trans. Jane Zielonko (New York: Alfred A. Knopf, 1953), pp. 118–19, 122.

12. "Never before in the history of mankind has hope been stronger than man, but never also has it done so much harm as it has in this war, in this concentration camp. We were never taught how to give up hope, and this is why today we perish in gas chambers" (pp. 121–22).

13. See Jan Kott's Introduction to the Penguin edition of *This Way for the Gas, Ladies and Gentlemen,* p. 20, and Milocz, pp. 129–34.

14. Piotr Rawicz, "The Companion of a Dream," *European Judaism* (Winter 1970/71): 2.

15. Jerzy Kosinski, *The Painted Bird,* Second Edition (Boston: Houghton Mifflin Company, 1976), p. xii. The author has provided a lengthy Introduction to this edition of the novel.

16. Piotr Rawicz, *Blood from the Sky,* trans. Peter Wiles (New York: Harcourt, Brace & World, 1964), p. 316.

17. A. Anatoli (Kuznetsov), trans. David Floyd (London: Jonathan Cape, 1970), pp. 13–17; and "The Memories," *New York Times Book Review,* April 9, 1967, p. 45. Kuznetsov is almost too emphatic in making his point, which he reiterates in several author's interpolations between chapters as well as in the preface. Here is a sample passage: "I am writing [this book] as though I were giving evidence under oath in the very highest court and I am ready to answer for every single word. This book records only the truth—AS IT REALLY HAPPENED" (p. 14).

18. Charlotte Delbo, *None of Us Will Return* (Boston: Beacon Press, 1978), p. 128; Elie Wiesel, *Legends of Our Time* (New York: Holt, Rinehart and Winston, 1968), p. viii; Gerald Green, *Holocaust* (New York: Bantam Books, 1978); Jean-François Steiner, *Treblinka,* trans. Helen Weaver (New York: Simon and Schuster, 1967); Manès Sperber, *. . . than a tear in the sea,* trans. Constantine Fitzgibbon (New York: Bergen-Belsen Memorial Press, 1967).

19. Carlo Levi, *The Watch* (New York: Farrar, Straus and Yoring, 1951), pp. 70–71.

20. Arnost Lustig, *A Prayer for Katerina Horovitzova,* trans. Jeanne Němcová (New York: Harper and Row, 1973), pp. 50–51.

4. *Poetics of Expiration*

1. Paul Celan, *Der Meridian* (Frankfurt am Main: S. Fischer Verlag, 1961), p. 15; translation by Erna Baber Rosenfeld.

2. Charles Olson makes this point in his essay on "Projective Verse," collected in *The Poetics of the New American Poetry,* ed. Donald Allen and Warren Tallman (New York: Grove Press, 1973), p. 150.

3. See M. H. Abrams, "The Correspondent Breeze: A Romantic Metaphor," in *English Romantic Poets: Modern Essays in Criticism,* ed. M. H. Abrams (New York: Oxford University Press, 1960), pp. 37–54.

4. Dan Pagis, *Selected Poems,* trans. Stephen Mitchell (Oxford, England: Carcanet Press, 1972), p. 26.

5. From the poem "*Soviel Gestirne*" ("So Many Stars"), in Paul Celan, *Speech-Grille and Selected Poems,* trans. Joachim Neugroschel (New York: E.P. Dutton & Company, Inc., 1971), p. 171; unless otherwise noted, all translations of Celan are taken from this volume. Citations will be noted in the text within parentheses.

6. Previously unpublished translation by Erna Baber Rosenfeld. In the German text of this poem, the verb in the second line is "*bespricht,*" which has been translated elsewhere as "conjures" (M. Hamburger) or "incants" (J. Neugroschel); both are literally correct but off the mark poetically; Celan himself

saw the translation given in this chapter and approved "breathes" as his own preferred translation.

7. Paul Celan, *Selected Poems,* trans. Michael Hamburger and Christopher Middleton (Middlesex, England: Penguin Books, 1972), p. 106.

8. Ibid., p. 90.

9. Nelly Sachs, *The Seeker and Other Poems,* trans. Ruth and Matthew Mead and Michael Hamburger (New York: Farrar, Straus and Giroux, 1970), p. 19. All citations will be noted in the text within parentheses.

10. *Der Meridian,* p. 17.

11. Nelly Sachs, *O The Chimneys: Selected Poems,* trans. Michael Hamburger, Christopher Holme, Ruth and Matthew Mead, and Michael Roloff (New York: Farrar, Straus and Giroux, 1967), p. 277.

12. Ibid., p. 103.

13. Ibid., p. 181.

14. Elie Wiesel, *Legends of Our Time* (New York: Holt, Rinehart and Winston, 1968), p. 2.

15. Ibid., p. 5.

16. Translation by Erna Baber Rosenfeld.

5. Contending with a Silent God

1. Elias Canetti, *The Human Province,* trans. Joachim Neugroschel (New York: Seabury Press, 1978), pp. 1–2. All subsequent citations will be noted in the text within parentheses.

2. Collected in Richard Rubenstein, *After Auschwitz: Radical Theology and Contemporary Judaism* (Indianapolis: Bobbs-Merrill, 1966), p. 152.

3. Paul Celan, *"Ansprache anlässlich der Entgegennahme des Literaturpreises der Freien Hansestadt Bremen,"* in *Ausgewählte Gedichte* (Frankfurt am Main: Suhrkamp Verlag, 1969), p. 127.

4. Ibid., p. 146.

5. Celan saw and approved this previously unpublished translation, by Erna Baber Rosenfeld, and himself supplied the English phrase "Pseudo-You" for the German *"Aber-Du."* All English translations of Celan's poems that appear in this chapter are by Erna Baber Rosenfeld; most were reviewed and approved by the poet.

6. Michael Hamburger, trans., *Hölderlin* (New York: Pantheon Books, 1952), p. 165.

7. I. L. Peretz, "Cabalists," in *Great Jewish Short Stories,* ed. Saul Bellow (New York: Dell, 1963), pp. 124–25.

8. Unless otherwise indicated, all references to Nelly Sachs's poetry are to the versions collected in the following two volumes: *O The Chimneys* (New York: Farrar, Straus and Giroux, 1967) and *The Seeker and Other Poems* (New York: Farrar, Straus and Giroux, 1970). These are cited in the text within parentheses by the abbreviations C and S, followed by page numbers.

9. The three poems quoted in their entirety appear here in previously unpublished translations by Erna Baber Rosenfeld; all three were seen and approved by the poet.

10. Collected in Emil Fackenheim, *Quest for Past and Future: Essays in Jewish Theology* (Boston: Beacon Press, 1970), p. 315.

6.   The Poetry of Survival

1. Joseph Leftwich, ed., *The Golden Peacock: A Worldwide Treasury of Yiddish Poetry* (New York: Thomas Yoseloff, 1961), p. 515.

2. Cynthia Ozick, *The Pagan Rabbi and Other Stories* (New York: Alfred A. Knopf, 1971), pp. 74–75. All subsequent citations will be noted in the text within parentheses.

3. Irving Howe and Eliezer Greenberg, eds., *A Treasury of Yiddish Poetry* (New York: Holt, Rinehart and Winston, 1969), pp. 53–54.

4. A full-length study of Jacob Glatstein is being prepared by Professor Janet Hadda (to be published by Twayne), but as of this writing there are no biographical or critical books about Glatstein for the English reader. For a list of works in English by and about Glatstein, see Janet Hadda's "Selected Bibliography" in *Yiddish*, I, i (Summer 1973): 63–70.

5. English readers interested in the subject will find useful the introductory essays by Irving Howe and Eliezer Greenberg in *A Treasury of Yiddish Stories* (New York: The Viking Press, 1965), *A Treasury of Yiddish Poetry* (1969), and *Voices from the Yiddish: Essays, Memoirs, Diaries* (Ann Arbor: University of Michigan Press, 1972). Sol Liptzin's *The Flowering of Yiddish Literature* (New York: Thomas Yoseloff, 1963) and *The Maturing of Yiddish Literature* (New York: Jonathan David Publishers, 1970) and Charles Madison's *Yiddish Literature: Its Scope and Major Writers* (New York: Frederick Ungar Publishing Company, 1968) are occasionally informative but on the whole less satisfactory.

6. For Glatstein's assessment of *Die Yunge* and the development of the *Inzikhistn*, see his "A Short View of Yiddish Poetry," trans. Joseph Landis, *Yiddish*, I, i (Summer 1973): 30–39, which reprints material from the first two numbers of *In Zikh* (1920). Additional material from the manifesto is translated by Chana Faerstein and appears in her fine article "Jacob Glatstein: The Literary Uses of Jewishness," *Judaism* XIV, 4 (Fall 1965): 414–31, to which I am indebted for some of the quotations in this chapter.

7. Max Weinreich's monumental two-volume study of the history of the Yiddish language is being prepared for publication in English translation by YIVO and the University of Chicago Press. Maurice Samuel's learned and affectionate study, *In Praise of Yiddish* (New York: Cowles Book Company, 1971), is full of valuable insights.

8. Faerstein, "Jacob Glatstein."

9. *The Selected Poems of Jacob Glatstein*, trans. Ruth Whitman (New York: October House, 1972), pp. 59–60. All subsequent citations will be noted in the text within parentheses. See also Jacob Glatstein, *Poems*, trans. Etta Blum (Tel Aviv: I. L. Peretz Publishing Company, 1970).

10. *A Treasury of Yiddish Poetry*, p. 331; translation by Nathan Halper.

11. Ibid., pp. 331–32.

7.   The Immolation of the Word

1. William Shirer, *The Rise and Fall of the Third Reich* (New York: Simon and Schuster, 1960), p. 241. For detailed documentation of the Nazi book burnings, see Josef Wulf, *Literatur und Dichtung im Dritten Reich* (Gütersloh: Sigbert Mohn Verlag, 1963), pp. 40–59.

2. In his play *Almansor* Heine wrote: "Das war ein Vorspiel nur, dort wo man Bücher / Verbrennt, verbrennt man auch am Ende Menschen."

3. Shirer, *Rise and Fall*.

4. George Steiner, *Language and Silence: Essays on Language, Literature, and the Inhuman* (New York: Atheneum, 1967), p. ix.

5. For Heidegger, see Raul Hilberg, *Documents of Destruction* (London: W. H. Allen, 1972), pp. 17-18, and Joachim Remak, *The Nazi Years: A Documentary History* (Englewood Cliffs, N.J.: Prentice-Hall, 1969), pp. 58-59.

6. See Richard Grunberger, *The 12-Year Reich: A Social History of Nazi Germany, 1933-1945* (New York: Holt, Rinehart and Winston, 1971), and George Mosse, *Nazi Culture: Intellectual, Cultural, and Social Life in the Third Reich* (New York: Grosset and Dunlap, Universal Library, 1968).

7. Victor Klemperer, *LTI: Die unbewältigte Sprache, Aus dem Notizbuch eines Philologen* (Munich: Deutscher Taschenbuch Verlag, 1969), pp. 220-23; translation by Erna B. Rosenfeld.

8. See, for instance, Cornelia Berning, *Vom 'Abstammungsnachweis' zum 'Zuchtwort': Vokabular des Nationalsozialismus*, (Berlin: Walter de Gruyter, 1964); Nachman Blumenthal, "On the Nazi Vocabulary," "Action," and "From the Nazi Vocabulary," in *Yad Vashem Studies*, I, IV, and VI (Jerusalem 1957, 1960, 1967); Shaul Esh, "Words and Their Meaning: 25 Examples of Nazi-Idiom," in *Yad Vashem Studies*, V (Jerusalem 1963); Heinz Paechter, *Nazi-Deutsch: A Glossary of Contemporary German Usage* (New York: Frederick Ungar Publishing Co., 1944); and Dolf Sternberger, Gerhard Storz, and Wilhelm E. Suskind, *Aus dem Wörterbuch des Unmenschen* (Hamburg: Claasen Verlag, 1968).

9. Michael Hamburger, *From Prophecy to Exorcism* (London: Longmans, 1965), pp. 22-23.

10. Sidney Rosenfeld, "Karl Kraus: The Future of a Legacy," *Midstream* XX, 4 (April 1974): 76, 77.

11. Karl Kraus, *Die Dritte Walpurgisnacht* (Munich: Kösel-Verlag, 1967), pp. 121, 122-23. Kraus wrote this book in 1934 but, with the exception of printing excerpts in *Die Fackel* of October of that year, withheld it from publication; it was first published in 1952 (Kraus himself died in June 1936).

12. See Grunberger, pp. 360-61.

13. Eugen Kogon, *The Theory and Practice of Hell: The German Concentration Camps and the System Behind Them*, trans. Heinz Norden (New York: Berkley Publishing Company, 1975), p. 64.

14. Elie Wiesel, *Night*, trans. Stella Rodway (New York: Avon Books, 1969), p. 49.

15. Elie Wiesel, "Why I Write," in *Confronting the Holocaust: The Impact of Elie Wiesel*, ed. Alvin Rosenfeld and Irving Greenberg (Bloomington: Indiana University Press, 1978), p. 201.

16. Primo Levi, *Survival in Auschwitz*, trans. Stuart Woolf (New York: Collier Books, 1973), pp. 112-13.

17. Rolf Hochhuth, *The Deputy* (New York: Grove Press, 1964); this edition of the play includes a sixty-five page postscript called "Sidelights to History." In its British edition, the play is called *The Representative*, a translation that is more accurate to the original German phrase *"Der Stellvertreter."* All citations will be noted in the text within parentheses.

18. See *The Storm over the Deputy*, ed. Eric Bentley (New York: Grove Press, 1964), p. 53, for the playwright's explanation of why he chose to write a

verse drama. Later references to this book will be cited in the text within parentheses.

19. Rolf Hochhuth, *Der Stellvertreter* (Reinbek bei Hamburg: Rowohlt Verlag, 1963), pp. 107, 108, 109.

20. A translation of Gerstein's account of the extermination process at Belzec appears in Lucy Dawidowicz, ed., *A Holocaust Reader* (New York: Behrman House, 1976), pp. 104–109.

21. Hochhuth's symbol clearly derives its identification from a Biblical source, most likely I John 3:10–12: ". . . the distinction between the children of God and the children of the devil: no one who does not do right is God's child, nor is anyone who does not love his brother. For the message you have heard from the beginning is this: that we should love one another; unlike Cain, who was a child of the evil one and murdered his brother."

22. A. Roy Eckardt makes an even more sweeping charge, tracing the roots of the Nazi genocide against the Jews back to Christian Scriptures themselves: "The New Testament remains the major dogmatic and existential barrier to any victory over antisemitism. . . . Every instance of Christian antisemitism in postbiblical history is directly or indirectly traceable to the events or reputed events recorded in the New Testament. The foundations of Christian antisemitism and the church's contribution to the Nazi Holocaust were laid 1900 years ago; the line from the New Testament through the centuries of Christian contempt for Jews to the gas ovens and crematoria is unbroken." See his *Your People, My People: The Meeting of Jews and Christians* (New York: Quadrangle, 1974), p. 13.

23. Quoted by Nachman Blumenthal, "On the Nazi Vocabulary," *Yad Vashem Studies,* I (Jerusalem, 1957), p. 51.

24. Jorge Luis Borges, *Labyrinths* (New York: New Directions, 1964), p. 146; the story is translated by Julian Palley.

25. Quoted by John Toland in *Adolf Hitler* (New York: Doubleday, 1976), p. 292.

8. Exploiting Atrocity

1. Peter Weiss, *The Investigation,* trans. Jon Swan and Ulu Grosbard (New York: Atheneum, 1966), "Note." All subsequent citations will be noted in the text within parentheses.

2. "The Material and the Models: Notes toward a Definition of Documentary Theatre," *Theatre Quarterly* I (January–March 1971): 42, 43.

3. Paul Gray, "A Living World: An Interview with Peter Weiss," *Tulane Drama Review* II (Fall 1966): 108.

4. Otto Best, *Peter Weiss,* trans. Ursula Molinaro (New York: Frederick Ungar Publishing Co., 1976), pp. 83–84.

5. Bernd Naumann, *Auschwitz: A Report on the Proceedings against Robert Karl Ludwig Mulka and Others before the Court at Frankfurt* (London: Pall Mall Press, 1966).

6. "The Material and the Models," p. 43.

7. Quoted in Ian Hilton, *Peter Weiss: A Search for Affinities* (London: Oswald Wolff, 1970), p. 47; from a Stockholm newspaper, *Dagens Nyheter,* September 1, 1965.

8. Best, pp. 91–92.

9. Oliver Clausen, "Weiss/Propagandist and Weiss/Playwright," *New York Times Magazine*, October 2, 1966, p. 132. For a forceful argument against the universalizing tendency illustrated by Weiss's words, see Cynthia Ozick, "A Liberal's Auschwitz," in *The Pushcart Press, I*, ed. Bill Henderson (New York: Avon Books, 1976), pp. 149–53: "Blurring eases. Specificity pains. We have no right to seek a message of ease in Auschwitz, and it is moral ease to slide from the particular to the abstract. We have no right, in the nourishing name of 'life,' in the perilously ennobling name of 'humanity,' to divest the Jews of Europe of their specifically Jewish martyrdom" (p. 153).

10. This same static, immobile quality characterizes Weiss's descriptive essay on Auschwitz, *"Meine Ortschaft,"* which appears in English translation as "My Place" in the *Chicago Review*, XIX (Winter 1978): 143–51.

11. The quotations from Styron are taken from several of the author's essays and interviews that deal with the Holocaust, including "Auschwitz's Message," *The New York Times*, June 25, 1974; "Introduction" (by Styron) to Richard Rubenstein's *The Cunning of History* (Harper Colophon edition, 1978); "An Interview with William Styron," *Contemporary Literature*, 20 (Winter 1979): 1–12; and "A Talk with William Styron," *The New York Times Book Review*, May 27, 1979.

12. William Styron, *Sophie's Choice* (New York: Random House, 1979), p. 73. All subsequent citations will be noted in the text within parentheses.

13. See Yehuda Bauer, *The Holocaust in Historical Perspective* (Seattle: University of Washington Press, 1978), pp. 30–49.

14. Rudolf Höss, *Commandant of Auschwitz*, trans. Constantine FitzGibbon (New York: World Publishing Company, 1959), p. 201.

15. Ibid., p. 202.

16. The filmscript is contained in *The Screenplays of Lina Wertmüller*, trans. Steven Wagner (New York: Quadrangle, 1977), pp. 268–334. All references are to this text.

17. John Simon, "Wertmüller's 'Seven Beauties'—Call It A Masterpiece," *New York* 9:5 (February 2, 1976): 24–31. For another and much harsher evaluation of the film, see Bruno Bettelheim, "Surviving," *The New Yorker* 52:24 (August 2, 1976): 31–52. Bettelheim, in an extended polemic, takes strong issue with the notion of survivorship portrayed in *Seven Beauties* and in Terrence Des Pres's *The Survivor*. (For Des Pres's evaluation of the film, see his "Bleak Comedies: Lina Wertmüller's Artful Method," *Harper's* 252 [June 1976]: 26–28.)

18. *The Screenplays of Lina Wertmüller*, p. xvii.

19. Jay Cocks, "Charnel Knowledge," *Time*, January 26, 1976, p. 76.

20. William S. Pechter, "Obsessions," *Commentary*, May 1976, p. 76.

21. Quoted in Ernest Ferlita and John R. May, *The Parables of Lina Wertmüller* (New York: Paulist Press, 1977), p. 29.

22. Ibid., pp. 29–30.

23. Leslie Epstein, *King of the Jews: A Novel of the Holocaust* (New York: Coward, McCann & Geoghegan, Inc., 1979), p. 268.

24. Quoted in Leonard Tushnet, *The Pavement of Hell* (New York: St. Martin's Press, 1972), pp. 169–70.

25. Brian Murdoch, "Transformations of the Holocaust: Auschwitz in Modern Lyric Poetry," *Comparative Literature Studies*, 11, 6 (1974): 123–50.

26. Quoted in Charles Newman, ed., *The Art of Sylvia Plath* (Bloomington: Indiana University Press, 1971), p. 64; from an interview with the poet.

27. Richard Ellmann and Robert O'Clair, *Modern Poems* (New York: W. W. Norton and Company, 1976), p. 456.

28. Arthur Oberg, *Modern American Lyric: Lowell, Berryman, Creeley and Plath* (New Brunswick, New Jersey: Rutgers University Press, 1978), p. 146.

29. Newman, pp. 64–65.

30. Ibid.; p. 65.

31. Ibid.

32. Ibid., pp. 231, 236.

Epilogue

1. Jorge Semprun, *The Long Voyage* (New York: Grove Press, 1964), pp. 189–90.

2. *Survival in Auschwitz*, p. 79.

3. *The Human Province*, p. 9.

4. Elie Wiesel, *A Beggar in Jerusalem*, pp. 113–14.

Bibliography

The list of titles that follows constitutes a selected bibliography of Holocaust literature and some of its attendant historical and interpretive material. Designed for readers who would like to gain a knowledge of works in English or English translation, it is not intended to be exhaustive. It includes most of the primary works referred to in the preceding chapters and also others of interest that may not have been part of the focus of this book. Titles are listed under the following headings:

    I.   Diaries, Journals, and Memoirs
   II. Fiction
 III. Poetry
 IV. Drama
   V. Anthologies, Essay Collections, and Literary Criticism
 VI. Other (chiefly historical and theological)

A great deal of literature, not listed here, exists in foreign languages and still awaits translation. In addition, new works are constantly appearing. For additional bibliographical help, readers should consult *Guide to Jewish History under Nazi Impact* (1960), edited by Jacob Robinson and Philip Friedman, and the annual volumes published by Yad Vashem (Jerusalem) and YIVO (New York).

I. Diaries, Journals, and Memoirs

Barkai, Meyer. *The Fighting Ghettos.* Philadelphia: J. B. Lippincott Co., 1962.
Berg, Mary. *Warsaw Ghetto: A Diary.* Translated by Norbert and Sylvia Glass. New York: L. B. Fisher, 1945.
Bettelheim, Bruno. *The Informed Heart.* Glencoe, Ill.: Free Press, 1960.
Bezwinska, Jadwiga, ed. *Amidst a Nightmare of Crime.* Oświeçim, Poland, 1973.
————. *KL Auschwitz Seen by the SS: Höss, Broad, Kremer.* Oświeçim, Poland, 1972.
Birenbaum, Halina. *Hope Is the Last to Die.* Translated by David Welsh. New York: Twayne, 1971.

Fenelon, Fanya [handwritten] Playing for Time (1980) [handwritten]

Buber-Neumann, Margarete. *Under Two Dictators*. Translated by Edward Fitzgerald. New York: Dodd, Mead and Co., 1949.

Cohen, Elie. *The Abyss: A Confession*. Translated by James Brockway. New York: W. W. Norton & Co., 1973.

———. *Human Behavior in the Concentration Camp*. Translated by M. H. Braaksma. New York: W. W. Norton & Co., 1953.

Delbo, Charlotte. *None of Us Will Return*. Translated by John Githens. New York: Grove Press, 1969.

Donat, Alexander. *The Holocaust Kingdom*. New York: Holt, Rinehart and Winston, 1965.

Flinker, Moshe. *The Diary of Young Moshe*. Jerusalem: Yad Vashem, 1971.

Frank, Anne. *The Diary of a Young Girl*. Translated by B. M. Mooyaart-Doubleday. New York: Pocket Books, 1952.

Frankl, Viktor E. *Man's Search for Meaning: An Introduction to Logotherapy*. Translated by Ilse Lasch. New York: Washington Square Press, 1963. (This is a revised and enlarged version of *From Death-Camp to Existentialism*, Beacon Press, 1959.)

Friedländer, Saul. *When Memory Comes*. Translated by Helen R. Lane. New York: Farrar, Straus and Giroux, 1979.

Friedman, Philip. *Martyrs and Fighters*. London: Routledge & Kegan Paul, 1954.

Gefen, Aba. *Unholy Alliance*. Israel: Yuval Tal Ltd., 1973.

Gilboa, Yehoshua. *Confess! Confess!* Translated by Dov Ben Aba. Boston: Little, Brown & Co., 1968.

Goldstein, Bernard. *The Stars Bear Witness*. Translated by Leonard Shatzkin. New York: Viking Press, 1949.

Goldstein, Charles. *The Bunker*. Translated by Esther Malkin. Philadelphia: Jewish Publication Society, 1970.

Gray, Martin. *For Those I Loved*. Translated by Anthony White. Boston: Little, Brown & Co., 1972.

Hart, Kitty. *I Am Alive*. New York: Abelard-Schuman, 1962.

Heimler, Eugene. *Night of the Mist*. Translated by André Ungar. New York: Vanguard Press, 1959.

Heyman, Éva. *The Diary of Éva Heyman*. Translated by Moshe M. Kohn. Jerusalem: Yad Vashem, 1974.

Hilberg, Raul; Staron, Stanislaw; and Kermisz, Josef. *The Warsaw Diary of Adam Czerniakow*. New York: Stein and Day, 1979.

Höss, Rudolf. *Commandant of Auschwitz*. Translated by Constantine FitzGibbon. New York: World Publishing Company, 1959.

Kaplan, Chaim A. *The Warsaw Diary of Chaim A. Kaplan*. Translated by Abraham Katsh. New York: Collier Books, 1973. (Previously published as *Scroll of Agony*, Macmillan, 1975).

Katz, Josef. *One Who Came Back*. Translated by Hilda Reach. New York: Herzl Press and Bergen-Belsen Memorial Press, 1973.

Katznelson, Yitzhak. *Vittel Diary*. Translated by Dr. Myer Cohen. Israel: Beit Lohamei Hagettaot and Hakibbutz Hameuchad Publishing House, 1972.

Klein, Gerda Weissman. *All But My Life*. New York: Hill and Wang, 1957.

Kogon, Eugen. *The Theory and Practice of Hell*. Translated by Heinz Norden. New York: Farrar, Straus and Company, 1950.

Korczak, Janusz. *Ghetto Diary*. New York: Holocaust Library, 1978.

Fenelon, Fanya, Playing for time (1980 [handwritten]

Michelson, Frida. I Survived Rumbula (1979)
Novitch, Miriam. Sobibor (1980)

Kraus, Ota, and Kulka, Erich. *The Death Factory: Documents on Auschwitz.*
    Translated by Stephen Jolly. Oxford: Pergamon, 1966.
Kuper, Jack. *Child of the Holocaust.* Garden City: Doubleday & Co., 1968.
Leitner, Isabella. *Fragments of Isabella: A Memoir of Auschwitz.* New York:
    Thomas Y. Crowell, 1978.
Lengyel, Olga. *Five Chimneys: The Story of Auschwitz.* Translated by Paul B.
    Weiss. Chicago: Ziff-Davis, 1947.
Levi, Primo. *The Reawakening.* Translated by Stuart Woolf. Boston: Little,
    Brown & Co., 1965.
————. *Survival in Auschwitz.* Translated by Stuart Woolf. New York: Collier
    Books, 1969. (Previously published as *If This Is a Man,* The Orion Press,
    1959.)
Lewinska, Pelagia. *Twenty Months at Auschwitz.* Translated by Albert Teichner.
    New York: Lyle Stuart, 1968.
Mark, Ber. *Uprising in the Warsaw Ghetto.* Translated by Gershon Freidlin. New
    York: Schocken Books, 1975.
Maurel, Micheline. *An Ordinary Camp.* Translated by Margaret S. Summers.
    New York: Simon & Schuster, 1958.
Meed, Vladka. *On Both Sides of the Wall.* Israel: Beit Lohamei Hagettaot and
    Hakibbutz Hameuchad Publishing House, 1973.
Nyiszli, Miklos. *Auschwitz: A Doctor's Eyewitness Account.* Translated by Tibere
    Kremer and Richard Seaver. Greenwich, Conn.: Fawcett Crest, 1960.
Rabinowitz, Dorothy. *New Lives: Survivors of the Holocaust Living in America.*
    New York: Alfred A. Knopf, 1976.
Ringelblum, Emmanuel. *Notes from the Warsaw Ghetto.* Translated by Jacob
    Sloan. New York: McGraw-Hill, 1958.
Rosen, Donia. *The Forest My Friend.* Translated by Mordecai S. Chertoff. New
    York: Bergen-Belsen Memorial Press, 1971.
Rousset, David. *The Other Kingdom.* Translated by Ramon Guthrie. New York:
    Reynal and Hitchcock, 1947.
Rudashevski, Yitskhok. *The Diary of the Vilna Ghetto.* Translated by Percy
    Matenko. Israel: Beit Lohamei Hagettaot and Hakibbutz Hameuchad Publish-
    ing House, 1973.
Schnabel, Ernst. *Anne Frank: A Portrait in Courage.* Translated by Richard and
    Clara Winston. New York: Harcourt, Brace, Harbrace Paperback Library,
    1958.
Senesh, Hannah. *Hannah Senesh, Her Life and Diary.* New York: Schocken
    Books, 1972.
Sereny, Gitta. *Into that Darkness.* New York: McGraw-Hill, 1974.
Szmaglewska, Seweryna. *Smoke over Birkenau.* Translated by Jadwiga Rynas.
    New York: Henry Holt, 1947.
Tillion, Germaine. *Ravensbrück.* Translated by Gerald Satterwhite. New York:
    Doubleday, Anchor Books, 1975.
Trepman, Paul. *Among Beasts and Men.* New York: A. S. Barnes & Co., 1978.
Unsdorfer, S. B., *The Yellow Star.* New York: Thomas Yoseloff, 1961.
Vrba, Rudolf, and Bestic, Alan. *I Cannot Forgive.* New York: Bantam Books,
    1964.
Wechsberg, Joseph, ed. *The Murderers Among Us: The Wiesenthal Memoirs.* New
    York: McGraw-Hill, 1967.
Wells, Leon. *The Janowska Road.* New York: Macmillan, 1963. (Reprinted as
    The Death Brigade, The Holocaust Library, 1978.)

Senger, V. The Invisible Jew (1980)

Tiffanger, Abel The Opel 1976

Wiechert, Ernst. *Forest of the Dead*. Translated by Ursula Stechow. New York: Greenberg, 1947.

Wiesel, Elie. *Night*. Translated by Stella Rodway. New York: Hill and Wang, 1960.

Zylberberg, Michael. *A Warsaw Diary 1939–1945*. London: Valentine-Mitchell, 1969.

Zywulska, Krystana. *I Came Back*. Translated by Krystyna Cenkalska. London: Dennis Dobson, 1951.

Appelfeld, A. Badenheim 1939 (1980)
Arieti, M. The Parnas (1979)

II. FICTION

Abish, Walter. "The English Garden." In *In the Future Perfect*. New York: New Directions, 1977.

Aichinger, Ilse. *Herod's Children*. Translated by Cornelia Schaeffer. New York: Atheneum, 1963.

Amichai, Yehuda. *Not of This Time, Not of This Place*. Translated by Shlomo Katz. New York: Harper & Row, 1968.

Anatoli, A. (Kuznetsov). *Babi Yar*. Translated by David Floyd. London: Jonathan Cape, 1970.

Arnold, Elliot. *A Night of Watching*. New York: Charles Scribner's Sons, 1967.

Bartov, Hanoch. *The Brigade*. Translated by David Segal. Philadelphia: Jewish Publication Society, 1967.

Bassani, Giorgio. "A Plaque on Via Mazzinio." In *Five Stories of Ferrara*. Translated by William Weaver. New York: Harcourt Brace Jovanovich, 1971.

———. *The Garden of the Finzi-Continis*. Translated by William Weaver. New York: Harcourt Brace Jovanovich, 1977.

Becker, Jurek. *Jacob the Liar*. Translated by Melvin Kornfeld. New York: Harcourt Brace Jovanovich, 1975.

Bellow, Saul. *Mr. Sammler's Planet*. New York: Viking Press, 1970.

Ben-Amotz, Dan. *To Remember, To Forget*. Translated by Eva Shapiro. Philadelphia: Jewish Publication Society, 1968.

Bor, Josef. *The Terezin Requiem*. Translated by Edith Pargeter. New York: Alfred A. Knopf, 1963.

Borges, Jorge Luis. "Deutsches Requiem" and "The Secret Miracle." In *Labyrinths, Selected Stories and Other Writings*. Edited by Donald A. Yates and James E. Irby. New York: New Directions, 1964.

Borowski, Tadeusz. *This Way for the Gas, Ladies and Gentlemen*. Translated by Barbara Vedder. New York: Viking Press, 1967.

Bryks, Rachmil. *A Cat in the Ghetto*. Translated by S. Morris Engel. New York: Bloch Publishing Company, 1959.

———. *Kiddush Hashem*. Translated by S. Morris Engel. New York: Behrman House, 1977.

Buczkowski, Leopold. *Black Torrent*. Translated by David Welsh. Cambridge, Massachusetts: MIT Press, 1969.

Chaneles, Sol. *Three Children of the Holocaust*. New York: Avon Books, 1974.

del Castillo, Michel. *Child of Our Time*. New York: Dell, 1958.

Epstein, Leslie. *King of the Jews*. New York: Coward, McCann & Geoghegan, 1979.

Forsyth, Frederick. *The Odessa File*. New York: Viking Press, 1972.

Fuks, Ladislav. *Mr. Theodore Mundstock*. Translated by Iris Unwin. New York: Orion Press, 1968.

Gary, Romain. *The Dance of Ghengis Cohn*. Translated by the author and Camilla Sykes. New York: World Publishing Company, 1968.

Gascar, Pierre. *Beasts and Men and the Seed*. Translated by Jean Stewart and Merloyd Lawrence. New York: Meridian Books, 1960.

Gouri, Haim. *The Chocolate Deal*. Translated by Seymour Simckes. New York: Holt, Rinehart and Winston, 1968.

Grade, Chaim. *The Seven Little Lanes*. Translated by Curt Leviant. New York: Bergen-Belsen Memorial Press, 1972.

Green, Gerald. *Holocaust*. New York: Bantam Books, 1978.

Grynberg, Henryk. *Child of the Shadows*. London: Valentine, Mitchell, 1969.

Hersey, John. *The Wall*. New York: Alfred A. Knopf, 1950.

Hilsenrath, Edgar. *Night*. Translated by Michael Roloff. New York: Doubleday & Co., 1966.

————. *The Nazi and the Jew*. New York: Manor Books, 1977. (Previously published as *The Nazi and the Barber,* Doubleday & Co., 1971.)

Jabès, Edmond. *The Book of Questions*. Translated by Rosmarie Waldrop. Middletown, Conn.: Wesleyan University Press, 1976.

————. *The Book of Yukel* and *Return to the Book*. Translated by Rosmarie Waldrop. Middletown, Conn.: Wesleyan University Press, 1977.

Kanfer, Stefan. *The Eighth Sin*. New York: Random House, 1978.

Kaniuk, Yoram. *Adam Resurrected*. Translated by Seymour Simckes. New York: Atheneum, 1971.

Karmel, Ilona. *An Estate of Memory*. Boston: Houghton Mifflin Co., 1969.

Karmel-Wolfe, Henia. *The Baders of Jacob Street*. New York: J. B. Lippincott Co., 1970.

Ka-Tzetnik 135633 (Yehiel DeNur). *Atrocity*. New York: Lyle Stuart, 1963.

————. *House of Dolls*. New York: Pyramid Books, 1969.

————. *Star Eternal*. Translated by Nina DeNur. New York: Arbor House, 1971.

————. *Sunrise over Hell*. Translated by Nina DeNur. London: W. H. Allen, 1977.

Klein, A. M. *The Second Scroll*. Canada: McClelland and Stewart, 1966.

Kosinski, Jerzy. *The Painted Bird*. Second edition with an introduction by the author. Boston: Houghton Mifflin Co., 1976.

Langfus, Anna. *The Whole Land Brimstone*. Translated by Peter Wiles. New York: Pantheon Books, 1962.

Levi, Carlo. *The Watch*. New York: Farrar, Straus and Yoring, 1951.

Lind, Jakov. *Landscape in Concrete*. Translated by Ralph Manheim. New York: Grove Press, 1966.

————. *Soul of Wood and Other Stories*. Translated by Ralph Manheim. New York: Fawcett Crest, 1966.

Lustig, Arnošt. *A Prayer for Katerina Horovitzova*. Translated by Jeanne Němcová. New York: Harper & Row, 1973.

————. *Darkness Casts No Shadow*. Translated by Jeanne Němcová. Washington, D.C.: Inscape Publishers, 1978.

————. *Diamonds of the Night*. Translated by Jeanne Němcová. Washington, D.C.: Inscape Publishers, 1978.

————. *Night and Hope*. Translated by George Theiner. Washington, D.C.: Inscape Publishers, 1976.

Malaparte, Curzio. *Kaputt*. Translated by Cesare Foligno. New York: E. P. Dutton & Co., 1946.

Morante, Elsa. *History, A Novel.* Translated by William Weaver. New York: Alfred A. Knopf, 1977.

Prager, Moshe. *Sparks of Glory.* Translated by Mordecai Schreiber. New York: Shengold Publishers, 1974.

Rawicz, Piotr. *Blood from the Sky.* Translated by Peter Wiles. New York: Harcourt, Brace & World, 1964.

Rosen, Norma. *Touching Evil.* New York: Harcourt, Brace & World, 1969.

Rudnicki, Adolf. *Ascent to Heaven.* Translated by H. C. Stevens. New York: Roy Publishers, 1951.

Samuels, Gertrude. *Mottele.* New York: Harper & Row, 1976.

Schaeffer, Susan Fromberg. *Anya.* New York: Macmillan, 1974.

Schwarz-Bart, André. *The Last of the Just.* New York: Atheneum, 1961.

Segal, Lore. *Other People's Houses.* New York: New American Library, 1973.

Semprun, Jorge. *The Long Voyage.* Translated by Richard Seaver. New York: Grove Press, 1964.

Shaw, Robert. *The Man in the Glass Booth.* Middlesex, England: Penguin Books, 1969.

Singer, Isaac Bashevis. *Enemies: A Love Story.* Translated by Aliza Shevrin and Elizabeth Shub. New York: Farrar, Straus and Giroux, 1972.

————. *The Slave.* Translated by Cecil Hemley and the Author. New York: Farrar, Straus and Cuddahy, 1962.

Sperber, Manès. *. . . than a tear in the sea.* Translated by Constantine Fitzgibbon. New York: Bergen-Belsen Memorial Press, 1967.

Spiraux, Alain. *Time Out.* Translated by Frances Keene. New York: Times Books, 1978.

Steiner, George. "The Portage to San Cristobal of A.H.," *The Kenyon Review,* n.s., I, 2 (Spring 1979): 1–120.

Steiner, Jean-Francois. *Treblinka.* Translated by Helen Weaver. New York: Simon & Schuster, 1976.

Stern, Daniel. *Who Shall Live, Who Shall Die?* New York: Lancer Books, 1963.

Styron, William. *Sophie's Choice.* New York: Random House, 1979.

Tomkiewicz, Mina. *Of Bombs and Mice.* Translated by Stefan Grazel. New York: Thomas Yoseloff, 1970.

Uhlman, Fred. *Reunion.* New York: Penguin Books, 1978.

Uris, Leon. *Mila 18.* New York: Doubleday & Co., 1961.

Wallant, Edward L., *The Pawnbroker.* New York: Macfadden Books, 1964.

Wiesenthal, Simon. *The Sunflower.* Translated by H. A. Piehler. New York: Schocken Books, 1976.

Wiesel, Elie. *The Accident.* Translated by Anne Borchardt. New York: Hill and Wang, 1962.

————. *A Beggar in Jerusalem.* Translated by Lily Edelman and the author. New York: Random House, 1970.

————. *Dawn.* Translated by Anne Borchardt. New York: Hill and Wang, 1961.

————. *The Gates of the Forest.* Translated by Frances Frenaye. New York: Holt, Rinehart and Winston, 1966.

————. *The Oath.* Translated by Marion Wiesel. New York: Random House, 1973.

————. *The Town Beyond the Wall.* Translated by Stephen Becker. New York: Holt, Rinehart and Winston, 1967.

Tissauges, Abel *The Ogre* (1976)

III. POETRY

Bryks, Rachmil. *Ghetto Factory 76*. Translated by Theodor Primack and Prof. Dr. Eugen Kullman. New York: Bloch Publishing Company, 1967.

Celan, Paul. *Selected Poems*. Translated by Michael Hamburger and Christopher Middleton. Middlesex, England: Penguin Books, 1972.

———. *Speech-Grille and Selected Poems*. Translated by Joachim Neugroschel. New York: E. P. Dutton & Co., 1971.

Feldman, Irving. *The Pripet Marshes and Other Poems*. New York: Viking Press, 1965.

Gershon, Karen. *Selected Poems*. New York: Harcourt, Brace and World, 1966.

Glatstein, Jacob. *Poems*. Translated by Etta Blum. Tel Aviv: I. L. Peretz Publishing House, 1970.

———. *The Selected Poems of Jacob Glatstein*. Translated by Ruth Whitman. New York: October House, 1972.

Hecht, Anthony. *The Hard Hours*. New York: Atheneum, 1967.

Heyen, William. *The Swastika Poems*. New York: Vanguard Press, 1977.

Hill, Geoffrey. *Somewhere Is Such a Kingdom, Poems 1952–1971*. Boston: Houghton Mifflin Co., 1975.

Klein, A. M. *Collected Poems*. Toronto: McGraw-Hill Ryerson, 1974.

Kolmar, Gertrud. *Dark Soliloquy: The Selected Poems of Gertrud Kolmar*. Translated by Henry A. Smith. New York: Seabury Press, 1975.

Kovner, Abba. *A Canopy in the Desert*. Translated by Shirley Kaufman, with Ruth Adler and Nurit Orchan. Pittsburgh: University of Pittsburgh Press, 1973.

———. *Selected Poems of Abba Kovner and Nelly Sachs*. Translated by Shirley Kaufman and Nurit Orchan. Middlesex, England: Penguin Books, 1971.

Levi, Primo. *Shema: Collected Poems of Primo Levi*. Translated by Ruth Feldman and Brian Swann. London: Menard Press, 1976.

Milosz, Czeslaw. *Selected Poems*. New York: Seabury Press, 1973.

Pagis, Dan. *Selected Poems*. Translated by Stephen Mitchell. Oxford: Carcanet Press, 1972.

Pilinszky, Janos. *Selected Poems*. Translated by Ted Hughes and Janos Csokits. New York: Persea Books, 1976.

Plath, Sylvia. *Ariel*. New York: Harper & Row, 1965.

Radnoti, Miklos. *Clouded Sky*. Translated by Steven Polgar, Stephen Berg, and S. J. Marks. New York: Harper & Row, 1972.

Reznikoff, Charles. *Holocaust*. Los Angeles: Black Sparrow Press, 1975.

Różewicz, Tadeusz. *"The Survivor" and Other Poems*. Translated by Magnus J. Krynski and Robert A. Maguire. Princeton: Princeton University Press, 1976.

Sachs, Nelly. *O the Chimneys: Selected Poems*. Translated by Michael Hamburger, Christopher Home, Ruth and Matthew Mead, and Michael Roloff. New York: Farrar, Straus and Giroux, 1967.

———. *The Seeker and other Poems*. Translated by Ruth and Matthew Mead and Michael Hamburger. New York: Farrar, Straus and Giroux, 1970.

Sklarew, Myra. *From the Backyard of the Diaspora*. Washington, D.C.: Dryad Press, 1976.

Snodgrass, W. D. *The Führer Bunker*. Brockport, N.Y.: BOA Editions, 1977.

Taube, Herman. *A Chain of Images*. New York: Shulsinger Brothers, 1979.

Wiesel, Elie. *Ani Maamin: A Song Lost and Found Again.* Translated by Marion Wiesel. New York: Random House, 1973.

Yevtushenko, Yevgeni. *Selected Poems.* Translated by Robin Milner-Gullard and Peter Levi. Baltimore: Penguin Books, 1964.

IV. DRAMA

Amichai, Yehuda. *Bells and Trains.* In *Midstream,* October 1966, pp. 55–66.

Amir, Anda. *This Kind Too.* Translated by Shoshana Perla. New York: World Zionist Organization, 1972.

Borchert, Wolfgang. *The Outsider.* In *Postwar German Theatre, An Anthology of Plays.* Translated and edited by Michael Benedikt and George E. Wellwarth. New York: E. P. Dutton & Co., 1967, pp. 52–113.

Eliach, Yaffa, and Assaf, Uri. *The Last Jew.* Translated by Yaffa Eliach. Israel: Alef-Alef Theater Publications, 1977.

Frisch, Max. *Andorra.* Translated by Michael Bullock. New York: Hill and Wang, 1964.

Goldberg, Leah. *The Lady of the Castle.* Translated by Ted Carmi. Tel Aviv: Institute for the Translation of Hebrew Literature, 1974.

Goodrich, Frances, and Hackett, Albert. *The Diary of Anne Frank.* New York: Random House, 1956. (Based upon *Anne Frank: The Diary of a Young Girl.*)

Hochhuth, Rolf. *The Deputy.* Translated by Richard and Clara Winston. New York: Grove Press, 1964.

Lampell, Millard. *The Wall.* New York: Alfred A. Knopf, 1961. (Based upon the novel of the same title by John Hersey.)

Meged, Aharon. *The Burning Bush.* Translated by Shoshana Perla. New York: World Zionist Organization, 1972.

Miller, Arthur. *Incident at Vichy.* New York: Viking Press, 1965.

Sachs, Nelly. *Eli: A Mystery Play of the Sufferings of Israel.* Translated by Christopher Holme. In *O the Chimneys.* New York: Farrar, Straus and Giroux, 1967, pp. 309–85.

Sartre, Jean-Paul. *The Condemned of Altona.* Translated by Sylvia and George Leeson. New York: Alfred A. Knopf, 1961.

Shaw, Robert. *The Man in the Glass Booth.* New York: Harcourt, Brace and World, 1967.

Sylvanus, Erwin. *Dr. Korczak and the Children.* In *Postwar German Theatre.* Translated and edited by Michael Benedikt and George E. Wellwarth. New York: E. P. Dutton & Co., 1967, pp. 115–57.

Tomer, Ben-Zion. *Children of the Shadows.* Translated by Hillel Halkin. New York: World Zionist Organization, n.d.

Weiss, Peter. *The Investigation.* Translated by Jon Swan and Ulu Grosbard. New York: Atheneum, 1966.

Wiesel, Elie. *The Trial of God.* Translated by Marion Wiesel. New York: Random House, 1979.

———. *Zalmen, or the Madness of God.* Translated by Nathan Edelman and adapted for the stage by Marion Wiesel. New York: Random House, 1974.

V. ANTHOLOGIES, ESSAY COLLECTIONS, AND LITERARY CRITICISM

Abramowitz, Molly. *Elie Wiesel: A Bibliography.* Metuchen, N.J.: Scarecrow Press, 1974.

Bilik, Dorothy Seidman *Immigrant-Survivors* (1981) BIBLIOGRAPHY

Alexander, Edward. *The Resonance of Dust: Essays on Holocaust Literature and Jewish Fate.* Columbus: Ohio State University Press, 1979.

Alter, Robert. "Confronting the Holocaust." In *After the Tradition.* New York: E. P. Dutton & Co., 1969, pp. 163–80.

Alvarez, A. "The Literature of the Holocaust." In *Beyond All This Fiddle.* New York: Random House, 1969, pp. 22–33.

Bentley, Eric, ed. *The Storm over the Deputy.* New York: Grove Press, 1965.

Best, Otto F. *Peter Weiss.* Translated by Ursule Molinaro. New York: Frederick Ungar Publishing Co., 1976.

Betsky, Sarah Zweig, ed. *Onions and Cucumbers and Plums: 46 Yiddish Poems in English.* Detroit: Wayne State University Press, 1958.

Burnshaw, Stanley; Carmi, Ted; and Spicehandler, Ezra, eds. *The Modern Hebrew Poem Itself.* New York: Holt, Rinehart and Winston, 1965.

Canetti, Elias. *The Human Province.* Translated by Joachim Neugroschel. New York: Seabury Press, 1978.

Cargas, Harry James. *Harry James Cargas in Conversation with Elie Wiesel.* New York: Paulist Press, 1976.

———, ed. *Responses to Elie Wiesel: Critical Essays by Major Jewish and Christian Scholars.* New York: Persea Books, 1978.

Dawidowicz, Lucy, ed. *A Holocaust Reader.* New York: Behrman House, 1976.

Des Pres, Terrence. *The Survivor: An Anatomy of Life in the Death Camps.* New York: Oxford University Press, 1976.

Ezrahi, Sidra. "Holocaust Literature in European Languages." In *Encyclopedia Judaica Yearbook 1973.* Jerusalem: Keter Publishing House, 1973, pp. 104–19.

Friedlander, Albert, ed. *Out of the Whirlwind: A Reader of Holocaust Literature.* New York: Schocken Books, 1976.

Glatstein, Jacob; Knox, Israel; and Margoshes, Samuel, eds. *Anthology of Holocaust Literature.* Philadelphia: Jewish Publication Society of America, 1968.

Haft, Cynthia. *The Theme of Nazi Concentration Camps in French Literature.* The Hague: Mouton, 1973.

Halperin, Irving. *Messengers from the Dead: Literature of the Holocaust.* Philadelphia: Westminster Press, 1970.

Hamburger, Michael. *From Prophecy to Exorcism.* London: Longman's, Green and Co., 1965.

Howe, Irving, and Greenberg, Eliezer, eds. *A Treasury of Yiddish Poetry.* New York: Holt, Rinehart and Winston, 1969.

———. *Voices from the Yiddish: Essays, Memoirs, Diaries.* Ann Arbor: University of Michigan Press, 1972.

Korman, Gerd, ed. *Hunter and Hunted: Human History of the Holocaust.* New York: Dell, Delta Books, 1974.

Langer, Lawrence. *The Age of Atrocity: Death in Modern Literature.* Boston: Beacon Press, 1978.

———. *The Holocaust and the Literary Imagination.* New Haven: Yale University Press, 1975.

Leftwich, Joseph, ed. *The Golden Peacock: A Worldwide Treasury of Yiddish Poetry.* New York: Thomas Yoseloff, 1961.

———. *The Way We Think: A Collection of Essays from the Yiddish.* 2 vols. New York: Thomas Yoseloff, 1969.

Mintz, Ruth Finer, ed. *Modern Hebrew Poetry.* Berkeley: University of California Press, 1966.

Murdoch, Brian. "Transformation of the Holocaust: Auschwitz in Modern Lyric Poetry." *Comparative Literature Studies,* II, 6 (1974): 123–50.

Rosenfeld, Alvin H., and Greenberg, Irving, eds. *Confronting the Holocaust: The Impact of Elie Wiesel.* Bloomington: Indiana University Press, 1979.

Steiner, George. *In Bluebeard's Castle.* New Haven: Yale University Press, 1971.

———. *Language and Silence.* New York: Atheneum, 1967.

Wiesel, Elie. *A Jew Today.* Translated by Marion Wiesel. New York: Random House, 1978.

———. *Legends of Our Time.* Translated by Steven Donadio. New York: Holt, Rinehart and Winston, 1968.

———. *One Generation After.* Translated by Lily Edelman and the Author. New York: Random House, 1970.

VI. Other

Arendt, Hannah. *Eichmann in Jerusalem.* New York: Viking Press, 1970.

———. *The Origins of Totalitarianism.* New York: World Publishing Co., 1958.

Bauer, Yehuda. *The Holocaust in Historical Perspective.* Seattle: University of Washington Press, 1978.

Berkovitz, Eliezer. *Faith after the Holocaust.* New York: Ktav Publishing House, 1973.

Dawidowicz, Lucy. *The War against the Jews 1933–1945.* New York: Holt, Rinehart and Winston, 1975.

Dimensions of the Holocaust: Lectures at Northwestern University (Elie Wiesel, Lucy Dawidowicz, Dorothy Rabinowitz, Robert McAfee Brown). Evanston: Northwestern University, 1977.

Eckardt, A. Roy. *Elder and Younger Brothers.* New York: Charles Scribner's Sons, 1967.

———. *Your People, My People.* New York: NYT/Quadrangle, 1974.

Fackenheim, Emil. *Encounters between Judaism and Modern Philosophy.* Philadelphia: Jewish Publication Society, 1973.

———. *God's Presence in History.* New York: New York University Press, 1970.

———. *The Jewish Return into History.* New York: Schocken Books, 1978.

———. *Quest for Past and Future.* Boston: Beacon Press, 1970.

Fein, Helen. *Accounting for Genocide.* New York: Free Press, 1979.

Feingold, Henry L. *The Politics of Rescue.* New Brunswick: Rutgers University Press, 1970.

Fleischner, Eva, ed. *Auschwitz: Beginning of a New Era?* New York: Ktav Publishing House, 1977.

Grunberger, Richard. *The 12-Year Reich: A Social History of Nazi Germany, 1933–1945.* New York: Holt, Rinehart and Winston, 1971.

Gutman, Yisrael, and Rotkirchen, Livia, eds. *The Catastrophe of European Jewry: Antecedents, History, Reflections.* Jerusalem: Yad Vashem, 1976.

Hilberg, Raul. *The Destruction of the European Jews.* Chicago: Quadrangle Books, 1961.

———, ed. *Documents of Destruction.* London: W. H. Allen, 1972.

Jewish Resistance during the Holocaust. Jerusalem: Yad Vashem, 1971.

Kahler, Erich. *The Tower and the Abyss.* New York: Viking Press, 1967.

Levin, Nora. *The Holocaust: The Destruction of European Jewry, 1933–1945.* New York: Thomas Y. Crowell Company, 1968.

Littell, Franklin H. *The Crucifixion of the Jews*. New York: Harper & Row, 1975.

Milosz, Czeslaw. *The Captive Mind*. Translated by Jane Zielonko. New York: Alfred A. Knopf, 1953.

Morse, Arthur D. *While Six Million Died: A Chronicle of American Apathy*. New York: Random House, 1968.

Mosse, George. *The Crisis of German Ideology: Intellectual Origins of the Third Reich*. New York: Grosset & Dunlap, 1964.

————, ed. *Nazi Culture: Intellectual, Cultural, and Social Life in the Third Reich*. New York: Grosset & Dunlap, 1966.

Naumann, Bernd. *Auschwitz*. Translated by Jean Steinberg. New York: Praeger, 1966.

Pawełczyńska, Anna. *Values and Violence in Auschwitz: A Sociological Analysis*. Translated by Catherine S. Leach. Berkeley: University of California Press, 1979.

Poliakov, Leon. *Harvest of Hate: The Third Reich and the Jews*. Revised and expanded edition. New York: Holocaust Library, 1979.

Remak, Joachim, ed. *The Nazi Years: A Documentary History*. Englewood Cliffs, N. J.: Prentice-Hall, 1969.

Rosenbaum, Irving J. *The Holocaust and Halakhah*. New York: Ktav Publishing House, 1976.

Rosenfeld, Isaac. *An Age of Enormity*. New York: World Publishing Company, 1962.

Rubenstein, Richard. *After Auschwitz: Radical Theology and Contemporary Judaism*. Indianapolis: Bobbs-Merrill, 1966.

————. *The Cunning of History: The Holocaust and the American Future*. New York: Harper Colophon Edition, 1978.

Ruether, Rosemary. *Faith and Fratricide: The Theological Roots of Anti-Semitism*. New York: Seabury Press, 1974.

Shirer, William L. *The Rise and Fall of the Third Reich*. New York: Simon & Schuster, 1960.

Spiegel, Shalom. *The Last Trial*. New York: Schocken Books, 1969.

Suhl, Yuri, ed. *They Fought Back: The Story of the Jewish Resistance in Nazi Europe*. New York: Crown Publishers, 1967.

Thalmann, Rita, and Feinermann, Emmanuel. *Crystal Night*. Translated by Gilles Cremonesi. New York: Coward, McCann & Geoghegan, 1974.

Toland, John. *Adolf Hitler*. New York: Doubleday & Co., 1976.

Trunk, Isaiah. *Judenrat: The Jewish Councils in Eastern Europe under Nazi Occupation*. New York: Macmillan, 1972.